W THEM
BACK

Other books by Eddie Gibbs

Born Into Battle: 1 & 2 Thessalonians
Body Building Exercises for the Local Church
I Believe in Church Growth
The God Who Communicates
Ten Growing Churches (ed.)
Followed or Pushed?

Winning Them Back

Tackling the problem of nominal Christianity

EDDIE GIBBS

MARC
Tunbridge Wells

Unless otherwise indicated, biblical quotations are from the
New International Version.

ISBN 1 85424 208 3

British Library Cataloguing-in-Publication Data.

A catalogue record for this book is available
from the British Library.

Front cover photo inset: Cephas Picture Library

Dedication
To Andrew and Ashley

Production and Printing in England for
MONARCH PUBLICATIONS
PO Box 163, Tunbridge Wells,
Kent TN3 ONZ
Nuprint Ltd, Station Road, Harpenden
Herts AL5 4SE

Contents

*F*igures

INTRODUCTION

THIS EXPLORATION of the spiritual wilderness of nominality has been undertaken with some hesitancy, recognizing at the outset that it is a subject fraught with problems. Yet because it represents such a pervasive problem for all churches and traditions, especially in the western world, and as there is practically no literature dealing with it in a comprehensive fashion, I ventured to make a start.

The first problems which the student encounters is the loose way in which the term 'nominality' is generally used. Some religious commentators use it in the broadest sense to describe the post-Christian societies which are found in most of the western world. Others, including many church leaders preoccupied with what to do about membership losses, designate as 'nominal' those persons who retain a minimal contact with organized religion while remaining conspicuous by their absence from the church's public worship or involvement in fellowship groups or organizations dedicated to serving the community. In the following pages I will occupy a middle-ground position. The broader approach needs to be reduced to its most significant components, for without greater specificity the nominality condition cannot be accurately diagnosed or effectively treated. Whereas the narrow definition is far too restrictive for the complexity of nominality to be fully appreciated, with the result that attention will be focused on surface symptom rather than the underlying causes. Furthermore, the restrictive approach tends to sidestep the painful truth that churches must first recognize themselves to be part of the problem before they can begin to contribute to the search for solutions. Doctors are not immune from the conditions which afflict their patients!

My acceptance of a comprehensive definition of nominality means that the scope of the discussion broadens alarmingly. Major topics need to be discussed, each of which is extremely complex and taken together are beyond the competence of any one individual. Consequently, I have had to rely heavily on the expertize of specialists in areas outside my particular field, which is that of church growth and evangelism, and I am aware of the limitations and inadequacies of my reflections. Despite the drawbacks encountered in trying to encompass so much material, I hope that the particular value of this approach will be to draw together and interrelate, in a thought-provoking manner, a number of issues which are usually considered in isolation. These become inseparably intertwined when viewed in relation to the issue of nominality.

A further problem arises in attempting to answer the question whether or not nominal Christians were ever Christians in the first place. Should the term 'nominal Christian' be regarded as an oxymoron? Are some so-called 'nominal Christians' in reality pagans masquerading as believers, while others are self-deceived Pharisaical religious legalists? I believe that nominality represents a far more complex range of spiritual conditions. It embraces whose who lack spiritual vitality because they are spiritually undernourished and do not know where to find sustenance or feed themselves. It includes the reluctantly nominal who have become disillusioned through contact with professing Christians and congregations which failed dismally to live up to the message they professed. Then again, nominality it not a static state, but rather a fluctuating and selective condition. It is characterized by contradictory behaviour. The normally exemplary believer is not immune from inconsistencies and periods of spiritual lethargy, and the nominal Christian may produce flashes of deep spiritual insight and, during times of extreme adversity, demonstrate surprising resources of faith.

Just as in warfare confusion frequently reigns in the combat zone due to the ebb and flow of battle lines and local skirmishes, so the 'nominality zone' where church and world intermingle demonstrates similar characteristics. Within the nominality zone are people who are at the point abandoning the church or being ejected by the church. There are those who have become disorientated and are wandering around not knowing what to believe or where to go for help. There are those who have been deceived by the Enemy and are in the process of being enticed to the other side. There are those from the Enemy's side who became disillusioned and wanted to transfer over, but never quite made it. Lastly, there are those who have opted to take up permanent residence in the nominality zone in order to keep open their options. In reality, their position is the most dangerous and uncomfortable of all because they are liable to be fired on from both sides!

The descriptive terms 'nominal Christian' refers to all those who, for whatever reason, want to be known as Christians, even though they may have lost contact with the church, have serious doubts concerning beliefs basic to Christianity, be living lifestyles which are incompatible with the values of the Kingdom of God, or be failing to maintain an ongoing relationship with the Lord due to neglect of the means of grace which he has provided for our spiritual sustenance. At various stages of life people may find themselves wrestling with different sets of issues. Thus, the study of nominality inevitably entails working with confusion and contradictions. People cannot be pigeon-holed into neat categories. To use a medical analogy, 'nominality' describes an interacting combination of conditions rather than one 'disease' to be isolated for treatment.

Any assessment of nominality will also be influenced by one's theology of the church and understanding of saving grace. Those who regard the church as pastorally embracing the total community and representing it in a priestly capacity, are more tolerant of nominality. For them it is an inescapable fact of life rather than a problem to be energetically addressed. Whereas those who emphasize the concept of the gathered church tend to regard all non-attenders as in need of evangelization. Thus the missionary work of Protestants from conservative traditions is regarded as sect-like proselytism by the Roman Catholic hierarchies of Southern Europe, the Orthodox in Russia, or Lutherans in Scandinavia. From their perspective, they consider their non-active constituency, not as unbelievers in need of evangelizing, but as vulnerable Christians with a fragile faith, in need of pastoral care. This attitude is in marked contrast to freewheeling evangelists who regard them as people who are eternally lost and in urgent need of the Saviour!

In addition to all the above there is the problem of lack of data by which nominality can be studied and the impact of each of the elements measured and evaluated. With the able assistance of Peter Brierley, director of the Christian Research Association, I have undertaken a qualitative survey of nominality among a number of churches and their nominal fringe in the English-speaking world. Some of the preliminary findings of this limited study are incorporated in this volume and a summary included as an appendix.

With all its limitations, this study into the causes of nominality and suggestions for ways in which the churches might begin to respond is offered as a starter and stimulus to further research and reflection.

Eddie Gibbs
Fuller Theological Seminary,
Pasadena, California
July 1992

CHAPTER ONE

THE NOMINALITY PROBLEM DEFINED AND DESCRIBED

MANY CHURCHES AND ENTIRE denominations throughout the western world are experiencing numerical decline. In a number of instances the membership shrinkage is causing alarm due to its rapidity and persistence. At the local level dwindling congregations are fighting a rearguard action to postpone the closure of their churches. At the regional level ecclesiastical authorities struggle to maintain a visible presence in densely-populated areas by amalgamating parishes, closing redundant churches or joining forces with other struggling denominations. In the case of new urban locations, the developers may allocate only one site for the building of a worship centre. Such a planning policy forces the churches into ecumenical projects, which may involve different congregations sharing a common worship centre, or people of different traditions forming one worshipping congregation that may be enriched by the distinctive spiritual emphases represented by the constituent groups. Such joint ventures in ecclesiastical engineering do not appear to have stemmed the receding tide and some have argued that such policies have in fact contributed to it!

While the overall figures of church attendance may register decline in a nation or region, this shrinkage is not necessarily experienced by all the denominations located there. As one denomination declines, so another advances, or an independent church thrives. Furthermore, even within declining denominations there are almost invariably churches which are defying the overall trend by demonstrating that growth is possible.

If we enlarge our horizons to encompass the total churchgoing scene, it is evident that there are signs of hope and that we need to learn from growing churches. Where noteworthy numerical growth is taking place, these situations need to be analysed and the data interpreted.

This growth may be due in large measure to dissatisfied and disgruntled members abandoning their churches to worship elsewhere. If such is the case, then we must ask, 'If those attractive features had been present in their old churches, would they have remained, and would those churches have had sufficient impetus to attract new members?'

If, on the other hand, it can be demonstrated that these churches are growing largely through the attraction and incorporation of previously unchurched persons, we must ask, 'What are they offering which declining churches are not, and would the unchurched in other settings respond in the same way if the churches there were motivated and had the resources to respond in like manner?'

Then we must face the deeper question as to whether the methods used which have proved so successful in attracting people are themselves compatible with the good news of the Kingdom of God. We are not so much impressed by large numbers as by the transformation taking place in the lives of significant numbers of people.

If the great majority of those people joining the church are finding forgiveness in Christ, being supported by a community of believers, encouraged to explore the implications of their commitment to Christ in every aspect of their daily lives, and equipped for service, then the more people the better! That is the kind of church we can be confident God wants to grow. And we all need to learn from the models presented by such churches.

The purpose of this book is twofold. Firstly, it attempts to identify and examine the elements which contribute to the decline of the church. Why do people become irregular in their attendance? Why have so many transferred their local church and/or denominational allegiance? Why have formerly active church members dropped out altogether? Why do those who no longer attend still want to identify themselves as Christians, and those who have never attended call occasionally upon the services of the church to perform the 'rites of passage': baptisms, confirmations, weddings and funerals? What is the prognosis for the declining church in the short and long term? To what extent is the problem of church decline due to factors within the church itself and how far to the cultural milieu in which it finds itself? These are some of the questions which will occupy us in the following pages. Secondly, this book suggests some strategies to help the church confront more adequately the challenge of nominality within its own ranks and to win back the multitudes which have already voted with their feet by swelling the ranks of the lapsed and the notional 'believers'. Our discussion will also extend to reaching those who identify themselves as Christians without ever having been actively involved in a local church.

THE NOMINALITY SYNDROME

Most movements and organizations go through a life cycle if events are left to take their own course. And the Christian church as an institution is not automatically immune from this degenerative process. It may afflict not only local congregations but whole denominations. The movement goes forward on the vision of the founder and the commitment of those drawn around the pioneer. With the passing of the founder, the initial group inspire their successors by their first-hand testimony. The next generation is still in touch with the living tradition, but these people are now aged and dwindling in numbers. Also their memories may not be so reliable as they once were. The second and subsequent generations tend to be nurtured within the movement rather than converted into it from outside. Consequently, many take for granted the privileges of membership and some become fascinated by alternative life-styles advocated by people outside their community of faith. The movement which the founder launched degenerates into a machine and ends up as a monument.

This decline in level of commitment to the institution in terms of activities, relationships and values we term *nominality*. *Webster's Dictionary* defines 'nominal' as 'existing or being something in name or form only'. Thus for someone to be a nominal member of an organization signifies that the person is not actively involved. They may carry the title, but there is little or nothing of substance to back it up. Frequently, nominality is referred to as nominalism. However, the term 'nominalism' more properly refers to a medieval philosophical theory; therefore it would not be used for casual adherence to organizations or life-style inconsistencies.

In most organizations, nominality begins to emerge in the second generation and is likely to become endemic by the fourth generation. By this time the nominal person will either have given up all claims to membership or have been reactivated. The lifespan of an organization is between sixty and eighty years, by which time it will have reached the point of no return unless intervention strategies are in place. This time-span partly explains why Marxist societies crumbled in Eastern Europe more than seventy years after the Russian Revolution. As the majority of the population became nominally Marxist their nominality eventually turned into disillusionment and cynicism. They were then ready to experiment with other philosophical and economic alternatives. Nominality seldom lasts for more than four generations. It represents a transitional stage, not a permanent condition.

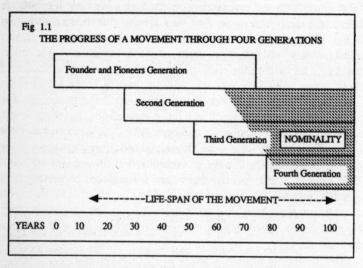

Fig 1.1
THE PROGRESS OF A MOVEMENT THROUGH FOUR GENERATIONS

Founder and Pioneers Generation

Second Generation

Third Generation   NOMINALITY

Fourth Generation

◄--------LIFE-SPAN OF THE MOVEMENT--------►

YEARS 0   10   20   30   40   50   60   70   80   90   100

Generational decline is evident in the history of Israel in the period following the Exodus from Egypt. As long as Joshua lived (110 years) 'the people of Israel served the Lord, and after his death they continued to do so as long as those leaders were alive who had seen for themselves everything that the Lord had done for Israel' (Josh 24:31; Judg 2:7 GNB). But the situation changed dramatically for the worse as the third generation came to adulthood. 'That whole generation also died, and the next generation forgot the Lord and what He had done for Israel.... Their fathers had obeyed the Lord's commands, but this new generation soon stopped doing so' (Judg 2:10,17 GNB).

DEFINING NOMINALITY

Nominality as a condition affecting institutions is more often described than defined. The most common way in which it is identified is in terms of declining attendance figures and level of involvement. Although this aspect of the problem is the one most easily measured, it does not contribute significantly to an understanding of the causes of the problem. The condition is complex both in relation to the symptoms and the causes. Therefore any definition must be comprehensive in order to embrace the various facets of nominality.

A working group of delegates to the Lausanne Congress held in Thailand in 1980 offered the following definition of nominality among protestant Christians.

> A nominal Protestant Christian is one who, within the Prot-
> estant tradition, would call himself a Christian, or be so
> regarded by others, but who has no authentic commitment
> to Christ based on personal faith. Such commitment
> involves a transforming personal relationship with Christ,
> characterized by such qualities as love, joy, peace, a desire
> to study the Bible, prayer, fellowship with other Christians,
> a determination to witness faithfully, a deep concern for
> God's will to be done on earth, and a living hope of heaven
> to come.[1]

The above definition demonstrates that nominality has to be defined in relationship to a norm. In terms of religious commitment what is normative will depend on the tenets of that religion. As far as Christianity is concerned, various traditions would emphasize different aspects. Some strands are more individualistic, while others emphasize corporate aspects. Some are more cognitive in their approach, while others or more experiential.

The Lausanne definition of nominality is written from an evangelical perspective which means that the need for a personal commitment to Christ is regarded as basic. The statement then defines what such commitment entails in terms of character formation, engaging in such religious activities as Bible reading and meditation, personal and corporate prayer, mutually beneficial interaction with other believers, and an insistence on the need to maintain a world awareness enlightened by an eschatological perspective.

Christians of traditions other than evangelical could identify with most, if not all, of that definition, although they might want to change the emphasis or make certain additions. It is significant that there is no mention of the sacraments, for example, which would be of special concern to Catholics, Lutherans and Episcopalians. Another omission in the definition is the contextual factors which contribute to the condition by encouraging double standards of belief and behaviour.

The value of the Lausanne definition is that it draws attention to the fact that nominality is concerned with more than lack of involvement with the worship and other activities of the local church. It challenges the person who may be familiar with the language of orthodoxy but is, or has become, a stranger to the inward realities of which that language speaks. On the one hand, there are those who continue to belong while they no longer believe; on the other, there are those who believe even though they cease to belong.

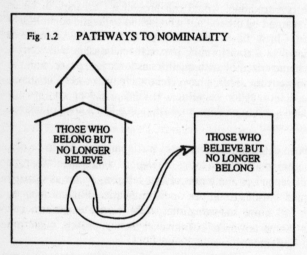

Fig. 1.2   PATHWAYS TO NOMINALITY

THOSE WHO BELONG BUT NO LONGER BELIEVE

THOSE WHO BELIEVE BUT NO LONGER BELONG

The Lausanne task group which studied nominality identified five types of nominal Christian which it categorized as follows:

1. Attends church regularly and worships devoutly, but who has no personal relationship with Jesus Christ.
2. Attends church regularly but for cultural reasons only.
3. Attends church only for major church festivals (Christmas, Easter etc.) and ceremonies (weddings, baptisms, funerals).

4. Hardly ever attends church but maintains a church relationship for reasons of security, emotional or family ties, or tradition.
5. Has no relationship to any specific church and never attends but yet considers himself a believer in God (in a traditional Christian sense).

This typology is helpful to the extent that it provides a classification identifying degrees of association with the local church, which is important when it comes to developing strategies for the re-evangelizing of the church's 'external constituencies'. Its limitation is in the narrowness with which nominality is depicted, which is not as comprehensive as the task group's definition. The value of this broader definition is that it raises issues which relate to the internal life of the church, and which must be addressed if the church is to embody more of the divine reality which it seeks to proclaim.

Care must be taken in assessing the reasons why people, who identify themselves as 'Christian' are not involved in a local church. Sometimes it is due to their refusal to take seriously the demands of Christian discipleship. At other times they may have left the church because they became either bored or disillusioned with institutionalized religion. A third possibility is that persons have come to faith outside a church context and have never been invited into the fellowship of a local church, or have not regarded organized religion as either meeting their needs or relating to their spiritual pilgrimage. David Barrett argues that

> Public declaration must therefore be taken seriously when endeavouring to survey the extent of Christianity. This definition covers many categories of Christian, including large numbers of groups and individuals who, while striving to follow Christ and being indisputably Christian, nevertheless refuse to identify themselves with any existing organized Christian church or denominations.[2]

THE CHURCH IN RELATION TO ITS SOCIAL CONTEXT

Churches can be categorized in one of two ways. They are either churches which people are 'born into' (*Gemeinschaft*) or churches which an individual chooses to join (*Gesellschaft*). The distinction was first made by Ferdinand Tonnes in relation to the stages of social evolution from the earlier communal, family-based, 'natural' *Gemeinschaft* society to the emerging individualized, contractual, 'mechanical' society of the

Gesellschaft.[3] The two forms of church correspond in their internal dynamic and relationship to the wider society. *Gemeinschaft* churches will be strongest in stable, homogeneous communities, whereas *Gesellschaft* churches will show greater growth potential in growing, heterogeneous societies. When churches which have traditionally operated on *Gemeinschaft* principles are transferred to areas where they lack their traditional support base, they have to adopt *Gesellschaft* operational characteristics if they are to establish themselves. We shall return to this perceptive distinction when we consider the influences of urbanization and secularization on the life of the church.

Sometimes the distinction is expressed in terms of 'church' versus 'sect'. The former identifies with the social context, whereas the latter stands over against society. The former maintain their numbers primarily by the process of socialization, while the latter do so predominantly by conversion. The former rely on attraction, expecting people to take the initiative in coming to them, while the latter take initiatives to reach people where they are, or at least invest effort and money in advertising their presence and communicating the message that they have something to offer which is significantly different from more traditional churches.

Smaller churches, especially those which represent recent movements with a concern for spiritual renewal, imagine that the nominality problem is largely confined to the traditional denominations which have gained the reputation of being liberal in their theology and left-wing in their social agenda. Such an assessment fails to recognize the fact that any movement, as it grows and becomes institutionalized, is prone to gather a following which does not match the enthusiasm and radical commitment of the pioneers. One only has to look at the founder and pioneers of Methodism, or trace the history of the early Pentecostal movement, to appreciate the personal sacrifice and extreme measures employed by these intrepid individuals. With the passage of time the movement became more sedate and respectable to the point of being embarrassed by its humble origins and disavowing aspect of the early 'extremism' which characterized the movement.

Whenever a movement grows in size and social influence to the point where its penetration, prestige and political 'clout' are unavoidably acknowledged by the community, then there is an increasing tendency for that movement to grow more by socialization than by conversion, whatever its theology of incorporation. In the minds of most North

American evangelicals, 'nominality' is primarily associated with the state churches of Europe: folk Catholicism in Italy, Spain and France, folk Lutheranism in Scandinavia, the Church of England with its invisible ranks of the 'church mystical' vastly outnumbering those dwindling survivors who consititute the 'church militant', and the Presbyterians who, despite their shrinking numbers, still proudly bear the title 'Church of Scotland'.

The situation in those countries does give cause for alarm, when only about 10 per cent of Catholics attend mass on any given Sunday, and between 3 and 5 per cent of Lutherans are in church. But North America has not remained immune from the nominality affliction. Since the mid 1960s most mainline denominations in the United States have experienced a serious fall-off in terms of both membership and attendance. Between 1985 and 1987 the United Methodists declined in membership by 18 per cent, the United Church of Christ by 20 per cent, the Presbyterians by 25 per cent, the Episcopalians by 28 per cent and the Christian Church (formerly Disciples of Christ) by 43 per cent.[4] Such has been the strength of the WASP (White Anglo-Saxon Protestant) cultural influence, at least until the early 1960s, that religious assent remained surprisingly orthodox. However, the warning signs are that the knowledge base of traditional Christian beliefs is alarmingly vague and narrow, and for 90 per cent of churchgoers belief is not translated into distinctive Christian values and life-style. Many professing Christians live lives which are indistinguishable from those persons who are not active churchgoers or who profess no Christian commitment. This state of affairs gives some substance to the cynical remark that 'Religion in North America is three thousand miles wide and three inches deep'. In a later chapter we will examine this assessment in greater depth when we consider the findings of religious surveys conducted in the US.

At the same time that nearly all the largest mainline churches in North America were in decline, others were experiencing significant growth. The Assemblies of God grew by 278 per cent to 2.2 million, Seventh-day Adventists by 85 per cent to 0.7 million, Southern Baptist Convention by 37 per cent to 14.7 million, and Roman Catholics by 16 per cent to 53.5 million. However, in the case of Roman Catholicism growth is mainly due to immigration from Central and South America. Furthermore, an increase in membership does not always translate into a corresponding increase in church attendance and involvement in the other activities of the church.

Irrespective of the theological stance of the church, in those regions where one church occupies a dominant position it has to battle with nominality. This is true for Lutherans in Minnesota or the Dakotas, Southern Baptists in Texas and Alabama, United Methodists in Tennessee, Mennonites in rural Pennsylvania, Catholics in Chicago or greater Los Angeles, Church of God Cleveland in Cleveland, Tennessee, or Mormons in Utah. When an individual lives in a community in which extended family members, together with a high percentage of neighbours, friends and work associates, are all associated with churches with the same denominational label, then there is a powerful social pressure for that person to belong to the church as part of his or her social identity. The candidate for membership will learn to verbalize the required formulas for acceptance into membership, but the genuineness and depth of that profession is difficult to assess precisely because of the strength of the social affirmation.

RELIGIOUS REWARDS AND COMPENSATORS

Religious sociologists Rodney Stark and William Bainbridge provide helpful insights into the various factors which motivate persons in their religious commitment. They distinguish between 'rewards' and 'compensators'. Rewards are tangible benefits, while compensators are intangible, at least in the short term.

A compensator is the belief that a reward will be obtained in the distant future or in some other context which cannot be immediately verified.[5] Compensators fall along a continuum from the specific to the general. This distinction is vital in differentiating between religion and magic. Magic deals in relatively specific compensators; religion always includes the most general compensators. Stark and Bainbridge argue that different social classes tend to get different things from religion. Privileged people will largely succeed in obtaining scarce rewards for themselves without the aid of religion. However, religion may serve their purposes by providing a social context in which to make contacts and to reinforce their position in a society in which the church plays an important civic role.

Those who are normally denied access to the privileged people who can distribute rewards and benefits to deserving cases may identify with churches in which such individuals are to be found. Otherwise, they will form their own churches which will emphasize other-worldly compensators over against tangible rewards. Eventually, even these churches may be able to add material benefits in terms of job opportunities and social standing within the ranks of the marginalized segments of the Christian community.

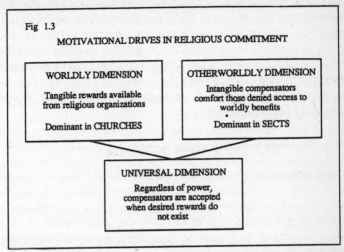

Fig 1.3

MOTIVATIONAL DRIVES IN RELIGIOUS COMMITMENT

WORLDLY DIMENSION

Tangible rewards available from religious organizations

Dominant in CHURCHES

OTHERWORLDLY DIMENSION

Intangible compensators comfort those denied access to worldly benefits

Dominant in SECTS

UNIVERSAL DIMENSION

Regardless of power, compensators are accepted when desired rewards do not exist

Pressed to an extreme, such an argument leads easily into scepticism regarding the motives of some people seeking church affiliation and membership. It does provide a needed reminder that people join churches for a variety of motives, both selfish and altruistic, material and social as well as spiritual. However, we must also keep in mind that the grace of God extends to those who initially come from less than the best of motives. The key factor is not the initial motive, but the quality of the care which is extended to the visitor and seeker.

At the deeper (or higher) level, wealth and prestige in the community, or lack of such social privileges, are irrelevant when facing guilt, loneliness, suffering, terminal illness and the greatest of all levellers, death.

When the news of the death of a certain wealthy person reached a group of his friends, one of them enquired, 'How much did he leave?' Another replied with one word which created shock waves among the mourners, 'Everything.'

Stark and Bainbridge concede that 'neither rich nor poor can gain eternal life in this world. All have equal need for compensators for this desire.'[6] From a Christian standpoint we might add the corrective that eternal life is not simply an intangible compensator, but is bestowed by

Jesus as an immediate gift, at least in provisional form; for whoever believes in the Son has eternal life (Jn 3:36, see also 5:24; 6:47; 1 Jn 5:11-13).

From the standpoint of our study of the emergence and spread of nominality, the importance of Stark and Bainbridge's argument is to highlight the fact that when the church is in a position to offer tangible rewards in the form of enhanced social position, employment opportunities, or economic gains, then there is the tendency to attract nominal adherents. The same is true when the prospect of obtaining intangible compensators is offered with the minimum of prerequisites or ongoing involvement and accountability.

THE DIMENSIONS OF NOMINALITY

Nominality describes not only a final state but also the process leading to that condition. People slide towards nominality by a variety of paths. We need, therefore, to identify the essential dimensions of 'religiousness' in order to identify where areas of weakness are located which, if unaddressed, will lead to increasing nominality. Religious sociologists Rodney Stark and Charles Y. Glock have suggested five dimensions through which 'religiousness' ought to be manifested.[7] These dimensions provide a helpful paradigm by which nominality can be monitored, embracing belief, practice, knowledge, experience and consequences.

The strength of religious convictions
This is the *belief* dimension comprising 'expectations that the religious person will hold a certain theological outlook, that he will acknowledge the truth of the tenets of the religion'. In terms of historic Christianity, there are a basic set of beliefs which are expressed in the *kerugma* (proclamation) and *didache* (teaching) of the early Church. These may be summarized as follows: the deity of Christ, his virgin birth, his ability to perform miracles and forgive sins, his substitutionary death, his resurrection from the dead, his ascension into heaven, the establishing of his kingdom here on earth in provisional form, his personal return to earth to consummate his kingdom, the resurrection of the body, the existence of heaven and hell, the giving of the Holy Spirit to his followers and the divine inspiration of the Scriptures.

Rather than speaking simply about religious beliefs, I have sharpened the category by referring to 'strength of religious convictions'. I have done this in order to draw attention to the fact that when adherents of a religion live within a social context in which such beliefs are assumed, then considerable social pressure is exerted to conform to that belief system. Where the church exerts a social influence, even people who are not church attenders are likely to remain surprisingly orthodox in their religious beliefs. Such is the case in North America, where Gallup Surveys indicate that a high percentage of the population as a whole remains loyal to traditional Christian teaching. Ninety-four per cent of the population believe in God or a Universal Spirit (1986), 86 per cent believe Jesus Christ is God (1991 Youth Survey), 65 per cent believe in life after death (1981), 71 per cent believe in heaven, while only 60 per cent believe in hell (1980).[8] When the pollsters go on to question how beliefs influence life it becomes clear that for many people 'belief' is little more than religious assent. They give conventional answers because they have never stopped to consider the implications of those stated beliefs for their manner of life. There is a disturbing gap between belief and personal commitment to those beliefs. People are vulnerable to social pressure not only to affirm belief but also to reject belief when a negative change in the social climate towards religion occurs.

Those same Gallup Polls also ask people whether they think religion is gaining or losing influence on American life. From a high of 69 per cent in 1957, opinion slumped to a low of 14 per cent in 1969 and 1970, followed by a temporary recovery to 48 per cent in 1985, then dropping again to 36 per cent in 1991. In answer to a related question, 'Can religion answer today's problems?', 81 per cent answered in the affirmative in 1957, but this dropped to 59 per cent in 1991. In terms of the importance of religion for daily living, 75 per cent said 'very important', in 1952, and 56 per cent in 1991. These three questions indicate that religion is playing a declining social role, which means that poorly founded and tenuously held beliefs are likely to be abandoned by a society which increasingly marginalizes and challenges the tenets of historical Christianity.

One further point needs to be made regarding the orthodoxy and strength of religious beliefs. These will vary somewhat according to the theological tradition of the church in question. Some denominations are more conservative and require a firm faith commitment to a body of doctrine, while others are more liberal and comprehensive in their approach. In the case of the latter, 'strong religious commitment' is more likely to be expressed in terms of commitment to ethical positions and social concerns rather than to traditional doctrines. Nominality has to be defined in regard to a normative body of beliefs within any given tradition. What is considered normative from the perspective of one tradition may be judged as nominal according to the criteria of another tradition! Whatever position is taken along the theological conservative/ liberal axis, beliefs must be clearly thought through in order to be promoted and defended in a societal context which increasingly regards religiously based beliefs as largely irrelevant.

The knowledge base of religious opinions and beliefs

'The Knowledge dimensions refers to the expectation that religious persons will possess some minimum of information about the basic tenets of their faith and its rites, scriptures and traditions.'[9] As we have already indicated, religious beliefs can be maintained on a seriously inadequate knowledge base so long as society provides adequate affirmation. The Gallup Poll surveys periodically ask three simple questions which reveal people's knowledge. They are: Who delivered the Sermon on the Mount? What are the names of the four Gospels? And where was Jesus born? In 1982, 42 per cent of the sample said that Jesus preached the Sermon on the Mount, 46 per cent could name all four gospels, and 70 per cent could name the town where Jesus was born. My own nominality survey conducted in 1991 showed that only 59 per cent of the sample knew who preached the Sermon on the Mount, only 49 per cent knew the meaning of 'Golgotha', and 55 per cent knew the occupation of Zacchaeus. It would appear also that many people who claim they believe in the divine inspiration of the Bible do not consider that belief significant enough to make them want to read it regularly in order to understand its teaching and apply it to their daily lives.

In terms of adherence to the tenets of historical Christianity, there should be a close correspondence between knowledge and belief. Stark and Glock indicate that this is not always the case:

> The knowledge and belief dimensions are clearly related since knowledge of a belief is a necessary precondition for its acceptance. However, belief need not follow from knowledge, nor does all religious knowledge bear on belief. Furthermore, a man may hold a belief without really understanding it; that is, belief can exist on the basis of very little knowledge.[10]

When surveying the general public, questions must be kept basic.

However, when the sample is restricted to churchgoers questions can be more wide-ranging. Fifty-five per cent of Protestants claimed that, if they were asked, they thought they could recite the Ten Commandments. When asked to identify the Old Testament prophets from a list of Elijah, Deuteronomy, Jeremiah, Paul, Leviticus and Ezekiel, 43 per cent of Protestants gave the correct answer for all six, while only 22 per cent of Catholics got this high score.[11]

Level of commitment to a local church

This is one aspect of what Stark and Glock refer to as 'practice', namely attendance at worship services, taking communion, etc. For a more accurate study of nominality, I have graded the practice in terms of regular active attenders, regular passive attenders, occasional attenders, the lapsed, the nominal and the notional.

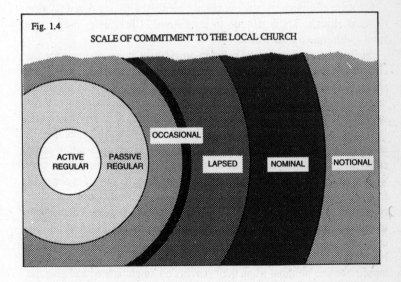

Fig. 1.4

SCALE OF COMMITMENT TO THE LOCAL CHURCH

ACTIVE REGULAR   PASSIVE REGULAR   OCCASIONAL   LAPSED   NOMINAL   NOTIONAL

Each of these terms is more precisely defined as follows:

Active Regular Attenders—People who attend worship services more than once a month, and do a job to contribute to the life of the local church.

Passive Regular Attenders—People who attend worship services more than once a month and do not do a job to contribute to the life of the local church.

Occasional Attenders—People who attend once a month or less, or only for major festivals or special services.

Lapsed Members/Attenders—People who at one time were either regular or occasional attenders, but who have ceased to attend for one year or more, and have not transferred to another church.

Nominal—This is a more restrictive use of the term 'nominal' to indicate those persons who would identify with a particular denomination or regard a local church as their church even though they have never been regular or even occasional attenders. Their association may be through family links, cultural expectations, involvement in their childhood, or restricted to the rites of passage (baptism, confirmation, marriage, burial).

Notional—People who identify themselves as 'Christian' but have never been churchgoers, and would not identify with any denomination or local church. Their attitude to institutional Christianity may range from indifference to hostility.

Such a scale is of practical value in providing a measuring tool for the church's attenders in comparison to the 'external constituency', or 'no-shows', made up of the Lapsed and Nominal. Those churches which are large and influential in society may have a considerable 'external constituency' to which they still have access and which they desire to reactivate.

These categories also serve as a reminder that nominality, defined in terms of degrees of association with the local church, is not a static condition. There may be a tidal flow either in or out. Some people who were once active regular attenders become passive out of a sense of frustration and futility, or because they have been excluded, or their commitment has lessened for some other personal reason. People who have been passive regular attenders become occasional through conflicting interests and reordered priorities. Occasionals become lapsed through boredom, personality conflicts or burn-out, and the children of the lapsed become nominal when their parents no longer attend and give the impression that churchgoing is something which you grow out of at adolescence.

If a norm is established that church membership includes regular worship and active involvement in group life, then the effectiveness of the church's ministry to achieve that end can be measured on an annual basis. This is best done in terms of percentages.

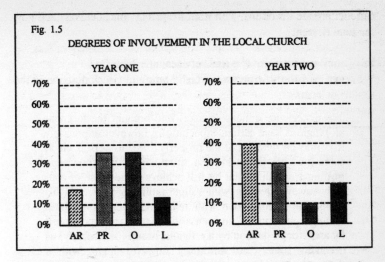

Fig. 1.5
DEGREES OF INVOLVEMENT IN THE LOCAL CHURCH

AR = Active Regular, PR = Passive Regular, O = Occasional and L = Lapsed.
Ensure that the four columns add up to 100 per cent. If the lapsed figure is
difficult to obtain, then work with the first three categories as your 100 per cent
base and distribute accordingly.

Repeating the exercise each year provides a ministry 'audit' to discover
how effective you were in attempting to incorporate the whole congregation in active involvement. One limitation in the measure is that it does
not tell you how individuals move from one category of involvement to
another. This would have to be registered in a file kept on each member/
attender, and the numbers correlated at the end of each year.

Personal acts of devotion
Devotional acts performed in private or within an intimate circle of
family and friends may include prayer, Bible reading, hymn singing or
other worshipful activities. The prominence given to such acts will
depend partly on the culture and theological tradition of the church, for
some are more corporate in their religious expression while others are
more individualistic. In some liturgical traditions, worship is more formal and clergy-dominated than in others. Yet every tradition makes
room for personal devotions, while most will encourage such practices.
    If such practices are regarded as essential or helpful, then there needs
to be some investigation to discover how many of the congregation

conduct private devotions, with what frequency, for how long, and how the time is spent.

Frequency and intensity of a sense of encounter with God

We come now to the *experience* which Stark and Glock describe in the following terms.

> The experience dimension takes into account the fact that all religions have certain expectations, however imprecisely they may be stated, that the properly religious person will at some time or other achieve a direct, subjective knowledge of ultimate reality; that he will achieve some sense of contact, however fleeting, with a supernatural agency....[T]his dimension is concerned with religious experiences, those feelings, perceptions, and sensations which are experienced by an actor or defined by a religious group (or a society) as involving some communication, however slight, with a divine essence, that is, with God, with ultimate reality, with transcendental authority.[12]

For a number of reasons this is the most difficult dimension to measure and evaluate. The first, and most obvious, consideration is its subjective nature. People may be self-deceived, their experience being no more than a self-induced emotional state. Secondly, their 'transcendental' experience may be a Satanic deception or demonic counterfeit. Thirdly, experiences vary enormously in kind. Attempts have been made to codify them in terms of: a non-involved awareness of a divine presence, a mutual acknowledgement, an ecstatic experience of bonding and loving embrace, a revelatory experience, a chastening, or a salvation experience. However the experience is described, it involves a measure of direct encounter with a divine presence.

Once again we encounter differing emphases according to theological tradition and cultural context. Some denominations, are more cerebral in their approach and suspicious of basing too much on the emotions, while other churches emphasize experience over knowledge. Mystics can be found within most traditions.

Within the North American Protestant culture there has been a widespread born-again movement which has emphasized the need for a direct encounter with God, resulting in self-surrender, the reception of forgiveness and the gift of the Holy Spirit. Some groups focus attention on the objective grounds for such an experience and play down the subjective, experiential aspects, while others emphasize the inner witness of the Holy Spirit to bring a subjective experience of forgiveness, a sense of wonder and unworthiness at being adopted into the family of God and, in some cases, the evidence of deliverance and the gift of heavenly languages.

A faith which influences the way people live their daily lives

This is the *consequence* dimension, which identifies the effects of religious belief, practice, experience and knowledge in a person's daily life.[13] The New Testament leaves no doubt that belief in the gospel has profound and far-reaching implications for living. Jesus said that the true believers will be known by the fruit of their lives. In the first instance fruit refers to aspects of character which are to take on a Christ-likeness. The fruit of the Spirit listed by Paul in Galatians 5:19-20 together provide a character portrait of Christ himself. The Christian disciple is to conform to that image. Character formation leads to life-style transformation, in terms of personal and social values and norms. The gospel's concern with the consequences of discipleship is not confined to personal morality, but extends to corporate and social standards as represented by the emphasis in the teaching of Jesus on the kingdom.

The consequences include concern for truth, justice, forgiveness and mercy. The teaching of Jesus regarding the kingdom places great emphasis on these qualities. They are characteristic of the kingdom. His kingdom must be sought in preference to material gain and personal power. In confronting the issues of contemporary society, general principles need to be translated into specific concerns: safeguarding the sanctity of life; upholding the intrinsic value of the individual; making oneself responsible and accountable to society; treating and preventing substance abuse; ensuring a socially responsible mass-media; providing equal opportunities to develop intellectual potential; ensuring access to self-fulfilling and productive employment; upholding ethical business practices and truth in advertising; racial tolerance; scaling down military expenditure in order to release urgently needed resources to combat hunger and disease and provide technical assistance to underdeveloped countries; commitment to the family of nations rather than an exclusive nationalism, etc. These are all kingdom concerns, and they need to be addressed by the body of Christ. This does not imply that every believer has to be equally informed and personally involved on every issue, which would be beyond the time and resources of any one person. Rather, groups within the church should be involved in these issues, providing information to the church as a whole, and when occasion demands calling on all the members to make public their commitment.

When believers are compared with non-believers in relation to ethical standards, one would expect to find that believers hold to higher standards than society as a whole. Gallup Surveys revealed that there was no statistical difference between churchgoers and non-churchgoers in relation to racial prejudice and materialism. It was only when the one in ten 'highly spiritually committed' were compared with the broader sample that significant differences began to show up. The most religious are much more likely than the least religious to believe sex between single people is morally wrong (74 per cent versus 11 per cent). The most religious are more likely to find pornographic movies immoral (87 per cent versus 46 per cent). The most religious are much more inclined to believe smoking marijuana is morally wrong (87 per cent versus 30 per cent). The most religious are more adamant in considering homosexuality morally wrong (87 per cent versus 54 per cent).[14]

Fig 1.6   NOMINALITY RATING

	very weak ←--------→ very strong
BELIEF	1 2 3 4 5 6 7 8 9 10
KNOWLEDGE	1 2 3 4 5 6 7 8 9 10
PRACTICE: PUBLIC WORSHIP	1 2 3 4 5 6 7 8 9 10
PRIVATE DEVOTION	1 2 3 4 5 6 7 8 9 10
EXPERIENCE	1 2 3 4 5 6 7 8 9 10
CONSEQUENCE	1 2 3 4 5 6 7 8 9 10

Many pollsters have attempted to produce a nominality scale, using some or all of the dimensions of religiosity mentioned above. The problem with this approach is that there is no necessary correlation between the various dimensions, so that the score given to any individual is of little practical value. The many factors involved make measurement extremely difficult. There is, in addition, the element of subjectivity, and also the possibility of a bias due to respondents giving the expected answers in a cultural context which affirms religious values. Despite these limitations, it is still helpful to assess the nature and extent of nominality in a given context, and the 'bias' factor can be taken into consideration when evaluating the results. The 'Nominality Rating' shown on page 30 provides a subjective self-assessment of each of the dimensions. It can be utilized on an individual basis or applied to a congregation.

In the course of this chapter we have endeavoured to indicate the extent and complexity of the nominality problem. In the two chapters which follow, we will first overview the biblical material which relates to the issue of nominality and then describe the principal causes of nominality which arise in the contemporary social context.

NOTES

1. 'Christian Witness to Nominal Christians Among Protestant Christians', *Thailand Report* (Lausanne Occasional Papers No. 23; 1980), p 5.
2. David Barrett, *World Christian Encyclopedia* (Oxford University Press; Nairobi, 1982), p 47.
3. See Krishan Kumar, *Prophecy and Progress—The Sociology of Industrial Society* (Penguin Books; London, 1978, 1986), pp 59, 69, 70.
4. Source: National Council of Churches. The membership in 1987 of the above-mentioned bodies was: United Methodists 9.1 million, United Church of Christ 1.7, Presbyterian 3.0, Episcopalian 2.5, and Christian Church 1.1 million.
5. Rodney Stark and William Sims Bainbridge, *The Future of Religion: Secularization and Renewal and Cult Formation* (University of California Press; Berkeley, 1985), p 6.
6. Stark and Bainbridge, *The Future of Religion*, p 11.
7. Rodney Stark and Charles Y. Glock, *American Piety: The Nature of Religious Commitment* (University of California Press; Berkeley, 1968).
8. *Religion in America—1992-3* (The Princeton Religion Research Centre, Princeton, NJ, 1993).
9. Stark and Glock, *American Piety*, p 16.
10. Ibid.
11. Ibid, pp 144, 156.
12. Ibid, p 15.
13. Ibid, p 16.
14. R&F Inc., 1981, p 23. Quoted in Stark and Glock, *American Piety*.

CHAPTER TWO

BIBLICAL INSIGHTS INTO THE NOMINALITY PROBLEM

A S HAS ALREADY BEEN noted in passing, there is nothing in Scripture that exactly corresponds to the nominality problem experienced by the contemporary church. Under the Old Testament dispensation, Israel lived as a theocracy, with religious requirements codified as an essential aspect of national law, much as is the case in Islamic nations today. Also, we have to remember that the Holy Spirit had not yet been given in the widespread and permanent manner possible following Our Lord's ascension and the Pentecostal outpouring. Nevertheless, we can learn from the constant warnings given by God to his people against persistent disobedience to his commands, against their faith being subverted by allegiance to false gods, and against misplaced trust in the power of other nations to save them from military conquest.

The period covered by the four Gospels represents a transition period in the unfolding of salvation history. Still the Spirit has not yet been given. But the power of the presence of the kingdom, realized in the ministry of Jesus and in the representatives whom he sent out in his name, was very much in evidence. Yet the frequent occurrences of miracles at this time were not of themselves sufficient to safeguard against religious complacency or outright rejection of the message of Jesus and his claims to be the Son of God. Although the disciples witnessed so much and experienced the power of God in their ministry performed in the name of Jesus, they were not thereby rendered immune from subsequent denial and desertion of the Lord. As we shall see, Jesus recognized their vulnerability and gave them a great deal of teaching to forewarn them of the temptations and opposition which they would have to face.

In the Epistles also we find frequent warnings against departing from the truth of the gospel or failing to live up to its moral standards. These letters were, for the most part, written within a few years of the founding of the churches addressed—in the case of the Thessalonian correspondence, within months of the birth of the church in that city. These admonitions tell us that temptations to be diverted, drift away, or become openly disobedient are ever-present problems. Most of the letters pre-date the Gospels, so that the latter's emphasis on the dangers of nominality may reflect the experience of the early church, which stimulated the authors' memory of the teaching of Jesus as they became aware of its application to contemporary situations.

In this chapter we will explore the insights provided by both Old and New Testaments and apply their lessons to the church today. Such insights provide sensitive indicators by which symptoms can be detected early on and preventive measures taken. As with many physical ailments, the longer a spiritual malady remains undetected and neglected the harder it is to treat.

NOMINALITY IN THE OLD TESTAMENT— A CHRONIC PROBLEM

The Old Testament record makes a clear distinction between the *faithless majority* which is deserving of the judgement of God (Is 10:20-22; Rom 9:27) and the *faithful remnant* which represents God's guarantee for the future.[1]

This remnant is not depicted as a beleaguered small group, merely battling for survival, but as a seed which will eventually flourish. The remnant which returns from the exile eventually will become numerous, prosperous and productive (Jer 23:3). They will take root below and bear fruit above (2 Kings 19:30, 31; see also Is 4:2,3). Micah also envisions a time when the scattered remnant will be brought together as a flock so that 'the place will throng with people' (Mic 2:12 NIV).

Bearing such scriptures in mind, we must at the outset beware of a *remnant theology* which justifies and even idealizes smallness to the extent of accepting widespread nominality as inevitable and irreversible.

Rather, remnant teaching causes us to take seriously the Old Testament warnings about nominality, recognizing that it is a constant danger

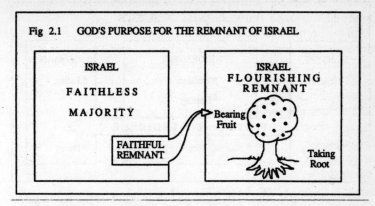

Fig 2.1 GOD'S PURPOSE FOR THE REMNANT OF ISRAEL

and that continuing vigilance is required. Sometimes God uses drastic measures to deal with it, but he never totally abandons his people. In this lesson we shall identify a variety of causes of nominality among the people of God in Old Testament times.

Desiring to return to the security of servitude
Having been delivered from Egypt by God's miraculous interventions, the children of Israel soon find themselves facing uncertainty, danger and hardship in the Sinai desert. After their miraculous Passover deliverance from Egypt and just three days after their journey through the parted waters of the Red Sea, the people begin to grumble (Ex 15:24). They made unfavourable comparisons by emphasizing the good aspects of their time in Egypt, especially the rich and varied diet they had enjoyed there! (Ex 16:3-12; Num 11:4-15.) They continued to give voice to their discontent, blaming Moses for the hardships which they were enduring (Ex 17:1-7). Eventually their disillusionment resulted in other individuals emerging to challenge his leadership and in the people themselves demanding a leader to take them back to Egypt (Num 12:1,2; 14:1-4,29; 16:ll,41).

In addition to putting the Lord to the test by doubting his material provision to sustain them in a desolate wilderness at the outset of their journey, the children of Israel later balked at the possibility of his military power enabling them to take the fortified cities in the Promised Land. Ten of the twelve men of the reconnaissance party sent to spy out the Promised Land were of the opinion that the people who occupied the

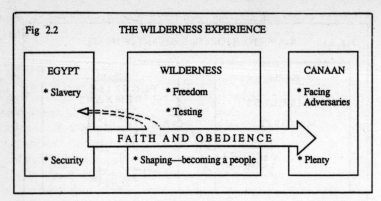

Fig 2.2 THE WILDERNESS EXPERIENCE

EGYPT	WILDERNESS	CANAAN
* Slavery	* Freedom	* Facing Adversaries
	* Testing	
FAITH AND OBEDIENCE		
* Security	* Shaping—becoming a people	* Plenty

land were too powerful to be dislodged (Num 13:28-33). Their negative attitude so demoralised the people that their only desire was to find an alternative leader and retrace their steps to Egypt (Num 14:1-4,29).

The consequences of the people's persistent rebellion were dire indeed. In response to Moses' pleas, Israel was spared from destruction in the wilderness. However, they were disqualified from entering the Promised Land. An entire generation would pass away before the order was given to cross the Jordan.

> The Lord replied (to Moses), 'I have forgiven them, as you asked. Nevertheless, as surely as I live and as surely as the glory of the Lord fills the whole earth, not one of the men who saw my glory and the miraculous signs I performed in Egypt and in the desert but who disobeyed me and tested me ten times—not one of them will ever see the land I promised on oath to their forefathers. No one who has treated me with contempt will ever see it.' (Num 14:20-23).

The temptation to rethink one's position and to dig up in unbelief what one has sown in faith may be termed a *post-decision evaluation*. In response to this negative tendency God provided strong leadership to bring his people through the wilderness and into the Promised Land. First Moses and then Joshua challenged the people to believe in God's adequacy, whatever the circumstances.

The Christian life also entails a pilgrimage of life-long duration which will include 'wilderness' experiences. Jesus himself entered into the wilderness of Judea immediately following his baptism and the anointing of the Spirit. It was the Spirit himself who led Jesus into the wilderness where he was tempted by the devil (Mk 1:9-12). Saul did not become Paul the Apostle until after his time in the wilderness of the Transjordan (Gal 1:17).

Teaching which represents the Christian life as problem-free, offering painless, instant fulfilment and guaranteed prosperity, creates the pre-conditions for later disillusionment and regression. On the material level Egypt had more to offer than the wilderness. The great difference was that in Egypt the people of Israel were slaves, whereas in the wilderness they were free. But freedom entails accepting risks and shouldering responsibilities. A life of pilgrimage means the absence of familiar landmarks because we have not passed that way before. It also means the acceptance of uncertainties, the essence of the life of faith for which the wilderness serves as a training ground.

Transference from the first to the second and subsequent generations

The nominality problem is accentuated when the second generation becomes the dominant group. Unlike the pioneers, who experienced the alienation, hardships and deliverances, the second generation has been nurtured all along within the religious community. This second genera-tion learns of God's mighty acts through receiving the tradition rather than from firsthand experience (Josh 24:31; Judg 2:7,10,17). For them, life cannot be divided into a 'before' and 'after' with the frontier-crossing moment of a dramatic conversion experience.

It is evident from Scripture that the frequency of the occurrence of miraculous events is associated with decisive periods in the unfolding of salvation history. The absence of miraculous interventions does not necessarily indicate lack of faith at that moment or a more general spiritual decline. God does not have to announce his presence by regu-larly interrupting the course of nature! However, it is quite another matter when God ceases to address his people. Apparently there were times during the history of Israel when 'the word of the Lord was rare; there was no open vision' (1 Sam 3:1; cf Ps 74:9; Lam 2:9; Ezek 7:26). Usually, times of famine of hearing the word of God were the conse-quence of the defiance of God's people (Amos 8:11).

Religion becomes secondhand when a generation arises which refuses to hear from God or to whom God has become silent. In extreme cases the Lord appears to abandon his people. Israel felt 'widowed' (Is 54:4) during its exile in Babylon. But the Lord comes to reassure his people that he was only 'playing dead'. He had simply abandoned them for a time so that they would come to realise how much they missed him, and their need of him (Is 54:6-7). The church throughout its two thousand year history has gone through cycles of decline, realization, renewal, and restoration. The important issue is to recognize that as soon as the second generation becomes the dominant group in the life of the church, nominality becomes a growing problem, unless that generation has its own authentic experience of God.

Yielding to social pressure to follow the ways of the peoples among whom they lived

The land which the Lord gave Israel to possess was not unoccupied territory. It had been heavily populated for centuries by a variety of tribes (Num 13:28,29; Deut 7:1). Thus, from the outset, the people of God had to learn to live in close proximity with peoples who did not share their religious faith or their moral standards. They had to face two principal temptations.

(a) *The temptation to adopt their life style*. In anthropological terms this is known as *enculturation*. Israel's occupation of Canaan after years of slavery in Egypt and a generation-long period of wandering through the Sinai wilderness represented ways of life in marked contrast to their settled existence in their newly occupied territory. It is clear that the conquest of the land during the campaigns led by Joshua did not completely drive out the Canaanite tribes. The question then became, 'Who would influence whom?' Intermarriage presented a particular problem and it inevitably led to syncretism (Josh 23:11-13; Deut 7:3,4; Ezra 9:2; Neh 13:23-27; Mal 2:10ff). Idolatrous worship, child sacrifices and divination all found their way into Israelite society despite the Lord's constant warnings against such practices (Deut 18:9ff; 2 Kings 17:15; 21:2; 2 Chron 36:14; Jer 10:2). Failure to respond to the Lord's warnings of national calamity eventually brought about the downfall of first the Northern and then the Southern Kingdoms. These defeats were a direct consequence of Israel's having denied its calling to live a separate and distinctive life-style (Lev 20:24,26).

In the previous chapter we encountered this issue in regard to churches which exist in comfortable conformity with the broader society, in contrast to those religious groups which, like sects, stand out against the surrounding culture. We will consider the relationship of church and society in a more comprehensive manner when we address the issue of secularization. At this stage it will suffice to say that when society exerts a greater influence on the church than its own distinctive message exerts on its members—a message centred on the gospel of the kingdom and the lordship of Christ—then the conditions are set for the spread of nominality.

(b) *The temptation to match their power through authoritarian, self-promoting leadership.* Following the breakdown of the loose tribal federation, known technically as the amphictionic league, which was the form of government during the period of the Judges, Israel hankered after a king to weld together the tribes on a firmer and more permanent basis. There was some justification for their request, because greater cohesion was becoming increasingly necessary in order to maintain their position in the face of threats from powerful enemies. A king would strengthen their national security by establishing policies and leading the army in battle. In addition the people were concerned to know who would succeed Moses in exercising prophetic leadership throughout the nation, especially as his sons had proved themselves unworthy through their misconduct.

But Israel's model of kingship is that of the surrounding Canaanite tribes and Samuel recognizes the danger to Israel if it modelled its concept of kingship on the dictatorial and self-indulgent styles of leadership which prevailed among those peoples. God, therefore, cautions his people through his prophet Samuel,

> This is what the king who will reign over you will do: He will take your sons and make them serve with his chariots... Some he will assign to be commanders of thousands and commanders of fifties, and others to plough his ground and reap his harvest, and still others to make weapons of war and equipment for his chariots. He will take your daughters to be perfumers and cooks and bakers. He will take the best of your fields and vineyards and olive groves and give them to his attendants. He will take a tenth of your grain and of your vintage and give it to his officials and attendants. Your menservants and maidservants and the best of your cattle and donkeys he will take for his own use. He will take a tenth of your flocks, and you yourselves will become his slaves. When that day comes, you will cry out for relief from the king you have chosen, and the Lord will not answer you in that day (1 Sam 8:11-18; see also 10:19; 12:12-20).

For Israel, the concept of theocracy had to be maintained and expressed in changing social and political circumstances through the human institutions best suited to those times. There was nothing wrong in principle with the move towards kingship; indeed, provision had already been made for such an eventuality (Deut 17:14-20). The problem was that the demand of the people was occasioned by the rejection of the Lord as their leader. In order to preserve the theocratic basis of Israel under this new form of governance, Samuel would rather speak in terms of a *nagid* (prince) than a *melek* (king) (Sam 9:16).

Before long Samuel's fears were realized when the simple leadership style of Saul became increasingly lavish during the reign of David, and even more so during the reign of his son Solomon (1 Kings 10:14-29; 11:1-8). On the death of Solomon, a delegation of leaders pleaded with Rehoboam to be less demanding than his father, as the people had become overburdened by the increased taxation required to finance Solomon's many building projects and to sustain his lavish courts. Unfortunately Rehoboam rejected the advice of his older and wiser counsellors in favour of the viewpoint of his younger leaders. The latter urged him to surpass Solomon in the demands he made on the people, thereby increasing their influence as the newer members of Rehoboam's administration. His misguided decision resulted in the tragic rebellion of the northern tribes under the leadership of Jeroboam (1 Kings 12:1-24). All of the subsequent line of northern kings, without exception, 'did evil in the sight of the Lord', leading their people in apostasy encouraged by the need to establish rival sanctuaries to Jerusalem in Dan and Bethel, and eventually in Samaria.

Within the church context, over-demanding leadership can lead to burnout among the lay leaders which results either in their transferring to other churches or, more often, dropping out of church life altogether. Members and attenders with discernment are cautious of pastors who seem to be concerned primarily with building an ecclesiastical empire to enhance their own image. Leaders themselves are jeopardizing the spiritual basis of their authority when they succumb to such temptations. The many lessons from the Old Testament of leaders who made ship-wreck of their lives need to be taken to heart. Saul fell from divine favour through disobedience (1 Sam 13 and 15), which in turn led to increasing jealousy of his successor whom God had already selected as his replacement (1 Sam 15:28,29). David went through a period of spiritual crisis and severe depression as a result of lust which led to murder. And Solomon, for all his wisdom, was foolish enough to be overwhelmed by his flamboyant tastes and need for status symbols more in keeping with an Eastern potentate than a humble servant of the Lord. Furthermore, he entered into marriage relationships with foreign women in order to establish and strengthen alliances with the surrounding nations (1 Kings 11:1-8).

Feeling insecure through having to face unfamiliar circumstances

The people of Israel became especially vulnerable from the time of their occupation of the Promised Land, which entailed a radical change of life-style from being a nomadic food-gathering people to becoming a settled people dependent on agriculture. Could the Lord of Hosts who, in the recent past, had caused them to be victorious in battle now be depended upon to ensure an abundant harvest?

Unlike Mesopotamia or Egypt (Deut 11:8-17), Israel had no significant rivers and was therefore dependent upon the seasonal rains, the 'former rains' which fell between October and January, and the 'latter rains' which fell during April and May (Joel 2:23; Zech 10:1). The former were necessary to prepare the ground for sowing and the latter to swell the ears of grain for harvesting.

The fact that Israel was dependent on rain from heaven to ensure the productivity of the land taught the people of Israel a spiritual lesson: even though they had now left the wilderness for the land 'flowing with milk and honey', they would have to continue to look to Yahweh for provision. They could not take the productivity of the land for granted. Their previous experiences in Canaan during the patriarchal period served as a warning of the area's susceptibility to periodic droughts (Gen 12:10; 26:1; 42:1; 2; 43:1). The sending of the rains depended on Israel's obedience to their Lord, with the threat that if the people persistently refused to listen to his word then those vital rains would be withheld (Lev 26:3-5, 18-20; Deut 11:14-17; 28:12,23,24; Jer 5:23-25).

The Canaanite and Phoenician baals were regarded as nature gods associated with the fertility of the ground and the provision of harvest (Hos 2:5,8). This highlights the significance of the decisive challenge presented by Elijah to the prophets of Baal. Phoenician baal worship had been patronized by King Ahab through the influence of his Sidonian queen Jezebel. In response to the nation's promotion of pagan worship, the Lord withheld dew and rain both as a punishment for their rebellion and to demonstrate the powerlessness of the baals. The three-and-a-half years of drought came to an end only after Elijah successfully challenged the prophets of Baal on Mount Carmel (1 Kings 18:17-40).

Israel was guilty of a misplaced dependency: looking to the Canaanite nature gods for provision and to other nations for protection (Hos 7:8-12). If such a temptation existed in a pre-scientific age, it exists today in a more potent, if different, form. Now the tendency is not so much to run to alternative gods, as to exert our self-sufficiency by looking for technological solutions to our environmental problems. There is nothing wrong in using our God-given research capabilities and inventive genius. But when such paths are pursued in an attitude of self-sufficiency and lack of consideration for other environmental factors, then our short-term solutions often carry embedded long-term negative consequences. Furthermore, we end up living in two worlds—one governed by moral absolutes and revelation and the other by moral relativity, expediency and resourcefulness. Nominality often grows out of a misplaced dependence on our self-sufficiency.

Developing a false sense of security occasioned by material prosperity

Abraham became very wealthy in livestock and in silver and gold through the blessing of God on his life (Gen 13:2). Prosperity is one of the covenant blessings according to the teaching of Deuteronomy, where it occurs as a dominant theme (Deut 5:33; 29:9). It should be recognized that the term 'prosper' does not always signify material blessings, but is applied also to a successful outcome to God-inspired plans relating to every aspect of life. But there is a stern warning not to forget the Lord while enjoying the abundance which he provides (Deut 6:10-12). Indeed, the promised prosperity is dependent on the obedience of God's people, being careful to follow his word (Deut 28:63). Breaking his commands will lead to their dispossession of the land itself.

Prosperity is not necessarily evidence of the Lord's pleasure, for the godly are faced with the problem of the wicked also prospering (Ps 73:3; Job 9:24; Jer 12:1; Mal 3:15). Material prosperity can prove to be spiritually perilous as it so easily leads to self-indulgence, ostentation and greed, rather than to thanksgiving to God and renewed commitment (Deut 31:20; 32:15). Whatever its material circumstances, Israel must never lose its sense of dependency on God for its protection and provision.

Problems arise when prosperity achieves the status of a doctrine. As soon as the argument is used that obedience *guarantees* material blessings, then such benefits become a matter of rights to be claimed. The Scriptures do not universalize the promise to this degree. The prophet

Habakkuk provides a biblical example of someone whose faith is maintained in the absence of expected blessings. In the face of impending national calamity his faith rises above circumstances.

> Though the fig-tree does not bud
> > and there are no grapes on the vines,
> though the olive crop fails
> > and the fields produce no food,
> though there are no sheep in the pen
> > and no cattle in the stalls,
> yet I will rejoice in the Lord,
> > I will be joyful in God my Saviour.
> > (Hab 3:17,18)

Along with the Apostle Paul, the servant of God must learn to be content in all circumstances, in times of need as well as in times of plenty. Changing circumstances serve to remind Paul of his need to draw continually from the physical strength and material provision which God supplies, without taking either for granted (Phil 4:11,12).

People who have become involved in a prosperity teaching which promises them guaranteed material rewards for their spiritual commitment are likely to experience the sense of disappointment more appropriately associated with those who have been taken in by the misleading promises of the promoters of pyramid-selling schemes. If people feel that God has not kept his side of the bargain, then they are likely to turn to other means to enhance their financial and material aspirations.

Substituting ceremonial religion for sacrificial service

In the writings of the Prophets and the Psalms we find repeated warnings against offering sacrifices while continuing to live disobedient lives. Such empty acts of worship are abhorrent to the Lord. Amos thunders against the empty ceremonialism which characterized the worship in Israel in his day.

> I hate, I despise your religious feasts;
> > I cannot stand your assemblies.
> Even though you bring me burnt offerings and grain offerings,
> > I will not accept them.
> Though you bring choice fellowship offerings,
> > I will have no regard to them
> Away with the noise of your songs!

> I will not listen to the music of your harps.
> But let justice roll on like a river,
>> righteousness like a never-failing stream!
>>> (Amos 5:21-24; cf. Is 1:10-15)

Empty worship had become combined with syncretism, which inevitably entailed a denial of the uniqueness of the revelation granted to the Jews (Deut 29:18; Hos 11:1-4; Jer 2:4-8; Ezek 23:30).

For worship to be acceptable it must be supported by upright conduct and merciful dealings with our fellow human beings and by fidelity towards the Lord (Hos 6:6). Isaiah specifies some of the serious social evils which must be attended to first, including justice for the oppressed, concern for the fatherless and compassion for the widow (1:16,17). Worship cannot be made a substitute for good conduct. Rather, the worship of God's people is the expression of a dedicated life. Every act of worship is a fresh self-offering (Ps 40:6-8). The psalmist appeals for spiritual sacrifices to be offered in the form of consecrated living (141:2). The nature of true sacrifice is summed up in the majestic words,

> You do not delight in sacrifice, or I would bring it;
>> you do not take pleasure in burnt offerings.
> The sacrifices of God are a broken spirit;
>> a broken and contrite heart, O God, you will not despise.
>>> (Ps 51: 16,17)

God does not need our offerings in the sense that he is dependent on us, because all that we bring to him already belongs to him (Ps 50:7-15). Our offering to God is in grateful acknowledgement that all we have is through his bountiful provision.

Wherever empty and hypocritical worship prevails, nominality is present both within the church and among those who have turned away through boredom or disillusionment. The renewal of the local church in its life of worship is a vital element both in preventing nominality and in the restoration of those who have drifted into nominality.

Succumbing to defeatist and apathetic attitudes

Israel was a small nation in a vulnerable location. It was frequently intimidated by its more powerful neighbours. The country's physical location made it strategically desirable as well as militarily indefensible. Caught within the pincer pressure of the nations to the east (Syria, Assyria, Babylonia and Persia) and the presence of Egypt to the south, it was only by the grace of God that Israel continued to survive as a nation, although it is described as the 'fewest of all peoples' (Deut 7:7). It turned in vain to Egypt for protection, which would prove to be no stronger than 'a splintered reed of a staff' (2 Kings 18:21; Is 36:6; Ezek 29:6,7). Judah erred in not consulting the Lord before entering into foreign alliances (Is 30:1-18). They preferred to put their trust in Egypt's horse-power than in the Lord's protective power (Is 31:1-3).

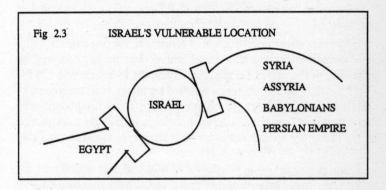

Fig 2.3   ISRAEL'S VULNERABLE LOCATION

SYRIA
ASSYRIA
ISRAEL   BABYLONIANS
PERSIAN EMPIRE

EGYPT

When Israel came under divine judgement in the form of a succession of military defeats which resulted in deportation to Babylon, she had to face the mocking of her captors, demanding derisively, 'Where is your God?' (Ps 42:3; 79:10; 115:2). During their long years in exile the situation became increasingly painful. The mood of the people is expressed in the psalmist's lament.

> By the rivers of Babylon we sat and wept
>   when we remembered Zion.
> There on the poplars
>   we hung our harps,
> for there our captors asked us for songs,
>   our tormentors demanded songs of joy;
> they said, 'Sing us one of the songs of Zion!'
>   (Ps 137:1-4)

God is prepared to allow his people to face the humiliation of mockery as part of his punishment; a kind of shock treatment to make them aware of the tragedy of their present situation (Ezek 22:4,5). But such severe punishment in no way signified that Israel had been finally rejected by

God. The Lord the redeemer of Israel, reassures his people in their exile experience that

> For a brief moment I abandoned you,
> > but with deep compassion I will bring you back.
> In a surge of anger
> > I hid my face from you for a moment,
> but with everlasting kindness
> > I will have compassion on you ...
> > (Is 54:7,8)

Fifty years after the destruction of Jerusalem, the first batch of exiles were permitted to return to Israel where they began work on the rebuilding of the ruined Temple, completing the foundations in 536 BC (Ezra 3:8-10). Further progress was halted for fifteen years on account of suspicion aroused among the Samaritans and other neighbours, who successfully petitioned the king of Babylonia to halt the construction work. This order was not rescinded until Darius the Great became king of Persia in 522 BC (Ezra 4:1-5,24).

From that time work progressed slowly and was abandoned for months at a time because the returned exiles were preoccupied with making lavish home improvements. In response to the scolding of Haggai and the urging of Ezra, work eventually recommenced to restore the foundations of Solomon's Temple on which Zerubbabel's Temple would then be built. As the new construction began to take shape some of the old priests who remembered the glory of the first Temple, destroyed sixty-six years before, wept at the contrast, while those who did not share those memories rejoiced at what had been accomplished (Ezra 3:12). To the former the present foundations seemed as nothing in comparison (Hag 2:3).

In churches with long histories there are usually a group of older members with long memories who are prone to make unfavourable comparisons by idealizing the past. Such attitudes contribute to the lowering of morale, reinforcing defeatist attitudes and intensifying sluggishness. People begin to think that it is not worth while to make an effort to rectify the situation. Proverbs depicts the *sluggard* as one who has succumbed to animal laziness, 'hinged to his bed' (Prov 26:14), offering preposterous excuses to explain procrastination (26:13; 22:13). The sluggard will not begin (6:9, 10; 20:4), finish (12:27; 19:24; 26:15) or face things (22:13; 26:16). He is restless (13:4; 21:25, 26), helpless (15:19) and useless (18:9; 10:26).[2] A sluggish attitude characterizes the life of many church members, which represents an incipient nominality. Eventually the lack of active involvement will lead to non-attendance on the part of a significant percentage of the apathetic and bored church members.

As a summary of the Old Testament's descriptions of nominality, we cannot do better than quote Jeremiah's complaint to the Lord that there were many people in his day whose lives did not correspond to their words: 'You are always on their lips but far from their hearts' (Jer 12:2b). Yet despite their flirtation with pagan gods, they still expected Yahweh to come to their rescue in time of need (Jer 2:26-28).

NOMINALITY IN THE GOSPELS—AN INCIPIENT PROBLEM

Nominality in relation to the Gospels is described as 'incipient' because it took some time to develop, and many of the New Testament documents which describe the beginnings of the Christian movement were written within a few years of the events related. There are numerous indications in the teaching of Jesus, however, that serious problems lay in the future and his disciples needed to be forewarned about them. They could not assume immunity from the condition of nominality because they represented a radical renewal movement within Israel.

In preparation for hearing the gospel, nominality in Israel, which took the form of misplaced confidence and aspirations, had to be dealt with. The main thrust of the ministry of John the Baptist was to awaken Israel out of its spiritual stupor. He not only spoke with the authority of the Old Testament prophets, his diet and clothing were deliberately chosen to remind his hearers of the confrontational ministry of Elijah (Mt 3:4; cf. 2 Kings 1:8; Lk 1:17), a resemblance that they readily recognized (Jn 1:21) and to which Jesus himself drew attention (Mt 11:14). John warned his audience that it was not sufficient for them to think that all was well because they could claim Abraham as their father (Mt 3:9). In order to shake their complacency he announced the coming of the kingdom as *threat* rather than *promise*. The axe of God's judgement is already poised to cut at the roots of the barren trees, which will be chopped for firewood (Mt 3:10). It is on the lips of Jesus that the message becomes the '*good news* of the kingdom'. But the threat element is only replaced by the good news emphasis when people have prepared themselves by genuine repentance (Mk 1:15). Entry into that kingdom will be through a highly significant initiation—a baptism of the Holy Spirit and power—which signifies both a purifying and an empowering (Mt 3:11). Although John the Baptist as a prophet was filled by the Holy Spirit, he could not empower others. Such was the limitation of the old dispensation. It was only through the ministry of Jesus that others would eventually be empowered.

Nominality anticipated in the teaching of Jesus

As we consider our Lord's teaching in regard to the nominality issue, there are two preliminary considerations which must be borne in mind:

Believers must learn to live alongside unbelievers (Mt 13:24-30; 36-43). There are always tares (darnel) to be found among the wheat. While the weeds are young they look almost identical to the wheat. In rabbinic tradition tares were regarded as degenerate corn. The particular application of this parable is not to unbelievers in the professing church, for the 'field' is interpreted as referring to the 'world' (v 38). The tares do not simply 'happen', but are intentionally sown by 'the enemy' among the wheat, warning that Satan acts strategically. The 'sons of the kingdom' cannot live alongside the 'sons of the evil one' on a basis of mutual compatibility. The key question is, Who will influence whom? Is our heart set on identifying with the Lord, or on association with the world?

Spiritual fruitfulness depends on responsive listening to the word of God (Mk 4:1-20). Nominality among the people of God causes a deafness to spiritual truth. Once we have been exposed to the good news of the kingdom of God it is our responsibility to take appropriate action. When Jesus declares, ' He who has ears, let him hear' (v 9), he is acknowledging that the hearer has the final word in the reception or rejection of the message.[3]

The parable of the sower describes four kinds of soils. The hard and unreceptive soil, represented by the path, had become hard through the impact of other people's feet. The shallow soil represents the impetuous but short-lived. As soon as circumstances become uncongenial they shrivel up. The thorny soil represents cluttered lives where anything is allowed to flourish. The good soil represents the conditions needed for a lasting response. In one sense Jesus is teaching that there will be a variety of results whenever the seed of the gospel is broadcast, but the question also arises as to whether better results could be achieved with the unproductive soils if the farmer cultivated the soil and dealt with the problems which were preventing it being fruitful. Elsewhere, I have tried to show how Jesus himself dealt with the types of soil which he describes so that some fruit eventually results.[4] In the course of his ministry Jesus had to deal with a variety of spiritual conditions which represented forms of nominality.

Those who are spiritually complacent. As we have already noted, this issue was one which John the Baptist addressed. Jesus also highlighted the problem when he contrasted the spiritual responsiveness and faith of Gentiles with the scepticism of the Jews. Israel's faithfulness is contrasted with the Roman centurion's belief in Jesus' power to heal his servant.

> I tell you the truth, I have not found anyone in Israel with such great faith. I say to you that many will come from the east and the west, and will take their places at the feast with Abraham, Isaac and Jacob in the kingdom of heaven. But the subjects of the kingdom will be thrown outside, into the darkness, where there will be weeping and gnashing of teeth. (Mt 8:10-12).

This saying is repeated in another context in Luke's Gospel (Lk 13:22-29). On this occasion Jesus is *en route* to Jerusalem when he responds to a question posed by an unnamed individual as to whether only a few people would be saved. As opposition to Jesus mounted, it appeared that many were having second thoughts. Jesus responds by declaring that the door into his kingdom is narrow, so that many who try to get through will never make it, either because they are prevented by the baggage of their self-righteousness or because they have left it too late.

He also warns those who have known him socially that it will be no use appealing that 'We ate and drank with you, and you taught in our streets', for he will respond, 'I don't know you or where you come from. Away from me, you evildoers' (Lk 13:26,27). In fact there is spiritual peril in becoming over-familiar with signs and wonders and remaining unresponsive. The cities of Korazin, Bethsaida and Capernaum were all within five miles of each other and were at the very centre of Jesus' Galilean ministry. Jesus shames Korazin and Bethsaida with the thought that 'If the miracles that were performed in you had been performed in Tyre and Sidon, they would have repented long ago, sitting in sackcloth and ashes' (Lk 10:13,14), and censures Capernaum as being worse than Sodom (Mt 11:23,24). As happened with the frequent miraculous interventions in the Exodus period, the miracles which accompanied the ministry of Jesus did not of themselves guarantee a positive response. The Jewish leaders who had witnessed many of his miraculous signs and wonders only demanded more of the same (Mt 12:38; 16:1).

Those who enjoy the benefits of association without making the decisive act of incorporation (Mt 13:31). Though the kingdom of heaven begins insignificantly as 'a grain of mustard seed', it demonstrates an impressive capacity for growth until it becomes 'the largest of garden plants' (up to ten feet in height), at which stage the birds come and perch in its branches to enjoy its shade. Some New Testament interpreters regard the 'birds' as an alien element or evil influence. Growing churches may be increasing in nominality through attracting people whom they fail to incorporate, or who refuse to get involved. Other expositors interpret the birds as a reference to the Gentiles who will eventually be attracted to the gospel. In either case, those who are attracted and benefit from association need to be incorporated as active members who are totally identified, by establishing close relationships with other believers which will provide support, ensure accountability and provide a context for ministry. In short, 'birds' need to be transformed into 'branches'.

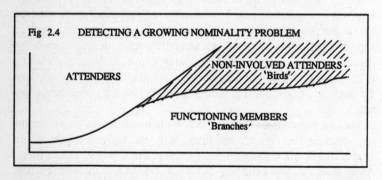

Fig 2.4   DETECTING A GROWING NOMINALITY PROBLEM

Those who become preoccupied with worldly pleasures and preoccupations. In the parable of the sower Jesus warns how 'the worries of this life, the deceitfulness of wealth and the desire for other things come in and choke the word, making it unfruitful' (Mk 4:19). The Lord challenges the rich young ruler to place his full reliance on God by selling all that he has and giving it to the poor as a prerequisite to becoming his disciple (Lk 18:18-29). In this young man's case, the wealth that he had either inherited or accumulated was more of an obstacle to spiritual progress than an evidence of God's blessing upon his life. Peter, Andrew, James and John had been required to face the same cost (Lk 5:11), as had Levi (Lk 5:27,28), as part of their response to Christ's challenge and invitation to follow him.

Our call to ministry or missionary service is liable to become dimmed on the day we place our first down payment on a house or buy our first stick of furniture! Material possessions, and desire for social prestige, concern for career advancement, preoccupation with financial security, can all get in the way of our progress in discipleship. Compromise on these points in defiance of the clear call of God will lead to a loss of spiritual vitality.

Those who substitute human traditions for the word of God. In an endeavour to uphold the letter of the law its intention and spirit maybe undermined. Through clever casuistry its ethical demands may be circumvented. Those who profess to be interpreters of the law become as useless and perilous as blind guides (Mt 23:16-22; Mk 7:1-23). A preoccupation with human traditions also has a tendency to result in a majoring on the minors (Mt 23:23-27) and a preoccupation with external appearances to the neglect of more substantive issues (Mt 23:2,26).

Those whose principal concern is to maintain traditional structures. New wine cannot be poured into old wineskins, or a new patch sewn on to an old garment (Mt 9:14-17). Jesus brings a newness which cannot be confined within old forms. Consequently, if the structures inhibit the expression and advance of the gospel, they will need to be replaced by those which facilitate the expression of life. Those who insist on preserving the old forms, even though they are demonstrably frustrating the embodiment of life and impending growth, will doom the institution to eventual fossilization.

Ecclesiastical structures should function like a skeleton or a scaffold rather than a corset! The *skeleton* is the internal structure holding together the parts of the body and facilitating movement. The skeleton grows as the body grows. The *scaffold* is an external structure, set in place in anticipation of new construction and subsequently dismantled.

Those who exalt ministry performance above the need for personal obedience (Mt 7:21-23). Jesus refers to people who make impressive claims regarding all that they have been able to achieve in his name through prophecy, exorcism and miracle working. Although they called upon him as 'Lord' to achieve results in their ministry, they did not yield to him as Lord of their personal lives. It is perilous to assume that because there is still spiritual power and impressive results in our ministry that all must be well with our souls. The Lord may continue to channel his grace through unworthy vessels because of his concern for the needy who come for help. The test of true believers is not to be found in their giftedness in ministry, but in their fruitfulness of character, as is made clear in the preceding verses (15-20). It is the quantity and quality of the fruit tree which is indicative of its health and vitality.

Those who wither in the face of hostility and persecution. Jesus repeatedly warned about mounting spiritual hostility. Those who lack deep roots will shrivel at the first sign of difficulty or opposition (Mk 4:16,17). Hostility may come from family members just at the time when their support is most needed, when 'all men hate you because of me' (Mt 10:21-39). While it is legitimate to flee one's persecutors, it is inexcusable to forsake one's faith. If Jesus himself suffered alienation from his family (who at one point seemed to have considered him mentally unbalanced—Mk 3:21, 31-32), and encountered persecution by his enemies, then his followers must not be surprised if they occasion misunderstanding and arouse antagonism.

But the followers of Jesus are not to be afraid when opposition intensifies into persecution, because the Lord is fully aware in every instance of what is happening and will testify to the Father on their behalf (Mt 24:10). Nevertheless, he foretells the day when 'Because of increasing wickedness, the love of most will grow cold' (v 12). By cooling off and compromising they will hope to escape betrayal and death. In their case, further persecution would not be worth the effort and would prove to be counterproductive. Ignore them. Leave them long enough and they will 'wither on the vine'.

Those who are deceived by false teaching. False teaching tends to proliferate when circumstances are difficult for the true believers. Those most attracted to pseudo-Christian sects which make exclusive claims, or other religions, are usually from the ranks of the nominal Christians. True believers are neither fooled by the seemingly harmless outward appearances presented by sects and cults in their media advertising (which may mask a reality which is far from wholesome) nor enticed by fantastic claims which eventually prove false or lead to self-destruction (Mt 24:4,5,11,23).

Nominality evidenced among Jesus' followers
The multitudes deserted him. In addition to the Twelve, it appears from
the gospel records that Jesus also had a wide circle of followers at
various stages in the discipleship process. Both Luke and John refer to
multitudes of disciples. The Pharisees were concerned that Jesus was
baptizing more disciples even than John the Baptist, who had a significant following (Jn 4:1 cf. 3:22,26). Luke makes it clear that the twelve
apostles were selected from a much larger group of disciples (Lk 6:13).
In addition to the Twelve, Luke tells the story of Jesus sending out
seventy (or seventy-two) to go ahead of him and prepare the people for
his coming (10:1ff). John reports that after the hard teaching recorded in
chapter 6 'from that time many of his disciples turned back and no longer
followed him' (6:66). One is left wondering how many of these former
disciples later returned. Jesus cautioned the crowds who followed him
that they could not become his disciples unless they loved him more than
their intimate family members and were prepared to take up their
crosses—ie be prepared to lay down their lives (Lk 14:25-27). When
Jesus made his triumphal entry into Jerusalem, who were those people
who spread out their cloaks and cried, 'Blessed is the king who comes in
the name of the Lord'? According to Luke, they were 'a whole crowd of
disciples' (Lk 19:37).

It appears that there was an ebb and flow in the numbers who
followed Jesus. Some followed from a distance, and these were particularly vulnerable. Jesus' long term strategy was to concentrate on the
training of the Twelve, who would form the foundations for the new
Israel. They would become the kind of leaders that the multitudes would
follow, and would themselves reproduce their own leadership qualities
and style. Without those foundation stones there could be no long term
future for the movement. When local churches make no provision for
training in discipleship by gathering people into groups where accountability is expected and support is provided, then those churches are in
similar jeopardy.

The individuals who wanted to follow Christ on their own terms. We
have already mentioned the instance of the rich young ruler (Lk
18:18-29). Two others also had serious problems in facing up to the
implications of discipleship: the *impetuous person* who had to be
reminded that he would no longer have the security of a home to return
to at night, and the *procrastinating person*, who had family priorities
which he made an excuse for a delayed response (Lk 9:57-62). Jesus

responds to the former by making him face the implications of becoming a disciple in terms of foregoing a permanent home. Jesus was constantly on the move, so following him would entail a life on the road, accepting whatever hospitality was offered. The latter seems to be making an excuse for the sake of appearances. In all probability his father was still alive, so that he was in effect postponing indefinitely the decision to follow Jesus, at least until his personal circumstances made it more convenient. Jesus' reply to him, to let the dead bury their own dead in order that he might go on at once to proclaim the kingdom of God, was his way of showing that he knew that the man was merely offering a lame excuse and that he needed to get his priorities sorted out because God's reign had been established on earth by the coming of Jesus Christ.

The Twelve who underwent a crisis of faith. Of Jesus' most intimate group of disciples, Judas betrayed him (Mt 26:14-16; 47-50), Peter disowned him (Mt 26:69ff) and they all deserted him at the crucial moment (Mt 26:31). It seems that they were so devastated that they contemplated returning to their former haunts and means of livelihood (Jn 21:3). Their experience makes it clear that close association with Jesus did not create immunity from nominality. Indeed, it would seem to be inevitable without the renewing and sustaining power of the Holy Spirit (Acts 1:8).

NOMINALITY IN THE NEW TESTAMENT CHURCH—AN EMERGING PROBLEM

The churches founded in New Testament times were as full of problems as many churches today. In fact any churches whose members are largely raw and recent converts from the pagan world produce even greater ministry demands and ethical problems than well-established churches full of members from families with a Christian heritage. We must avoid the tendency to idealize the New Testament churches.

However, the issues addressed in the New Testament were largely occasioned by the pagan environment out of which the new converts came. They constituted the unfinished business which the churches had to tackle in their teaching and disciplinary measures. This is a different dynamic from that occasioned by long-time, even lifelong, members being enticed back into the life-style of the world. There is little evidence of the kind of nominality problems experienced today because of the brief time-span between the founding of the New Testament churches and the correspondence addressed to them. Neither the date of the founding of every church nor the date of every letter can be identified with pinpoint accuracy, but the following represents a reasonable approximation. Paul's letter to the Thessalonians was written within the first year of the founding of the church in Thessalonica; the letters to Corinth and to Titus (Paul's servant whom he left in Crete to care for the church that was probably founded after Paul's first Roman imprisonment), within four years; the letters to Ephesus and Colossae within six years; the letters to Galatia within eight years (though possibly as early as two years, depending on whether the letter is addressed to the churches of North or South Galatia and whether it was written after the first or second of Paul's missionary journeys); and to Philippi and Timothy in Ephesus after ten or more years. Nominality is a condition arising out of spiritual neglect, and Paul's follow-up visits and letters dealt promptly, sensitively, but forthrightly with the problems beginning to arise within the young churches. If the churches had neglected to deal with issues of faith and conduct, then nominality would have begun to take hold as moral standards fell and spiritual vitality declined.

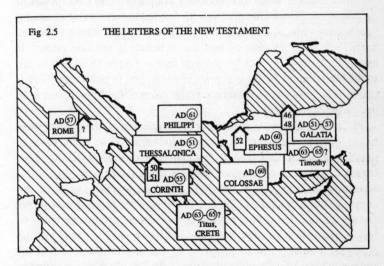

Fig 2.5   THE LETTERS OF THE NEW TESTAMENT

With the exception of Syrian Antioch, Corinth, and Ephesus, Paul and his associates only stayed for brief periods of time in most of the cities and towns where they founded new churches. This meant that the new believers were inadequately taught and had inexperienced leadership. To make up for this deficiency, Paul made follow-up visits, sent his assistants to check on progress and maintained an ongoing correspondence. For instance, Timothy was sent the Thessalonica (1 Thess 3:2,10) and Philippi (Phil 2:22,23) and Epaphroditus to Philippi (2:25). Among the emerging problems which Paul and his emissaries had to deal with, five were particularly important.

1. The teaching of false doctrine

In Galatia some were being diverted to 'another gospel', which sought to maintain that certain Jewish ceremonial practices required in Old Testament times were necessary for salvation. Paul vigorously opposes this teaching, recognizing that it undermined the basis of the gospel rooted in salvation by grace (Gal 1:6-9). His letter seeks to stem 'desertion' (v 6) from the ranks. They were behaving as though they were people 'bewitched' (3:1). Having begun in the Spirit, they are now trying to progress through human effort. Such a departure would prove futile from the outset. Nominality entails people having a form of religion but without the power which was previously availed to them. Paul appeals to the Galatians, 'Does God give you his Spirit and work miracles among you because you observe the law, or because you believe what you heard?' (3.5). A religion of legalism is bereft of spiritual power. It inevitably leads to hypocrisy, through human failure to live up to the standards required by the elaboration of the law to cover every eventuality. The only way to overcome gratification of the sinful nature is to live by the Spirit (5:16).

In Colossae some were questioning the uniqueness of Christ. They were falling prey to a mixture of extreme Judaism and an early form of gnosticism, which combined ceremonialism expressed in dietary regulations, observance of religious festivals and circumcision (2:11; 3:11), asceticism (2:21,23), angel worship (2:18) and a downgrading of the unique position of Christ (1:15-20; 2:2,3,9) with the possession of secret knowledge (2:2,3,18). Paul's reply is to emphasize the supremacy of Jesus Christ. He is the very image of God (1:15), the Creator (1:16), the pre-existent sustainer of all things (1:17), the head of the church (1:18) and the fullness of deity in bodily form (1:19; 2:9). As with the Galatian heresy, the philosophy being spread abroad in Philippi was hollow and deceptive (2:8), lacking any ability to restrain the old sinful nature (2:23).

The early church was no stranger to the religious pluralism which we are beginning to face in many parts of the western world. In the light of contemporary challenges to the uniqueness of Jesus Christ as the only begotten Son of God and Saviour of the world, the teaching of Colossians is particularly relevant. We in the West need to learn from the experience of those churches in the non-western world which have lived from their inception as minority groups in a religiously pluralist environment, or in a society dominated by non-Christian religious thought. As soon as the gospel is reduced to just one among many possible paths to salvation then the nerve-cord of mission is cut and the church begins to lose it distinctive witness.

In Corinth some were denying the resurrection of the dead. Paul deals with this problem in his first letter to the Corinthians (see Cor 15:12ff). He argues forcefully that if it be true that Jesus did not in fact rise from the dead, then their faith is futile (v 14,17); The apostles can be discounted because they are false witnesses (v 15); and the Corinthians are still in their sins (v 17). For other New Testament references to false teachers see 1 Thess 2:1-3; 1 Tim 1:3-7; 4:1-3; 2 Tim 3:1-8; 1 Jn 2:18,19,22-23; 2 Jn 7-11; Jude 3-4; 2 Pet 2; Rev 2:6,4,15,20. From these examples it is clear that false teaching presents a constant and serious threat to the continuing spiritual vitality of the church and that any departure from the gospel will inevitably lead to nominality and eventually to apostasy.

2. Demonstrating unacceptable character traits

Paul had to rebuke church members in Thessalonica for lax sexual standards (1 Thess 4:13), living unruly lives (2 Thess 3:6), refusing to work and interfering in other people's affairs (1 Thess 4:11; 2 Thess 3:10).

The church in Corinth was full of moral problems, which is not surprising when one considers the reputation of the city as promiscuous, tawdry and raucous, and the fact that the church had drawn into its fellowship new believers from the riff-raff of harbour-front society. Among their number were to be found the sexually immoral, idolaters, adulterers, male prostitutes, homosexual offenders, thieves, the greedy, drunkards, slanderers, swindlers. Paul bluntly reminds them, 'that is what some of you were. But you were washed, you were sanctified, you were justified in the name of the Lord Jesus Christ and by the Spirit of our God' (1 Cor 6:9-11).

Their presence in the fellowship was testimony both to the power of the gospel to rescue those who are perishing (1 Cor 1:18), and to the effectiveness of Paul's missionary methods. Yet they brought problems into the church fellowship which could not be ignored. There were party squabbles which needed to be resolved (1 Cor 1:10—4:21), cases of sexual immorality including an incident of incest, and legal wrangles between church members (chapters 5,6). Their worship times had degenerated into occasions for disorderly conduct, and their fellowship meals were marred by the greedy conduct on the part of some participants. Evidently the church in Corinth was not known for its social graces! People came 'rough hewn' for the sharp corners to be knocked off and the rough areas made smooth within the robust fellowship of the Church. While believers cannot, and for the sake of the spread of the gospel should not, cut themselves off from their former associates, they must ensure that moral problems within the church are dealt with promptly, otherwise their unhealthy influence will spread like yeast in dough. Paul goes so far as to counsel that believers who remain impenitent should be socially ostracized to make them realize the seriousness of their situation (1 Cor 5:6-11).

Similarly the Ephesian believers, who lived in a city known for its cult prostitution, are enjoined to 'no longer live as the Gentiles do, in the futility of their thinking', their minds darkened, their hearts hardened, giving themselves over to 'sensuality so as to indulge in every kind of impurity, with a continual lust for more. You however did not come to know Christ that way' (Eph 4:17-20).

Paul draws a sharp contrast between their former way of life and the way in which they should live as Christians in terms of a complete change of attire—putting off the old self and putting on the new (Eph 4:17-24). With even more radical imagery, Paul declares that it is like passing from death to life. The living death to which he refers is a life which is separated and alienated from God. Our response to the gospel demands a dramatic divine rescue operation, due to the strength and all-pervasive nature of the forces which bind us. The Ephesian believers in their preconversion existence followed the ways of this world, the ruler of the kingdom of the air and the spirit who is now at work in those who are disobedient (2:1,2). The seeming hopelessness of the human predicament is emphasized by stressing that the anti-God forces operated above us in the spiritual realm, around us in our social context, and within us in our sin-prone, sin-stained and sin-distorted nature.

Rather than living to satisfy every physical desire, the Ephesian believers were to submit themselves to God's shaping of their lives (2:10)

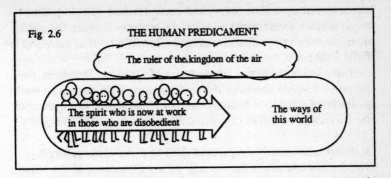

Fig 2.6   THE HUMAN PREDICAMENT

The ruler of the kingdom of the air

The spirit who is now at work in those who are disobedient

The ways of this world

after the pattern of Jesus Christ. In specific terms this meant them learning humility and patience and maintaining a submissive and loving attitude towards each other (4:2-3). They were to be open and honest in their conversation (4:25). Rather than getting what they wanted through theft, which was a logical course of action in a society which put so few restraints on instant self-gratification, they were to work hard to meet their own needs as well as to give to the needy (4:28). This is in a society where credit was not so readily available 'to take the waiting out of wanting', to quote an old slogan of one credit card company. Bouts of rage, hurling insults, coarse conversation and cutting remarks were not acceptable behaviour; rather they must show consideration and kindness to others in all their dealings with one another (4:29-32; 5:4). There must be no hint of sexual immorality among them (5:3), neither are they to become drunk, which has proved the road to ruin for so many (5:18).

Paul knows from personal experiences gathered during his three-year stay in Ephesus that the days were evil (5:16). He is sufficiently in touch with the situation to be very specific in the issues with which he deals. The believers will only remain secure and vital by being filled with the Holy Spirit, clothed with the protective armour of God, going on the offensive, wielding the sword of the Spirit, which is God's word, and being empowered and directed by Spirit-inspired prayer (5:18; 6:10-18).

The social environment is equally unhealthy for the believers in Crete. In writing to Titus, Paul evidences a low opinion of the Cretans. He quotes one of their own prophets who said, 'Cretans are always liars, evil brutes, lazy gluttons', and adds that he is in agreement with this assessment (Tit 1:12,13). Therefore he rebukes them. Paul identifies with them in terms of their former pattern of life when they were enslaved by all kinds of passions and pleasures which resulted in relationships characterized by malice, envy, and mutual hatred (Tit 3:3). Titus is urged to teach sound doctrine, respectful attitudes between the generations, the need to be submissive to authority and not getting entangled in futile arguments.

These examples drawn from church life in New Testament times provide a forcible reminder that new converts from the pagan world have a lot of growing to do after being born from above. Trying to repeat the born-again experience again and again is no answer to nominality.

3. Divisiveness caused by a partisan spirit or personal disagreements

The epistles contain numerous calls to unity, evidence of the tension existing between various groups and individuals.

Firstly, there was the widespread problem of *the strained relationship between Jewish and Gentile believers*, which was aggravated by the activities of 'Judaizers' who were hard on the heels of Paul in most places he visited, trying to ensure that the 'new way' remained a movement within Judaism. This would help restore relationships with the Jewish hierarchy which some were desirous of achieving, especially since a large number of priests had become obedient to the faith (Acts 6:7).

A further consideration which no doubt motivated the actions of the Judaizers was the need to ensure that the followers of Jesus Christ were regarded as a *religio licita* throughout the Roman world, thus protecting them from persecution. This sanction by Rome would best be achieved by ensuring that they remained a sect under the protective umbrella of Judaism, which enjoyed the privilege of the legal right to exist.

Paul mentions the Judaizers frequently. Many of them were from Jerusalem and may have included some of the recently converted priests reported in Acts (6:7). In countering their activities Paul is concerned to safeguard the essential place in the gospel of the forgiveness of God and the giving of the Spirit through God's free grace, over against the legal demands of the law. He is at pains to emphasize that the Gentile Christians have equal standing with their Jewish brethren and should not be treated as second class citizens. Furthermore, there was to be no Jewish cultural overloading of the gospel. This was made clear by the decision of the Jerusalem Council (Act 15).

Secondly, there was *the partisan spirit in Corinth*. When we read of the church in a given city in the New Testament, we must not think in terms of a single, centralized gathering, but rather of a federation of home based meetings. Where the believers met in the home of a wealthy person, the rooms could have been quite large and therefore able to accommodate a hundred or so people, while in more humble dwellings numbers would have been much smaller because of space restrictions. Such dispersion had made possible a dangerous degree of fragmentation, with various groups forming distinct parties and claiming as their leaders Paul, Apollos, Peter, and Chrestus (Christ?) (1 Cor 1:10-17). Paul urges them to stop arguing and to demonstrate the oneness that comes from Christ, to whom they all owe their primary allegiance.

Thirdly, Paul had to deal with *disagreements between individuals* in many of the churches, and he mentions two by name in Philippi. The issue is tactfully yet firmly addressed by Paul, naming Euodia and Syntyche, and urging them 'to agree with each other in the Lord' (Phil 4:2). In view of Paul's appeal for single-mindedness, the rejection of selfish ambition and the need for humility, perhaps the problem was more widespread (Phil 2:1-5). He calls for Christ-like attitude of complete self-giving as the antidote to the problem (Phil 2:6-12). In the light of all that Jesus has done on their behalf, there is no place for complaining or arguing (v 14).

Fourthly, *legal battles between church members* are a further problem in the Corinthian church which Paul addresses (1 Cor 6:1-8). The particular issue seems to be a civil lawsuit regarding a property transaction which had given rise to charges of cheating. Resorting to the civil courts only serves to damage the reputation of the church in the eyes of the pagan world. Unlike criminal matters which should be handled by the state (Rom 13:3-4), civil matters should be resolved within the fellowship.

The continuing need to ensure a climate of healthy relationships within local churches needs to be stressed, because at least one recent survey, conducted among non-churchgoers who were regular attenders at some point in their lives, shows that among the most common reasons for church drop-out is bad relationships with fellow-members or the pastor.

4. Loss of 'first love' with the passage of time
Paul complains to the Philippians that 'everyone looks out for his own interests, not those of Jesus Christ' (Phil 2:21). There is also the case of Demas who, because he loved this world, had deserted Paul and gone to Thessalonica (2 Tim 4:9). It is probable that both these references related to the situation in Rome, where the Christian church was under

close scrutiny by the Roman authorities. Just as in a marriage relationship there can be a cooling-off of affection, concern, and consideration between one partner and the other, so believers can lose the warmth and intimacy of the relationship they once enjoyed with Christ. This state of affairs had apparently become widespread in Ephesus by the time John addresses them in Revelation, some forty-three years after the founding of the church (assuming a date of AD 95, which is ascribed to Revelation by the majority of New Testament scholars, which gives time for the church to have produced a large percentage of second generation believers). Their hard work and concern for doctrinal purity had not proved sufficient to provide adequate safeguards. John seeks to deal with the condition by reminding them of the love they once had for the Lord and for one another, and urging them to return to the deeds of love they once joyfully undertook. If the condition remains unchecked, their 'lampstand' will eventually be removed.

This catalogue of problems besetting the church identifies issues which may contribute in a variety of ways to the onset of nominality among a segment of the total membership. It identifies doctrinal deviations and life-style inconsistencies which, if left undetected and untreated, act like corrosive acid, eating into those elements necessary for spiritual vitality and maturity.

5. Outright apostasy

The authors of the epistle to the Hebrews gives lengthy and solemn warning to those who are in danger of hardening their hearts and turning away from the living God (Heb 3:12ff.; 4:1ff; 10:26ff). Expositors differ as to whether people have in fact turned from the Lord as described, or whether the author is speaking hypothetically, but clearly, the text accepts the possibility of failing to possess one's spiritual inheritance and coming under the judgement of God (3:17-19; 10:26-31). Those who are in danger of distancing themselves are urged to 'draw near to God with a sincere heart in full assurance of faith ... [and] hold unswervingly to the hope we profess' (10:22,23). They are to 'spur one another on toward love and good deeds', and not to neglect to meet together (10:24,25).

This brings us to the end of our survey of factors operating among the people of God which lead to nominality, under the terms and conditions of the Old Covenant as well as the New.

The broad spectrum of issues and the frequency with which they are mentioned should alert us to the need for practical teaching, continuing vigilance and wise and firm intervention strategies to ensure that these matters are addressed not only after they have emerged within the fellowship, but as a precaution to make the church less vulnerable to infiltration. Due to the church being made up of forgiven sinners rather than perfected saints, no congregation will be immune from such influences. This means that the church must have a strong doctrine of restoration as well as salvation, and have appropriate disciplinary procedures and reincorporation programmes.

NOTES

1. The remnant doctrine runs throughout Scripture. In Gen 45:7, Joseph refers to all Israel as a remnant on the basis that the small group in Egypt constitutes God's seed which will eventually grow into a great nation and carry God's blessing to the world. Later in the Old Testament the 'remnant' is used to refer to those who survived the Syrian invasion of 701 BC, to the exiles returning from Babylonia after their prolonged exile and, later still, to those restored to the Promised Land who remain faithful to the Lord (Ezra 9:8). The prophets Jeremiah and Isaiah place strong emphasis on the remnant as the evidence of God's continuing gracious dealings with his people. See Jer 6:9; 23:3; 31:7; 50:20 and Is 1:9; 4:3; 10:20-23; 11:11, 16; 46:3.
2. For a perceptive and amusing word study on 'the sluggard', see Derek Kidner's commentary on Proverbs in the Tyndale Series (InterVarsity Press; Leicester, 1964).
3. Charles Kraft, *Communication Theory for Christian Witness* (Abingdon Press; Nashville) 83:98-105.
4. See Eddie Gibbs, *The God Who Communicates* (Hodder & Stoughton; London, 1985), Chap 2.

CHAPTER THREE

CHARACTERISTICS AND CAUSES OF NOMINALITY

W E TURN NOW TO the contemporary scene in seeking to broaden our understanding of the characteristics and causes of nominality. Due to its complexity, nominality may be triggered by a number of issues and be revealed by a wide range of indicators. For the purpose of analysis it is helpful to bear in mind that there are three principle sources: society at large, the church itself and individuals in their response to their immediate social context. These channels do not exist in isolation from each other, but overlap and interact. Seldom does nominality arise from a single source. The fact that there are usually multiple causes makes it more difficult to deal with. It has parallels in the field of medicine, where one disease may trigger chemical imbalances and cause other physical malfunctions.

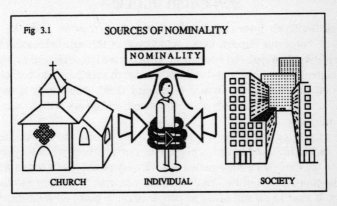

Fig 3.1   SOURCES OF NOMINALITY

NOMINALITY

CHURCH   INDIVIDUAL   SOCIETY

In this chapter we shall first examine the most common characteristics of nominality among people who are either former churchgoers who have ceased to attend, or who have never been actively involved or regular church attenders. These are the lapsed, 'nominal', and notional described on page 26. Then we shall identify those conditions within the life of local churches which, if neglected, are likely to give rise to nominality. Lastly, we shall focus on causes which arise within the life of the individual, due in part to the peer pressure to which that person is constantly exposed, as well as to personal choices for which the individual must accept personal responsibility.

When the church exists in isolation from society, there is a tendency for broader social issues not to be addressed, with the result that the church member is not adequately equipped to bear witness in the world. Furthermore, the layperson is often left to struggle in isolation, bereft of a supportive fellowship which understands the pressures he or she has to face. It is little wonder that so many people live 'schizophrenic' lives, operating by one set of presuppositions and principles in the church and home and by a different set of standards in the workplace. Jesus taught that wheat and weeds cannot exist side by side indefinitely, for eventually one will overwhelm the other (Mk 4:7). Furthermore, the world is represented in Scripture as enemy-occupied territory: 'the whole world is under the control of the evil one' (1 Jn 5:19). We underestimate to our peril the power and subtlety of our adversary.

CHARACTERISTICS OF NOMINALITY AMONG NON-CHURCHGOERS

People withdraw from churches for a variety of reasons. Some have become burnt out through over-commitment or through unreasonable expectations being placed upon them. Others have left because they had a disagreement with the pastor or other church members and became disgruntled. The major obstacle to winning these people back is that they know too much already about the church and do not want to relive a painful experience.

As for those who have never been actively involved in church life, they may have stayed away because on the rare occasions when they did attend the impression they gained was not very positive. For the casual visitor churches are of two kinds: the one you want to get into and the one you want to get out of—and people begin to make up their minds within the first seven minutes after their arrival! However, the fact that people have either left the church or never been involved should not be interpreted as evidence of their having abandoned their Christian faith. As we noted in the first chapter, Gallup Surveys conducted among the unchurched show that the majority continue to be orthodox in their stated beliefs.[1] The problem is that such beliefs are likely to have a grossly inadequate knowledge-base to support them, and their significance for daily living gradually becomes eroded with the passage of time and increased distancing from the community of faith.

Nominals want to be identified as Christians

Nominals who are no longer churchgoers strongly reject being considered irreligious or pagan. They will claim equal spiritual status with those who are active church members. Their non-attendance at church is justified by questioning the integrity of the institutional church, claiming that churchgoers are hypocritical and that their own separation from the church is evidence of their sincerity. Non-attenders, not surprisingly, play down the importance of church attendance and the need for involvement in a community of people who share their faith and from whom they can find stimulation and support.

Despite the fact that they no longer attend or now only maintain a distant or occasional contact with the church, a high proportion of non-attenders may still claim association with a particular denomination or local church. For example, in the Australian national census returns for 1981 many people identified themselves as 'Methodist' even though the Methodist Church has not existed since forming part of the Uniting Church in 1977!

Some churches have extremely large 'external constituencies', so that nominality is widespread throughout society. For other groups, which are nearly always much smaller, counter-culture, sect-like groups, the nominality problem is likely to be much less severe.

Churches regard their external constituencies in a number of ways. One approach is to look upon their inactive members as deserters to be castigated; another is to regard them as a community for which the church has an ongoing responsibility. Sometimes the position is rationalized by arguing that the confessing church acts on behalf of the non-attenders, who have as equal a right to belong as the actively committed but who are responding to the Lord's calling in a different way by committing themselves primarily to the affairs of the world. In

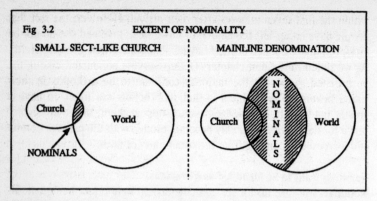

Fig 3.2   EXTENT OF NOMINALITY

SMALL SECT-LIKE CHURCH   MAINLINE DENOMINATION

this way of thinking the worshipping community is the 'representative church' acting by proxy for the much wider community of 'anonymous Christians'.[2] More generally, the floating membership is simply ignored until such times as they make an appearance at church, or approach the church to arrange for the baptism of their infants, marriage, burial, or practical help or emotional support during a family crisis. Additionally, those whose names remain on the church's membership roll are likely to be canvassed to continue or increase their financial support to maintain the ministries of their church.

They claim their ideals are based upon, or at least compatible with, the teachings of Christ

Nominality is sustained by a store of religious teaching which has been passed down from one generation to the next. Unfortunately, as the party game of Chinese Whispers (known as 'Telephones' in the US) demonstrates, the message tends to be increasingly distorted as it is passed along the line, until it bears no relationship to the original. Where the tradition of personal and home Bible reading has been maintained among the unchurched, as is the case in Norway and in segments of the population in North America, then the message can be preserved with greater accuracy and comprehensiveness over a longer period of time.

Until the beginning of the 1960s it was not unusual to find an almost puritanical code of ethics, in the popular sense of that term, among many unchurched artisans in Britain. In their homes no washing or housework was done on Sundays and the more boisterous games were disallowed. The majority of children were still sent to Sunday School and encouraged to join church-related youth organizations. Telling lies, bad language and blasphemy in particular were severely punished. I can remember many examples of these cultural taboos from my own upbringing in that particular social environment.

Although Christ's teaching may seldom be mentioned explicitly, he is still highly regarded as a good example and wise teacher. However, as society becomes increasingly secular, people become less concerned as to whether Jesus actually said and performed all that the Bible records about him. He is represented more as an ideal than a historic figure—a focal point for all that is good and wholesome. They know enough of his moral teaching to recognize the shortcomings and inconsistencies in the lives of professing Christians who identify with organized religion. By taking this approach they can stave off the challenges of enthusiastic churchgoers to become personally committed to Christ and get involved in the life of the church.

They are selective in their beliefs, religious practices and moral conduct
This is as true of those within the church who have succumbed to nominality as of those who no longer attend. However, with the latter there is much less chance of their selectivity being effectively challenged. Individuals, bereft of fellowship, are left to establish their own criteria for religious orthodoxy or behavioral standards. They pick and choose according to personal preference or peer group pressure. There is no corrective and challenge such as would be provided from Bible reading, through hearing Bible exposition and life-application from the pulpit or by discussion within a small group in which group members were endeavouring to hold each other accountable.

With the passage of time the spiritual resources accumulated from the past become distorted, diluted and eventually exhausted. This process is one of the reasons why nominality seldom endures for more than three or four generations. At that point it will either be removed by restoration and revitalization, or else the nominality will be replaced by spiritual indifference or outright apostasy.

They continue to demand occasional ministries from the church
Despite their own lack of participation, nominal Christians expect the church to maintain its presence and traditional range of services to the community, even though they do nothing to facilitate the church's continuing operation. The principle occasions when they make contact

with their ministers and pastors are when they want the baptism of their children, or to be married, of for a family member to be buried. These are popularly known as 'the hatched, matched and dispatched' constituency! They consider that the church's rites and ceremonies are available on demand to all. In Scandinavia and West Germany the entire population has these rights by law. Pastors cannot refuse to baptize, marry or confirm, because everyone is guaranteed these services from the church by the fact that they pay a church tax as part of their income tax contributions. Provision is made for individuals to contract out of this arrangement, but only a small percentage of the population take this option.

The external constituencies of the state churches of Europe are a silent and invisible army which is likely to become both visible and vocal as soon as a church closure is threatened, or a church burial ground needs to be disturbed to make landscaping easier or to make room for an extension to the church building. The more homogeneous the community and ancient the church building, the louder the protest which is likely to be raised.

When faced with a domestic crisis or community-wide emergency, nominal Christians will criticize the church whenever it fails to provide the expected pastoral care and material help. They will not accept the response of government and other secular service agencies as sufficient in themselves. Also, the church may be expected to host community events and provide facilities for local organizations to meet: school concerts, scout parades, Masonic events, etc. Nominals want the presence of the church on their terms—not too close and not for too long!

CAUSES OF NOMINALITY IN THE LIFE OF THE CHURCH

In the course of my travels among many congregations during the past twenty years and more, I have observed that there are ten common reasons which provide opportunities for nominality to arise within the life of the local church. By failing to recognize the signs and not applying adequate corrective measures, the church itself must accept a large measure of responsibility for the ensuing situation. The church must be prepared to recognize the fact that it may be as much a part of the problem as of the solution! This is not to imply that the church should necessarily accept total responsibility. Sometimes there are factors involved which lie outside the influence of the church leadership, or pastors and lay leaders may lack the insight and training to deal adequately with the situation. The nub of any particular problem may lie with the pastor, the leadership, or within the ranks of the congregation, as will be seen by the range of issues discussed in the following pages.

1. The congregation has never had the gospel clearly presented in the power of the Holy Spirit

The preaching to which they have been exposed has consisted of moral homilies rather than a radical gospel of repentance and the offer of new life in Christ. At other times, the preaching was judgemental and aggressive, insisting on adherence to the letter of the law rather than conveying the Spirit. Another aspect of this problem can be seen in some evangelical churches where gospel preaching and the challenge to commitment have become so routine as to have lost their impact. Responding to the 'altar call' had become just another ritual, or a manipulative ploy to meet the emotional needs of the overly impressionable, rather than providing an opportunity for individuals to make a significant response to the inner promptings of the Holy Spirit.

In yet other contexts the preaching has been so stylized and punctuated with religious jargon as to be unintelligible or irrelevant to large sections of the audience. The antiquated style and remote content of the presentation make it appear that the gospel message is addressing some other people in a distant age, rather than having anything directly to say to today's world or to the present audience personally.

2. The authority of the Bible has been undermined through rationalism and empiricism

At the outset we must make a distinction between the kind of 'liberalism' which represents an open spirit of enquiry in search of truth, from that which denies the very possibility of ever arriving at the truth in religious matters. Os Guinness expresses this last-mentioned position with the vivid imagery characteristic of his writing:

> In the talk of some liberals certainty is as elusive as the Loch Ness monster. Occasional sightings are reported, but no confirmation is ever possible. Dogma is now dubious and doubt dogmatic. Ambiguity covers everything like a Scottish mist, and in the end a suspicion arises naturally in the minds of others, if not their own: If faith is that ambiguous and that elusive, is there really anything there at all?[3]

Another prevalent attitude is that of the dogmatist with a closed mind, who rests his or her case on the 'assured results of scientific investigation'. This is less common than in previous decades, now that science is increasingly recognizing the limitations of its own explanations of the origins and principles by which the empirical world operates.

Some Christian liberals have allowed the philosophical assumptions which surreptitiously undergirded the scientific method, to provide the presuppositions and methodology for their own thinking. The secular theologies and 'God is dead' school of the 1960s are prime examples of such abdication to the secular mind-set. The only pieces of religious traditions allowed to survive are those which can be altered to fit these assumptions. Os Guinness outlines four steps in the process: the *assumption* that some modern insight is superior to what Christians now know and do; the *abandonment* of everything which does not fit this assumption; the *adaptation* of what remains of traditional beliefs to make them compatible with that assumption; and *assimilation*,

> where the leftover Christian assumptions are not only adapted to but absorbed by the modern ones. This is the fourth step (assimilation), where the original half-truth of liberalism (flexibility) develops into full-blown compromise or worldliness, and Christianity capitulates to some aspect of the culture of the day.[4]

Under such teaching, people have heard the necessity for new birth denied and have become confused as they heard the theological experts failing to agree among themselves regarding the foundational truths of historic Christianity.

Many liberal Christians in the years after World War II accepted the premise that it is the world which sets the agenda for the church, rather than the church going into the world with its own God-given agenda. Many eventually began to consider that the theological baggage they had taken with them was superfluous and therefore to be discarded. They based their socio-political theorizing and intervention strategies on other ideological premises and agendas.

This sad state of affairs arose for two main reasons. Firstly, a segment of the church ignored the social dimension of the gospel, so that those individuals who were determined to work out the implications of the gospel in particular contexts found themselves having to operate outside church structures and without the support of their fellow-Christians. As a consequence, they had to look for new friends and in so doing adopted their presuppositions and became infected by the anti-church stance and, in some cases, the anti-Christian position of their fellow-advocates.

Secondly, the gospel had been presented largely in terms of personal salvation and an eternal life which had more relevance to a future life in heaven than to daily living here on earth. Until the 1960s 'the kingdom of God emphasis' in the teaching of the Gospels had been largely ignored in evangelical circles. In neither evangelical nor the more liberal sections of the church had there been developed an integrated understanding of the gospel which related its personal and corporate dimensions and its incarnational and eschatological perspectives.

This division meant that neither those who emphasized separation from the world nor those who were committed to engagement with the world were provided with adequate biblical and theological foundations. The former needed to be released from an unbiblical narrowing of the gospel and isolation from the world. The latter needed a keener theological critique of their social engagement, a personal experience of the liberating and reconciling power of the gospel and a realization of the vital role played by the Holy Spirit, to enable them to maintain their distinctive witness as Christians in the world. Jesus provides the balance between separation and involvement in his great prayer for himself and his disciples recorded in John chapter 17. He has no intention of taking them out of the world. On the contrary, he sends them into the world on the same basis and to the same ends that he himself was sent into the world. They go as those who are 'sanctified', that is, as those with a prior allegiance to their Lord who maintain and seek to apply the truth of his word to every issue and situation which confronts them (Jn 17:15-19; see also Paul's advice on engagement with the world in 2 Cor 10:3-5).

3. The word of God has been proclaimed in a cold, abrasive and judgemental manner

Frustrated and angry preachers are prone to gravitate towards those passages of Scripture which describe and warn of God's justice and impending judgement on the impenitent. By playing the role of an austere prophet they imagine that God is on their side, which leads them to claim divine sanction for every stern pronouncement which, in reality, has more to do with their need to give vent to their pent-up feelings than with their calling as a herald of the word of God. This criticism is not intended to imply that the modern preacher can ignore teaching concerning the sombre consequences of rejecting the gospel, for such an emphasis has its rightful place in the course of declaring the whole counsel of God. The preacher is not at liberty to edit out of the text unpopular themes.

But the nature and certainty of divine judgement should never be preached without first having shed tears in the course of the preparation of the message. Righteous indignation must always be tempered by a heartfelt longing for the impenitent to change their ways, and a preparedness on the part of the pastor to go to any lengths to reach out effectively to the recalcitrant. Paul, who said many harsh things about the Judaism of his day, nevertheless writes regarding his fellow Israelites, 'I could wish that I myself were cursed and cut off from Christ for the sake of my brothers, those of my own race, the people of Israel' (Rom 9:3; see also Rom 10:1). Judgemental preaching knows nothing of this depth of soul-agony. And those who have sat and squirmed under such ministry have in reality rejected a caricature of the gospel and thereby missed out on the fundamental message of a God who so loved the world that he sent his only Son, not to condemn the world, but that the world might be saved through him (cf Jn 3:16,17).

4. Insensitive and over-aggressive personal evangelism
Some immature and over-aggressive Christians, having learned a particular approach to evangelism, have then inflicted their rote-learned sales pitch on unsuspecting individuals on every occasion which presented itself or which they artificially induced, with little regard to the needs or perceptions of the individuals they are addressing. Their approach smacks of the salesperson who manipulates the customer to achieve a sale at all costs. They display little awareness of, or interest in, the concerns and questions felt or raised by the individual. But such evangelists soon discover the truth of the old maxim that 'the person persuaded against their will is of the same opinion still'. There is all the difference in the world between gaining a scalp and winning a soul.

People who have been offended by such insensitive approaches, or have become uncomfortable where such was the accepted understanding of the nature of evangelism, have either moved to other traditions with which they feel more comfortable or dropped out of church altogether. They did not wish to be manipulated or forfeit their integrity, which they felt was being placed in question if they succumbed to pressure to join in an evangelistic programme based on such high-pressure selling techniques. In the context of teaching courses on evangelism, I have discovered that a significant percentage of seminaries had been put off evangelism by the insensitive ways in which they had been approached by those eager for their conversion. The urgency inherent in the need to proclaim the gospel must not be expressed in impatience. Even though Jesus said to Nicodemus, the enquiring Pharisee, that he must be born again, he did not then proceed to 'nail him to the wall'. The account in John 3 does not in fact indicate what response, if any, Nicodemus made on that occasion. But his subsequent appearances in John's narrative indicate that he was undergoing an attitude change which eventually led to him appealing for fairness on the part of the Sanhedrin in dealing with the Jesus case. In fact he counsels them to do precisely as he had done, 'hear him to find out what he is doing'. The last mention of Nicodemus is of his accompanying Joseph of Arimathea to take Jesus' body down from the cross, and bringing the expensive herbs and spices to prepare the body for the tomb provided by his companion (Jn 3:1-21; 7:50, 51; 19:39).

5. Unhappy experiences in church-related small groups

At a later stage we shall emphasize the strategic importance of small groups for the revitalization of the church in order to renew nominal Christians. But when such groups are established with unclear aims, when the leadership is poorly selected and inadequately trained, and when there are no co-ordinating structures and accountability requirements, then they can do a great deal of damage. Small groups develop a strong interpersonal dynamic, which can be either supportive or destructive.

Some individuals have felt unduly pressured by a group to the extent that their personality was being violated. For others, what they thought they had shared in strict confidence is later gossiped through the wider fellowship. When they find out, they feel betrayed by the group. Others have been embarrassed by having their ignorance on biblical matters unkindly exposed, or been expected to pray aloud before they felt ready to do so. Still others have been 'cold-shouldered', suffering 'sociological tissue rejection', ie, being made to feel that they did not belong in that particular group.[5]

However, when people are not in a primary group relationship they seldom make significant progress in the Christian life. They may become better informed through hearing sermons and lectures, but they are unlikely to grow spiritually. For such growth to take place, they need to be learning in an ongoing relationship with other believers. Left for too long in isolation, they will begin to wither spiritually and their gifts, God-given to be used for ministry, will begin to atrophy. This generalization does not usually apply to Christians involuntarily isolated through sickness or incarcerated through persecution. In their cases, they may prove the all-sufficiency of God's grace in the midst of adversity and emerge all the stronger as a consequence of their experiences during enforced, prolonged solitude.

6. Culturally irrelevant worship services

The two areas of concern here are the liturgical form of the service and the preaching style. People are either bored or offended by culturally-distanced methods of communication. The problem may be one of archaic language (eg the Anglican Prayer Book of 1662 and the King James Bible of 1611), or of alien forms and imported histories. Churches transplanted from Europe to North America, and even more when transported to the Third World, need to examine the way that public worship is conducted within their tradition in order to judge its appropriateness for the different social context.

The Church of England *Book of Common Prayer*, compiled in 1662, begins the morning service with these words of exhortation: 'Dearly beloved brethren, the Scripture moveth us in sundry places to ... confess our manifold sins and wickedness.' A non-churchgoing auto mechanic I took to that service only grasped one of those words, *manifold!* That was the only contact with his world. Liturgical purists often resist attempts to modernize language on the basis that modern English services are not written in language which is memorable. There may be some truth in this assessment, but the bottom line is that the words must communicate and the thoughts be expressed in a way with which people can readily identify. To their credit, the mainline churches, including Roman Catholic, Lutheran and Episcopalian, have modernized the language of their liturgies in recent years.

In passing, a word needs to be said on an aspect of culture which is frequently overlooked in connection with the use of printed liturgical forms. Whereas most churches are living in the Gutenberg age, society has moved into a post-Gutenberg age dominated by the electronic rather than the printed media. The majority of the urban population is uncomfortable handling big books with a high language level. Most would not read a serious book a year. Thus they feel intimidated when faced with a stack of books including prayer book, hymn book, Bible, and supplementary song books with contemporary compositions. They feel clumsy handling them, are often looking in the wrong book in search of the place where they are in the service. In a blue-collar culture these people are usually obvious because they lick their thumbs as they turn a page—hands roughened by manual work handle paper clumsily. Also by focusing too much attention on the printed page the communication dynamic is impaired through lack of eye-contact.

These are not arguments against liturgy, for the familiarity, predictability and congregational participation which a liturgy encourages can be turned to advantage. Such has been demonstrated by the charismatic movement's influence in both Roman Catholic and the liturgy-using Protestant churches. The key issue is the 'packaging' of liturgy, using service cards rather than bulky prayer books and substituting overhead projection for the printed page. The value of the overhead screen is that it forces us to look up and allows us to glance around.

Sometimes the problem is not so much that the language is archaic as that it is riddled with the religious jargon or technical vocabulary that has become part of the church's language. Such specialized language may have its use in establishing one's orthodoxy within a particular tradition and as a shorthand in communication among the initiated, but it becomes a serious obstacle to communication when people are present who are unfamiliar with 'churchspeak'.

The style and context in which the presenter is comfortable may not be appropriate to the one who receives. There is a need to move from the 'extraction' approach to identification with the listener. The divinely ordered model for Christian ministry is incarnational.

7. Too frequent changes of minister

Lack of continuity results when ministers are coming and going every two or three years.[6] While in theory this should mean a stronger lay commitment to keep things going, in reality it more often leads to people feeling abandoned. They reason that if the minister is not committed, then why should they be? Lyle Schaller, with tongue in cheek, comments about churches characterized by short pastorates: 'This often causes the congregation to develop a high level of competence in three areas: (a) giving parties to welcome the new minister, (b) watching the new minister get acquainted with the people and the parish, (c) giving parties to bid farewell to the departing minister'.[7]

Rapid pastoral turnover is a characteristic of many small rural churches and struggling urban churches in areas of social transition. It is precisely these difficult situations which require pastors with a strong sense of call and a long-term commitment to work for a significant turn around to take place in the church. All too often such churches can only attract the services of ministers who have failed to obtain an appointment to a more 'desirable' location with greater prospects. In reality the struggling churches are located on mission frontiers and need gifted leadership with specialist training to handle the challenges.

8. No effective procedures for incorporating newcomers

In the small, family-size church the problem is more one of attitude than organization, for small churches incorporate newcomers by a process of adoption. This happens spontaneously, if slowly, and even then not everyone can gain acceptance by the group. Visitors who are made to feel marginalized by the small church generally cease to attend within a brief period, unless they are part of the village, small town, or ethnic community. In the latter case they may hang on in an attitude of defiance or assumed indifference. A small church operates as a single extended family, so there are no different social groupings from which to choose within the church. The only alternative is to be either in or out!

In the larger church, the cause of non-incorporation of the newcomer is more organizational than attitudinal, because when a church grows beyond the singe-cell structure it ceases to incorporate people spontaneously. The larger the congregation, the more intentional and sophisticated must be the incorporation procedures.[8]

Churches which fail to recognize this social dynamic end up with a growing percentage of worship service attenders who are not involved beyond that one commitment, and perhaps attending an occasional special event. Their motivation for remaining within the fellowship is at a low level. It is those people who can too easily slip away without being missed.

9. Unresolved personal conflicts

Research conducted in the 1970s by John S. Savage revealed that a major cause of church members becoming inactive was anxiety produced by conflict with either the pastor, another family member, or another church member.[9] If their initial anxiety was not resolved it turned into anger. This in turn caused them to withdraw from those situations which stirred up their anxiety. Many of these people who dropped out because of personality conflicts found that the church never followed up to discover why they lost interest or dropped out. If no help came within six to eight weeks, they then began to invest their time in other, non-church-related, activities.

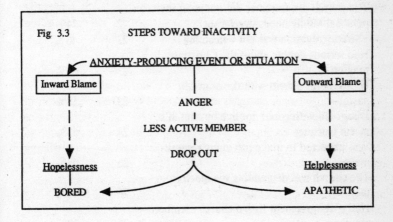

Fig. 3.3   STEPS TOWARD INACTIVITY

ANXIETY-PRODUCING EVENT OR SITUATION

Inward Blame   Outward Blame

ANGER

LESS ACTIVE MEMBER

Hopelessness   DROP OUT   Helplessness

BORED   ←→   APATHETIC

The Nominality Survey conducted by the author revealed an interesting breakdown by average age of the reasons for stopping attendance at church. The results were as follows:

Reasons stopped attending church	Average age	Percentage influenced by reason
The worship service was **boring**	20	63%
Moved out of the area and did not look for a new church	21	63%
There were few other people there of my age and background (**lonely**)	21	56%
The church programmes did not meet my personal/family needs (**irrelevant**)	22	74%
The congregation was **not welcoming**	22	46%
Had **serious doubts** about the Christian religion	23	65%
Had a **disagreement** with the minister/pastor	23	18%
Disagreed with/could not live by church's **moral teaching**	24	53%
Was expected to make too many **commitments**	26	43%
The church was **demanding too much** from me	26	42%
Had a **disagreement** with a church member/members	26	30%

See Table 9 in the Appendix.

10. Institutional degeneration

In concluding this section on causes within the church which contribute to nominality, we must recognize that every human organization is subject to a life cycle which can lead to decline, to the point where it lingers on in a final residual phase. In the case of organizations which are conservative in orientation, that residual phase can prove remarkably resilient. Its condition resembles that of the noble Wesley in the film *The Princess Bride* who, after having the life force drained from him, is declared 'mostly dead' by his dubious healer Miracle Max, but with the support of strong and loyal friends continues to be dragged around until the 'miracle cure' he has been given begins to work.

The passing of the church's fortieth anniversary is the danger point, because by that time the second generation has occupied most of the leadership positions and the pioneering spirit has been lost. This progression from expansion through a static state to eventual degeneration is not inevitable, but the symptoms must be recognized and treated appropriately.

In the following chapter we shall discuss in some detail the comprehensive nature of the issues needing to be addressed for the revitalization of the local church. And in chapter 5 onwards we shall turn our attention from institutional considerations to major contextual issues which have had such a profound and far-teaching influence on people's religious thinking and church participation.

WHY A PERSON'S RELATIONSHIP WITH CHRIST BECOMES DAMAGED OR DISTANT

The blame for so many people degenerating in their spiritual lives cannot all be laid at the door of the church or attributed to a hostile social environment. Individuals must also accept some of the responsibility for their unsatisfactory spiritual condition. In the following considerations, which relate to individuals in their relationship with God, we shall see the interaction between the individual, the life of the church and the broader social context.

They may be left unaware of Christ's claims upon their lives
Many churchgoers are spiritually nominal because they have never been taught the demands of the gospel of the kingdom nor personally challenged to consider and respond to Christ's claims upon their life. This state of affairs may have arisen because the ministry was either theologically inadequate or pastorally timid.

In the former case the need for, or reality of, the new birth is often denied. Sometimes this is due to an over-reaction against the 'decisionism' which characterizes much of North American evangelism; at other times it arises from a theology which accepts all humanity as being part of the family of God, without the need for a personal response to Christ's unique atoning work. In this view evangelization is not telling people that they need to be saved, but informing them that they have already been saved without them having realized the fact.

In the latter case, pastoral timidity is occasioned by a fear of rejection and especially of offending those loyal members who run the organizations and make significant financial contributions. Some pastors find it much easier to challenge the young people and newcomers about their need of Christ than those who are pillars of the church. In other circumstances, newcomers are simply welcomed on their own terms without anyone enquiring as to where they are in their spiritual pilgrimage for fear of frightening them off. In churches where visitors are more of a rarity than a regular occurrence there is a strong temptation simply to affirm, rather than to raise questions and present challenges. The result is that people drift out as easily as they drifted in. Dean Kelley convincingly argued, as a result of studying growing denominations, that a clear-cut message, a strong set of ethical codes and a high commitment correlated with high rates of growth, whereas low expectations led to low levels of commitment which sapped vitality and stunted growth.[10]

Many individuals are to be found in such churches who are ready to respond to the gospel by accepting Jesus Christ as Saviour, submitting to him as Lord and receiving the freedom-giving and joy-generating gift of the Holy Spirit, once the requirement to do so has been established and the steps have been carefully and sensitively explained.

They may be resisting Christ's claims upon their lives

Some have repeatedly rejected Christ's call to the point where they have become 'gospel hardened'. They oppose any emphasis on spiritual ministry, avoid religion becoming too personal and further protect themselves by insisting that religion is a private matter. Probing into the state of their soul is discouraged as a disrespectful intrusion. The options open to them, other than the privatizing of religion, are ceremonial religion, civil religion, or syncretistic religion. The first is more common in Europe whereas the second prevails in the United States. Both submerge spiritual conviction beneath national aspirations. The ceremonial religion in Europe tends to retain a traditional Christian basis whereas the civil religion of the United States is more vaguely deistic. The third option, syncretistic religion, is found in some forms of Freemasonry, religions such as Baha'i, and the New Age Movement. Where one or more manifestations of this third option are present, you find that the people involved in such movements have a broader theological agenda under which the gospel is subsumed. The result is theological fuzziness and confusion resulting in a lack of spiritual vitality and evangelistic urgency.

These situations are so serious and potentially explosive that a great deal of spiritual wisdom, pastoral fortitude and prayerful compassion will be required in dealing with them. Sometimes faithful ministers of the gospel have been forced out of such churches. So often, the prophet's lot, even more than that of the policeman immortalized in Gilbert and Sullivan's opera, 'is not a happy one'. Perhaps the pastor's ejection could have been avoided in some cases if he had gone about his task with greater sensitivity, but spiritual opposition can be so vehement that the outcome might be the same irrespective of the individual and the methods adopted. Jesus himself ended up not as a super-star but as a rejected and suffering Saviour. Jesus likened the people around him to children arguing what game to play. It did not matter whether the game was weddings or funerals, they still refused to participate. It made no difference whether God's messenger came as an austere prophet, as in the case of John the Baptist, or as a friend of publicans and sinners who obviously enjoyed life, as Jesus was regarded by the religious establishment (Lk 7:31-35).

They may be overly dependent on the spiritual vitality of other Christians

Such people are often weak and vacillating believers. They are extremely vulnerable to peer group pressure. Their security is in 'second hand' religion which they have never made their own, rather than in a personal relationship with Christ and an awareness that they are adopted sons and daughters. Their unhealthy self-preoccupation leads to self-deception rather than a realization of their true spiritual condition. They presume that they are more secure and credible than they are in reality. They survive only as long as they can lean upon others to help them through dull stretches or difficult times.

They are the products of introverted and over-protective groups which have not realized that the objective of discipleship is to lead individuals to spiritual maturity, not continuing dependency.

They may have atrophied as a result of never identifying their gifts or becoming involved in ministry

In one sense this state of inactivity cannot fairly be labelled 'nominality', but it can readily lead to disinterest and eventual dissociation. The longer a gift is left unidentified and neglected, the more difficult it becomes to activate. For people to grow in their spiritual lives they need to be personally advised in the development of their potential for ministry to others. They need to be given challenges which will stretch their faith and presented with situations beyond their present level of experience which will further develop their skills and leadership potential.

When people are given jobs which are inconsequential we should not be surprised that those who are able and busy decline to accept them in order to safeguard themselves from backing a loser or having their valuable time wasted. At other times church leaders are given broader responsibilities without corresponding authority and resources. The consequences are frustration and burnout, which lead us to our next point.

They may have become burnt-out as a consequence of over-commitment or lack of support

Over-zealous Christians who have been over-enthusiastic or pressurized to undertake a job which has proved too demanding on their time or level of ability begin to regret their decision to get involved. Sometimes the problem lies with the individual, at other times it is a consequence of poor management of volunteers by the church leadership. Consequently, burnt-out Christians look for a way out—and for them there is no half-way house. Their only safeguard against beginning a train of events which leads to the same outcome, is to drop out of church life altogether. Sometimes they even move house in order to dissociate themselves completely. This is a tragic decision made by more former church leaders than we want to recognize.

A study conducted by the Alban Institute on lay leader burnout identified the following principal causes: frustrating meetings, indefinite task descriptions, lack of evaluation, indeterminate terms of office, difficulties with delegating, unexpressed appreciation.[11] Of the respondents, who consisted of participants at a conference on burnout, fifty per cent felt some measure of dissatisfaction about the way their resources were expended in the church. If this data is in any way representative, and there are many indications around the church at large that it is not far off the mark, then it is clear that pastors need to improve their skills in the area of recruiting, motivating, managing and developing volunteers.

Morally compromised individuals through societal pressure or self-interest

Selective obedience will lead eventually to serious inconsistencies. No one can continue indefinitely trying to serve two masters. Compromised believers lose their joy and spiritual effectiveness and end up simply going through the motions for the sake of maintaining appearances. Some have resigned themselves to living by double standards in a futile endeavour to gain the best of both worlds. Others have been overwhelmed by outside pressures which they did not have either the spiritual discernment to challenge or the support of understanding Christian friends to help them survive. It will not do for those who see the discrepancies but have not themselves been exposed to the pressures to act in a judgemental manner. Many individuals need understanding and support before they can listen to criticism and advice about straightening out their lives.

Residual Christians

These are the second generation 'cultural Christians' who are living on the spiritual capital accumulated through previous generations. They may be familiar with religious language, while knowing little or nothing of the reality. For example, in Wales the great hymns of the revival of 1904 are still sung at rugby football matches and in the pubs. Welsh comedian Max Boyce, in his song 'Forty Thousand Instant Christians' provides a humorous commentary on the unforgettable phenomenon of Welsh rugby fans gathered in Cardiff Arms Park, the national stadium, striking terror into the hearts of the visiting team with the rendition of 'Guide Me, O Thou Great Jehovah' to the tune of *Cwm Rhondda*. Gather a crowd of Welshmen and you have an instant male voice choir! Stirring up half-buried memories of a remarkable outpouring of the Spirit in a previous generation is more likely to generate emotion than lead to repentance. The 'residual Christians' may eventually become renegades, renouncing their faith entirely.

CLASSIFICATION OF THE UNCHURCHED

The term 'nominal Christian' is a comprehensive title which includes a wide range of people who are not currently, or never have been, part of the institutional church. In his book, *The Unchurched—Who They Are and Why They Stay Away*,[12] J. Russell Hale, after touring the country in

1976 and interviewing many unchurched people, developed a helpful categorization which provides a fitting conclusion to this chapter. He lists the following:

Anti-institutionalists—Those who have rejected organized religion. Some fault the church for its conservatism while others have dissociated themselves on account of its liberalism! For others, their objections arose over the church's self-preoccupation and disregard of both evangelistic opportunities and social needs.

Boxed-in—Those who rebelled because they felt their lives were restrained or controlled by churches setting ethical standards to which they were not prepared to submit. Others opted out because they perceived themselves to have been either exploited or thwarted and were not prepared to be reduced to passivity and dependence.

Burned-out—This is a consequence of long term exposure to the church. Some mlook back to their childhood years and early adolescence, when they were forced to attend church services and other church activities which failed to capture their interest. For others, the burnout came much later in life as a consequence of their energies being utterly exhausted in serving the church, or from feeling that their talents were not recognized, their efforts not appreciated, or their time constraints not respected.

Floaters—In contrast to the Burned-out, these are the rootless individuals who move from church to church to ensure that they never become involved or make themselves vulnerable. When swapping and changing is done without any sense of loss, then the decision to go nowhere can be made equally painlessly.

They express no hostility toward the church and do not crave an acceptance by the churches that the Locked out feel is denied them. The Floaters prefer looseness and marginality and express relative satisfaction with their apathy.[13]

Hedonists—These are the pleasure seekers who give priority to leisure interests over spiritual commitment. They find their sporting and recreational activities more interesting and beneficial than church involvement. Sometimes it is triggered by an over-reaction to a legalistic and overly sombre attitude to life, so that people grow up feeling starved of fun and healthy pleasures.

Locked-out—They feel that the church has closed its doors to them because they were not of the right social background. They were discriminated against or simply ignored in the hope that they would get the message, conveyed by subtle innuendo or outright expressions of hostility, that they were not wanted.

Nomads—These are the people, so prevalent in urban societies, who are incessantly on the move. Some represent the chronic unemployed, desperately searching for jobs and willing to take anything on an interim basis until something offering better prospects comes along. Others are upwardly mobile, regarding each job as a further step up the professional ladder. Companies are far less committed to their work-force today, which lowers employee loyalty. People do not stay long enough to put down roots and become involved in community based activities and institutions. The average job in the United States does not last longer than seven years. Like the Floaters, the Nomads eventually fall away from the church when they fail to find a church which meets their expectations. Sometimes the Nomads fit the description 'the reluctantly unchurched'.

Pilgrims—These people are still engaged in a spiritual search. They may be examining the teachings of a number of religions, or distancing themselves from the Christian tradition in which they were nurtured in order to look at a broader spectrum from a more objective standpoint. The trouble with this approach is that religious 'knowledge' is only attained through personal involvement and not through distancing. By attempting to keep all their options open they are likely to end up committed to nothing, which is an all-too-comfortable position to adopt.

Publicans—This attitude is very commonly adopted by the unchurched. By charging churchgoers with being hypocrites and fakes, they justify their own non-participation. In the case of those who were formerly strongly involved in the church, it provides a handy defence mechanism by which they can handle their own residual feelings of guilt or regret. Of course, the church has never claimed to consist of perfect Christians; they meet as forgiven sinners committed to a life-long process of discipleship. Inconsistencies and self-deceptions have to be dealt with in the learning process. Charles Hadden Spurgeon is said to have counselled an individual in search of a church which measured up to his ideal, 'If ever you find the perfect church, don't joint it. Your arrival would spoil it!'

True unbelievers—From the standpoint of the topic of this book the category of True Unbeliever falls outside the range of Nominal Christians. But it needs to be included as a warning that 'nominality' may eventually lead to a complete renunciation of the faith. This category represents a small percentage of the population of the western world, especially in North America. But there is no room for complacency. The situation can suddenly change, for when opinions are lightly held they are likely to change with every shift in the wind direction. Among the true unbelievers will be the agnostics, the atheists and the deists for whom God is removed from this world's affairs. On the other hand there are the panentheists and outright pantheists, who stress the immanence of God to the point of identifying the whole of creation as a manifestation of deity. Technically this is referred to as 'monism'. Through the influence of westernized forms of Hinduism and, more recently, of the New Age Movement, this option has been gaining in popularity, especially with those espousing a strong environmental agenda.

Already we have met examples of these options and in the following chapters we shall come across many of them again as we explore the impact of a range of societal influences which have given rise to nominality.

NOTES

1. See Page 23
2. The term 'anonymous Christian' was coined by the Roman Catholic theologian Karl Rahner.
3. Os Guinness, *The Gravedigger File* (InterVarsity Press; Leicester, 1983) p 163.
4. Ibid, pp 199-205.
5. The term was coined by C. Peter Wagner in *Your Church Can Be Healthy* (Abingdon Press; Nashville, 1979) p 56. He writes: 'It is a social fact that some groups of people prefer the death or dissolution of their group to the alternative of accepting people whom they perceive as being incompatible.'
6. It must also be noted that some church boards hire and fire with great frequency in order to prevent power slipping from their own hands. This is particularly a characteristic of small introverted congregations which consist of tight-knit networks of families who were charter members and have been there for several generations.
7. Lyle E. Schaller, *Activating the Passive Church* (Abingdon Press; Nashville, 1981), p 57.
8. Arlin J. Rothauge, in *Sizing Up a Congregation*, distinguishes between four sizes of church, indicating the distinctive ways in which each incorporates newcomers. The four sizes are: the Family Church with up to 50 active members; the Pastoral Church with between 50 and 150; the Programme Church with 150-350 and the Corporation Church with 350-500 and over.
9. John S. Savage, *The Apathetic and Bored Church Member* (LEAD Consultants; Pittsford, New York, 1976). See also a popular summary of his

report in Win Arn (ed), *The Pastor's Church Growth Handbook* (Church Growth Press, Pasadena, 1979), pp 76-78.

10. Dean M. Kelley, *Why Conservative Churches are Growing* (Harper and Row; New York, 1977). His work has been criticized for ignoring the contextual factors which strongly influence growth and decline, but these cautions do not invalidate his study for our purposes here.

11. Roy M. Oswald with Jackie McMakin, *How To Prevent Lay Leader Burnout* (The Alban Institute Inc.; Washington DC, 1984).

12. J. Russell Hale, *The Unchurched—Who They Are and Why They Stay Away* (Harper and Row; San Francisco, 1980).

13. Ibid, p 130.

CHAPTER FOUR

THE RENEWAL OF THE CHURCH FOR THE RESTORATION OF NOMINAL CHRISTIANS

I N THE PREVIOUS CHAPTERS, which attempted to uncover something of the complexity of the nominality problem, we have at many points identified the church itself as one of the causes. Sometimes it contributes because its low level of spiritual life causes widespread disillusionment which, in turn, leads to low morale among the ranks of surviving church members and to many people simply voting with their feet. At other times, it has contributed unwittingly to the problem by failing to adapt to a rapidly changing society. It is still structured to meet the ministry demands of a churched culture, when in reality it should be developing new structures to tackle the missionary challenges of a predominantly unchurched culture.

RECOGNIZING THAT A SIGNIFICANT CULTURAL SHIFT IS UNDERWAY

The tendency of Protestant churches in North America to concentrate their energies on the middle-class, suburban segment of the population most closely associated with traditional values, has made them slow to realize the significance of this cultural transformation. In Europe and Australasia there has been a greater conceptual awareness of the marginalizing, or alienation, of the urban masses, but the churches' response to the situation has been hampered by the romantic notion of still being a church of the people, albeit only in a representative capacity now that the vast majority do not put in an appearance at corporate worship. Such an attitude most prevails where just one or two denominations account for the majority of the population, rather than a bewildering multiplicity of Christian groups competing to increase their segment of the 'religious market', as is the case in most parts of the USA. When one church is dominant it becomes a religious 'servicing agency' for a population content to receive its ministries on an occasional basis. Churches can thereby justify their existence and continue as they have always done, providing they have access to funding and trained personnel to make such services available to the general public.

However, with the passage of time, the continuing secularizing influences of the broader culture increase the distance between church and people to the point where fewer and fewer people turn to the church for the ceremonies which mark the 'rites of passage' or the counselling support to help through times of crisis. With the churches' waning influence in society and their fight for survival in the less responsive segments of urban society has come the growing realization that a church designed to meet the ministry needs of the 1950s and 1960s is unlikely to make it through the 1990s unless it is prepared to undergo some fundamental changes.

A number of authors have addressed the need for changes in the churches at the present time. Among them are Lyle Schaller,[1] Kennon Callahan, and George Barna. In his book *Effective Church Leadership*, Callahan begins three chapters with an attention-getting statement:

- The day of the professional minister is over, the day of the missionary pastor has come.
- The day of the churched culture is over, the day of the mission field has come.
- The day of the local church is over, the day of the mission outpost has come.[2]

Nearly all of today's ministers are the products of churches that nurtured them in past decades, and of seminaries that focused on the traditional theological disciplines in the preparation of their students for ministry. Once the graduates embark on ministry, they find themselves enmeshed by the expectations placed upon them by the institution they are paid to serve. For the most part, they serve the church faithfully in terms of sustaining the worshipping life of the congregation; they supervise programmes largely designed to serve the needs of existing members and provide pastoral support for the families who make up the congregation or are closely associated with it. Their major shortcoming is in the area of making a significant impact on the growing ranks of the dechurched and unchurched. They were not adequately trained for such a ministry, neither are the local churches motivated and structured to enable effective outreach ministry to take place. Callahan provides an accurate, if disconcerting, assessment when he maintains that

> Professional ministers are at their best (and they do excellent work), in a churched culture. But put them in an unchurched culture, and they are lost. In an unchurched culture, they do a remarkably decent job of presiding over stable and declining and dying churches. They maintain a sense of presence, dignity, decorum, and decency—with a quietly sad regret—much like a thoughtful undertaker who sees to keeping things in order throughout the funeral...[3]

George Barna, a market researcher who brings his skills to bear on the mission of the church, draws attention to the fact that a new day has dawned for the church of North America. His 1989 book, *The Frog and the Kettle*, warns that if the church does not realize that its environment is heating up it will, like the proverbial frog, end up dead in the water. In a follow-up volume, which distils lessons drawn from his consultant work with churches which are effectively responding to the missionary challenge of the 1990s, he concludes,

> The Church in America is in desperate need of a new model for the local church. We currently develop churches based on a model of ministry that was developed several hundred years ago, rejecting the fact that the society for which that model was designed no longer exists. The constant cry of the unchurched—'the church is irrelevant to the way I live'— cannot be addressed until the model itself is renewed to acknowledge that the times have changed. Our approach to meeting people's needs with the unchanging truths of the gospel must reflect our sensitivity to that change.[4]

This new model is required for pastoral reasons—to reactivate existing members to experience a more dynamic faith which is expressed in worship, fellowship and support for the members of the Christian community. It is also necessary for the equipping of the people of God for mission—to help them live the 'abundant life' and speak God's message in the world with the intention of winning back one-time church attenders and bringing to faith those who call themselves Christians without having personally experienced the new life which the gospel makes available.

THE DESIRE FOR CHURCH RENEWAL

As churches have come to recognize their ineptitude in the face of persistent numerical decline, admitting the futility of their efforts to turn the tide and recapture zeal for the gospel, there has been a growing concern for renewal. In the Scriptures the concept of renewal is very comprehensive for, by means of the gospel and the giving of the Spirit, all things are made new. Furthermore, renewal is impossible without divine intervention. It is first and foremost a sovereign gift of God. While it is supremely a work of God there is also a human aspect. The Spirit is not often given to those who do not want to receive. There must be a longing for a fresh vision of God and for the divine empowering of his church. Yet renewal is not given for self-indulgent ends. Rather, it is in order that God's name may be glorified in the world and his kingdom extended by renewed people bearing his message and manifesting his life as they live under the direction of the Holy Spirit.

Patterns of renewal

Spiritual degeneration, both individual and corporate, becomes more difficult to treat the longer the condition is neglected. As with any contagious, life-threatening ailment, it is vitally important to take preventive measures and to be vigilant to ensure early detection of the symptoms. Too often in the history of the church events have been left to take their course, to the point where the situation reaches catastrophic proportions, before steps are taken towards restoration. This leads to a cyclic pattern of spiritual life, when earlier treatment could have provided prompt intervention to turn the cyclic pattern into a wave pattern. Intervention strategies often prove ineffective either because they are not radical enough, treating symptoms rather than root causes, or because they are not sufficiently comprehensive. They only deal with one dimension of the problem.

Although the term 'renewal' is valuable in that it expresses the radical and all-embracing nature of the new covenant as well as the need for a process of ongoing renewal (Rom 12:2; 2 Cor 4:2; Tit 3:5), its impact has become blunted through over-use. It has also become identified in the minds of some church people with *charismatic* renewal, which means

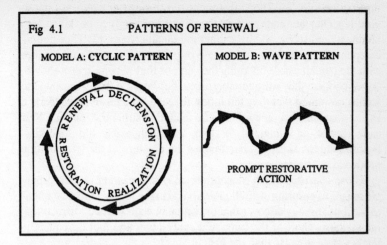

Fig 4.1   PATTERNS OF RENEWAL

MODEL A: CYCLIC PATTERN

RENEWAL DECLENSION
RESTORATION REALIZATION

MODEL B: WAVE PATTERN

PROMPT RESTORATIVE
ACTION

that it is dismissed too readily by those who reject the theology associated with the Charismatic Movement. At the other extreme, churches that have embraced the theology and spirituality of the Charismatic Movement tend not to recognize their need because they interpret 'renewal' in terms of an experience with which they are already familiar. For these reasons, some groups seeking new forms of church life which will more adequately respond to today's challenges are speaking in terms of *transformation*, which may apply equally to the charismatic and non-charismatic section of the Church. The difference will be in the nature of the issues which need to be addressed to enable the church to live in ways which significantly impact on its environment with a life-transforming message.

The transformation process
Transformation incorporates the two dimensions of spiritual renewal and structural redesign. One cannot be pursued without regard for the other if there is to be significant progress in the long term. Churches that want neither have confined themselves to a rut. When they reach the point, either through desperation or boredom, of wanting to escape from their '*rutualism*', they tend to move in one of two directions. Those groups which earnestly seek spiritual renewal may in due time experience *periodic revivals*. Such fresh movements of the Spirit go in one of

three directions. (1) They are terminated through determined opposition. (2) They are embraced by the parent body only to be 'killed with kindness' and suffocated by a thousand qualifications. (3) They find an independent existence as a separate organization in an uneasy alliance with the church whose offspring they are; or they become a new church, either because they were forcibly ejected or because they were made to feel so unwanted that they felt it best to leave. The lesson to be learned here is that spiritual renewal must be related to structural renewal. New wine cannot be contained for long within inflexible old wineskins. Before long the skins will burst under the pressure of the fermentation produced by the new wine.

Those churches which concentrate on *reorganization* as their principle means of ensuring institutional survival in the face of chronic numerical decline, usually discover that the actual benefits of their restructuring fall seriously short of the canvassed expectation and, not infrequently, the last state is worse than the first.

Within long-standing institutions a powerful dynamic is at work to ensure that any significant changes are short term and played down so that conditions return to normal. Radical movements combining renewal and reorganization have to negotiate the 'black hole' of institutional protectionism if they are to become expressions of *continuous transformation*. The older and more prestigious the organization, the more skill it has acquired in dealing with innovative ideas which, from time to time, have threatened its rigidly traditional assumptions, values, and priorities. 'Black holes' come in two forms. One type of 'black hole' is 'preservationism', which is characterized by an enormous capacity to absorb energy to preserve a reputation which has been gained over an extended period of time as the institution responded to the priority issues of former years. To be fair to institutions that have a track record of significant achievements, there is justification in their nervousness that new commitments may jeopardize that hard-earned reputation. The key issue is to find ways of responding to the current agenda without sacrificing existing strengths. The other form which 'black holes' take is 'restorationism', which, in this context, is defined as a commitment to recreate an ideal state or golden era as a foundational principal of a church's self-identification. Although the attempt will prove illusory, if not futile, it will absorb a great deal of energy as the church rallies around its patriarchal figures who are the guardians and exponents of its history and affirms its identity by vocalizing its distinctive 'tribal' terminology.

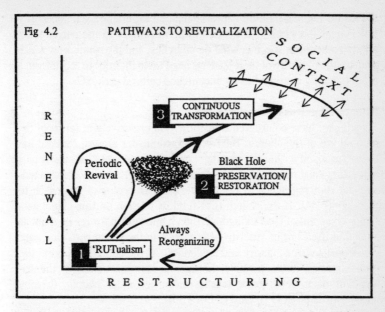

Fig 4.2   PATHWAYS TO REVITALIZATION

Would-be innovators are either safely contained and rendered harmless by the institution or they disappear without trace down the 'black hole' of 'preservationism' or 'restorationism'. Both of these are characterized by increasing isolation from the contemporary social context as well as from other branches of the Christian church.

Approaches to transformation
Transformation, which includes both spiritual renewal and organizational restructuring, need not, in most circumstances, be conceived primarily in revolutionary terms. Transformation implies changing of vital elements of the organization's value system which have been forged during its long history.

In any tradition there are valuable elements to be preserved. We need to ask what issues were originally being addressed which gave rise to the distinctives of any organization and which in course of time became a 'tradition'. Traditions are not respected by attempting to live in the past, but by learning from the past. Questions need to be raised as to whether the same needs exist now as when the institution was at its most formative period. If circumstances have changed significantly, then the institution must ask how its accumulated experience and concentration of resources might be applied more effectively to the current situation. To be more specific, what do churches, and the seminaries which prepare the majority of their leaders, need to do in order to move from a predominantly churched to an unchurched cultural context?

Defining the extent of transformation

Thus far we have considered transformation exclusively in terms of the internal life of the church. But, as Howard Snyder argues, renewal has to be conceived within the paradigm of the kingdom of God, ie, as part of a total global transformation.[5] In order to underline how comprehensive our thinking needs to be, he speaks of an ecological approach to theology (p 44). If the church is to fulfil its mission on this planet as a sign and servant of God's kingdom, then it must yearn for renewal not as an end in itself but in order to bear witness in the world with increased comprehensiveness, clarity and credibility. As the church embodies the transformation made possible through its identification with the triumphant risen Lord, grace reaches more and more people, thereby bringing greater glory to God (2 Cor 4:15).

Snyder points out that God's *'oikonomia'* describes his economy for the fullness of time. 'The economy of God is the manifestation of the Kingdom of God. It is reconciling and uniting of all things, visible and invisible, under authority of Jesus Christ' (p 51). 'Biblically, God's economy is to put all things in proper order within his *'oikos'*. This is the image involved in saying God has an oikonomia for the fullness of time to unite or reconcile all things in Jesus Christ (Eph 1:10)' (p 56).

The Scriptures refer to the world in both positive and negative terms. The world belongs to God by right of creation, providence and redemption, but at the present time it is under the sway of the evil one, who is described as the prince of this world. Believers in Christ must recognize that they no longer belong to this present world order, but in renouncing its values they are not to isolate themselves by becoming indifferent to world concerns. They are to perform as salt and light in the world, exerting a far wider influence than their relative lack of numbers would suggest. They are to function as 'the overwhelming minority'. They are to remain vitally involved with the affairs of this world and concerned about every aspect of the well-being of this planet as stewards of God's creation—a solemn responsibility placed upon God's covenant people from before the Fall (Gen 1:27, 28; 2:15, 19-20).

The church's message of reconciliation is directed toward itself with a view to bringing about a transformation which is evident both in the church's internal life and in its engagement with the world. This is the *normality* which must be striven for if *nominality* is to be effectively countered. Yet two cautionary words must be added. The first is the need to recognize that the kingdom has not come in all its fullness within the life of the church. The kingdom is present now here on earth, yet only in a provisional form. Its inauguration with the first coming of Christ has yet to be consummated by his glorious return. There is the constant tension of having to live with the 'now' and 'not yet' of the kingdom. The second point is related to this, namely that the church here on earth is composed of forgiven sinners who are still in the process of being saved. They are not yet perfected and as a consequence they are, in their personal lives as well as in the institutions of which they are part, liable to fall short of the ideal by demonstrating serious inconsistencies due to human frailty and demonic influence.

The Reformers were realistic in assessing the spiritual achievements of their day. They recognized that the renewal was partial, and that its permanence could not be guaranteed. They therefore spoke of the need for the church to be *semper reformanda*—always reforming. The church must accept blame for the prevalence of nominality when it lives content with its inconsistencies, or demonstrates its hypocrisy by castigating its erring members, or society at large, for the very sins and shortcomings which are tolerated in its own institutional life. The church on a renewal track declares in which direction it is heading, and freely acknowledges its shortcomings. People will be attracted by its honesty, recognizing that it is travelling in the right direction, without pretending to have arrived. After all, discipleship is a life-long pilgrimage. A disciple is a life in formation and never a finished product. There is no graduation ceremony this side of glory!

The transformation of the church must be in accordance with Snyder's comprehensive ecological model. The church does not have the option of being selective in terms of its global concerns, although its ministry commitments will of necessity be selective in accordance with the call of God and the resources which he has given to each local congregation to play a specific local role as part of the larger global enterprise. The various elements of transformation are represented in Fig 4.3, which seeks to express this comprehensiveness, and each item will be expanded and applied to the nominality context in the course of

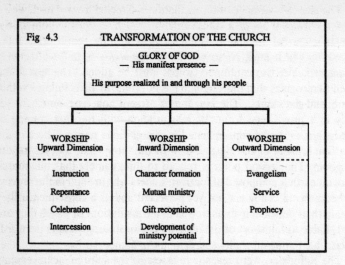

Fig 4.3   TRANSFORMATION OF THE CHURCH

this chapter. I wish to acknowledge my indebtedness to Howard Snyder for providing the general outlines of the model, which I have taken the liberty of adapting (for Snyder's original see *Liberating the Church*, p 82).

THE DIRECTION SETTING ROLE OF LEADERSHIP

Throughout the long and varied history of the church it is clear that significant periods of renewal and advance have been characterized by leadership which was of a high quality and level of commitment. While not excluding any from joining the ranks of the church, the Scriptures also set a high standard for leadership. Clearly leaders shoulder a heavy burden of responsibility which should cause them to cry out to God, 'Who is sufficient for these things?' But the Lord is the head of his church and, as such, he accepts ultimate responsibility and has promised to provide the necessary knowledge, wisdom, discernment, skills and strength to those who ask in humility and yield their lives as his obedient servants. Such promises do not guarantee that mistakes will not be made, that there will not be times of perplexity and frustration, or that failure will not be experienced. These varied experiences are part of the learning and maturing process, and the troughs are necessary to compensate for the high points to ensure that our dependence is still founded upon the Lord and not on human resourcefulness.

An essential characteristic of spiritual leadership is *authenticity*. Church leaders must embody what they teach. Transformed churches are characterized by a dedicated and enthusiastic leadership which knows where it is going, has a discipled impatience in wanting to move ahead, expresses its yearning to God in heartfelt intercession, marshalls all the resources it can identify towards the accomplishment of the vision, and gives God the credit for every significant step taken.

Build a sense of community among the leaders

Significant progress is unlikely to be made until the leaders demonstrate their commitment to one another in seeking the will of God and affirming one another's contribution towards that end. In the case of a new pastor, high priority should be given to cultivating relationships with the leadership team, both the paid and volunteer members. Leaders grow in their appreciation of the worth of each person as they provide personal support and affirm each other's distinctive gifts. Trust is built as the pastor takes time to learn the personal history, journey of faith, personality traits, areas of interest and giftedness in ministry, leadership track record and agendas of the individual team members.

Establish a philosophy of ministry

Renowned church consultant Lyle Schaller identifies one of the key causes of lethargy as the loss of a sense of direction. He offers the following prescription for churches so afflicted:

> In a majority of congregations afflicted with the complacency, lethargy, or passivity ... the most effective response requires a redefinition of the role of that parish. This approach is based on the belief that the life and ministry of most churches can be conceptualized as a series of chapters. Frequently each chapter is written around a distinctive role or identity of that congregation.[6]

In order to formulate a soundly based philosophy of ministry the following considerations need to be borne in mind. Biblical priorities need to be established. The ministry context needs to be investigated. Target groups need to be identified. Denominational distinctives need to be contextualized. And the God-given ministry resources within the congregation need to be activated.

Many churches have tried to take the easy way out by adopting a philosophy of ministry from another church. Such short cuts seldom work because the contexts, church histories and internal dynamics are not identical. Furthermore, the adopting of a statement crafted elsewhere means that there is not the sense of ownership that comes when a congregation has worked hard to develop a statement which accurately describes where they are, who they are, and the direction they want to take. A philosophy of ministry statement is more than a human product: it is the fruit of corporately seeking the will of God and emerging with a clearer sense of self-identity and purpose, which are essential prerequisites in serving as fellow-workers with God (2 Cor 6:1).

Bearing in mind the above caution, the following two examples are given to clarify what is meant by a 'philosophy of ministry'. You will notice how different they are in format. Sometimes they seem to state the obvious. But the important point to grasp is that their value is in the work which lies behind them. As the leadership of the congregation struggles to express what it is in business to achieve, so it establishes the key objectives which provide the parameters for the many activities which collectively constitute the ministry of that church. As we will see later, decentralization is crucial to the ministerial effectiveness of the church in winning the nominals in the 1990s; but without clear philosophy of ministry to provide both direction and cohesion, decentralization may lead to fragmentation and a loss of momentum.

Fig 4.4   **PHILOSOPHY OF MINISTRY**
Calvary Community Church, Thousand Oaks, California

CELEBRATE THE LIFE OF GOD
- through awarenes of and response to God's presence
- through communion and commitment to Jesus Christ
- through oneness and praise in the Holy Spirit

CULTIVATE PERSONAL GROWTH IN CHRIST
- through study of Bible doctrine
- through application of biblical principles to life
- through development of mature Christians who reflect the character of Christ

CARE ABOUT ONE ANOTHER IN CHRIST
- through sharing one another's joys, growth and needs
- through recognition, development and use of gifts of the Spirit by every believer
- through service and sacrifice to meet each other's needs

> **COMMUNICATE CHRIST TO THE WORLD**
> - through penetration of society
> - through reproduction of our life in Christ by evangelism
> - through disciplining by celebration, cultivation and caring
>
> *Reproduced by permission*

All Saints, Beverly Hills, California, is a church with a very different ecclesiastical and theological tradition. The following is the result of a day's deliberation of the vestry augmented by other lay leaders.

Fig 4.5   **PHILOSOPHY OF MINISTRY**
All Saints, Beverley Hills, California

All Saints is a community of disciples seeking to glorify God, to grow in Christ and to be empowered by the Holy Spirit.

We are called to proclaim Jesus Christ as Lord and Saviour, to be a place of worship, healing and prayer, and to further God's Kingdom in the world.

As we WORSHIP, we seek to celebrate God's presence, express God's love for us in Jesus Christ, and be renewed and empowered by the Holy Spirit through a broad variety of worship experiences and the offering of our daily lives.

In our DISCIPLESHIP ministry, we seek to call people to Christ, to grow in him and to live out the Good News.

In providing PASTORAL CARE, we seek to create a nurturing environment where brokenness can be healed and where people can discover their full potential in Christ.

Because we are called to SERVICE, we seek to identify specific needs, both spiritual and material, in the community, to act on these needs as God calls us and to become faithful stewards of God's creation.

Through EVANGELISM, we seek to share the Gospel with all people and to work for the extension of God's kingdom throughout the world.

The God-given genius of leadership is to achieve a firm grasp of the big picture. Leaders must be able to make sense of a complex and confusing picture and pick their way through the multiplicity of demands which surround them. They have to learn the discipline of standing back in order to gain perspective and take time to discern the wood from the trees. In the midst of the clamour of constant demands which tug at leaders from all sides, they have to learn to listen to the voice of God, to know what should be done and what should be left undone or left to another time. Such is the discipline which Jesus exhibited in the course of this three years of public ministry. It was a principle reason why he achieved so much within such a short space of time.

Once established, a philosophy of ministry needs to be reviewed every three years to ensure that it is still appropriate to the situation. The ministry context may change due to a population turnover resulting in a different ethnic composition, economic level or employment categories. The church itself may change significantly due to shifts in the community demographics, or new theological currents, or vision for new ministry involvements. If there is one thing worse than a church not having an agreed philosophy of ministry, it is a ministry statement designed to respond to *yesterday's* ministry needs and opportunities.

Formulate a vision statement
This is a brief, one sentence statement which crystallizes your self-identity and mission focus. It is the slogan which appears outside your church, in your bulletins, flyers and other forms of advertizing. In winning back the nominals, it is more important to state basic values or ministry emphasis than to provide a denominational label. Most lapsed and distanced church members are not attracted by denominational distinctions. They are not wooed by calls for 'tribal' loyalty. They are likely to be attracted to the churches which break through those negative stereotypes of organized religion which keep them away. A well-chosen vision statement can cause people to rethink and be attracted to churches which respond to their needs, providing the 'goods' are available as advertized!

DEALING WITH NOMINALITY AT THE LEADERSHIP LEVEL

Nominality is so entrenched in the life of some churches that a great deal of preparatory work needs to be done before embarking on the task of formulating a philosophy of ministry. We have already mentioned the importance of the senior pastors investing time to get to know their leaders on a personal level, to the point where they can share their journeys of faith with one another. Openness regarding the past provides the necessary foundation for corporate dreaming about the future. Otherwise we are liable to be haunted by nightmares generated by the past rather than inspired by dreams of future possibilities!

Identify the informal power structure
Especially in a church permeated with nominality, there tend to exist powerful individuals and pressure groups who influence decision-making despite the fact that they are not members of the committees responsible. Out of frustration, disillusionment or sheer exhaustion they have resigned from official positions, while continuing to influence the course of events from the sidelines. They have not relinquished their influence and their unseen presence is felt in the committees of the church where their spokespersons continue to serve or have been elected in their place; it is therefore important that the source of the viewpoints expressed is identified, if the church is going to make any progress through stormy waters. The individuals in question may need to be approached directly for their views to be solicited or their involvement invited, before the matter comes up for committee discussion.

It must also be recognized that organizational charts hide as much as they seek to make clear. The chart shows you how the work of the church has been divided into separate departments and the nature of the formal hierarchy of authority and responsibility. But the chart reveals nothing about the quality of relationships which exist along those lines of communication, nor of the frequency of meetings. The organizational chart below is represented in two ways. The first is the formal chart, while the second version tells you where special relationships have been established or where people do not relate so well. Barbara, the church secretary, has the closest relationship with Mary in Adult Education because they are both single and spend a great deal of leisure time together. John, the Pastor, whose commitment to the outreach ministries of the church contributed significantly to its rapid growth in the early days, has the closest professional affinity with Paul, whom he recruited to take over when his other church duties demanded more of his attention. Jerry does not see eye to eye with the Senior Pastor, but is able to voice his concerns at the Church Board level through a close friend of his who serves on the board. Rachel, in charge of children's ministry feels that John does not give sufficient attention to her department, so she ensures her concerns are heard at Board level through her close friend Helen, who is wife of the Board Chairman. Astute leaders ensure they are plugged into the informal communication channels as well as the formal!

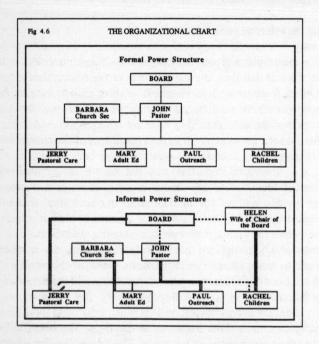

Fig 4.6   THE ORGANIZATIONAL CHART

Formal Power Structure

BOARD

BARBARA
Church Sec

JOHN
Pastor

JERRY
Pastoral Care

MARY
Adult Ed

PAUL
Outreach

RACHEL
Children

Informal Power Structure

BOARD

HELEN
Wife of Chair of
the Board

BARBARA
Church Sec

JOHN
Pastor

JERRY
Pastoral Care

MARY
Adult Ed

PAUL
Outreach

RACHEL
Children

Expose the church leadership to other church models

For many church leaders the only church they have ever known is the one in which they have moved through the ranks until they have been appointed to a leadership position within that congregation. Due to the conservative nature of many churches, a lengthy period of loyal service is required as a prerequisite for office. As a consequence, the leadership of many established congregations is unrepresentative of the broader community. Especially when the neighbourhood is characterized by rapid population turnover. Such leaders become out of touch with the actual ministry needs, and may even display hostile attitudes towards the 'outsiders' who are invading the community and changing its character.

It may prove helpful for such defensive leaders to visit other churches which display some of the ministry principles which the new pastor wishes to embody. One temptation to be resisted is the attempt to transpose the ministry model of some famous megachurch, which is usually not transferable because it is the result of an unusually gifted leader being in the right place at the right time. In other words, it is the product of a unique set of circumstances.[7] Do these large churches have anything to teach the small struggling church seeking direction and inspiration? Yes indeed. They can provide principles of ministry which may be transferable from one ministry context to another. But if the results are not so dramatic, it should not be concluded that the fault lies with the church attempting to translate the principles. It may be that their own ministry context is not so responsive or they may not have the same growth potential.

Sometimes the megachurch can prove too intimidating to provide an effective model from which principles can be drawn. When this is a danger, it is more helpful to take the leadership to visit a church with which they can more readily identify because it shares a similar ministry situation to their own, does not have superstar leadership, is of the same, or a related, church tradition, and is sufficiently ahead to provide ideas for the next steps, rather than being so remote as to require a space shuttle. If church leaders can meet with their counterparts in another church which is in a transformational mode, then much learning and significant attitude changes can be brought about within a short space of time.

Change the sequence in selecting lay volunteers for key positions in order to reorder priorities

The order in which appointments are made at the annual meeting indicates the relative importance assigned to each position. When the emphasis is placed on those tasks which relate to the internal ministries of the church, then the introverted stance of the church is reinforced. A change in the order in which appointments are made can jolt the congregation out of its mind-set and signal that the mission stance of the church is being taken seriously. Schaller emphasizes this point when he says:

> the priorities used in assigning influential lay volunteers to offices, committees, and boards may be the most influential single factor in determining the purpose and operational priorities of many congregations! Therefore, these assignments should be made in a manner that is consistent with the values and goals of that congregation.[8]

Any change in sequencing should normally be explained as expressing the programme priorities for the church in the coming year. The church members also need to be aware of the significance of that particular area of responsibility and of the gifts and experience required for effective leadership.

Leadership qualities to be sought
The effectiveness of the ministries of a local church depends on the quality of the leadership. Great care needs to be taken in the selection of future leaders in order to avoid perpetuating nominality in the congregation and to take steps to deal with the condition. Max De Pree, the chairman of Herman Miller Inc, an office furnishing company listed among the ten best managed companies in North America by *Fortune* magazine, provides the following list to serve as guidelines in leadership selection.
—has consistent and dependable integrity
—cherishes heterogeneity and diversity
—searches out competence
—is open to contrary opinion
—communicates easily at all levels
—understands the concept of equity and consistently advocates it
—leads through serving
—is vulnerable to the skills and talents of others
—is intimate with the organization and its work
—is able to see the broad picture (beyond own area and focus)
—is a spokesperson and diplomat
—can be a tribal storyteller (an important way of transmitting corporate culture)
—tells *why* rather than *how*[9]

Those involved in leadership selection soon come to realize that character flaws are more difficult to deal with than skill limitations. Therefore it comes as no surprise to discover that the Scriptures place such a great emphasis on spiritual qualifications for church leadership (1 Tim 3:1-16; Tit 1:7-9).

Leadership support
Once volunteer workers have been appointed to a task they should not be abandoned to sink or swim. They will need ongoing support in a number of areas. The demands of the job should be monitored to ensure

that they are not increasing to the point where they are in danger of becoming unmanageable. Sometimes the requirements of the area of responsibility are underestimated by the person assigning the task, and this mistake needs to be acknowledged and promptly rectified. The church leadership needs to be kept informed as to progress, resource requirements, ongoing problems and future plans. The individuals carrying the assigned responsibilities need pastoral support for themselves and their families. As the ministry grows, the volunteer may require further skill training to that he or she can continue to move the ministry forward. Leadership skills are acquired in response to the practical demands of ministry rather than in a theoretical setting of the classroom. Lessons are best learned on a need-to-know basis.

The effective senior pastor delegates with care and never abdicates leadership responsibility. Discipleship signifies that the church is in the people-building business rather than simply processing people to conform to a particular mould. It entails empowering people to do ministry by encouraging initiative, developing skills and helping individuals to learn by their mistakes. As George Barna perceptively comments, it entails treating volunteers like professionals—not 'cheap labour'.[10] Out of concern for the individual's needs, as well as for the well-being of their area of operation, meaningful and regular interactions should be scheduled.

Leaders of spiritually vibrant churches are ambitious for the people around them, rather than regarding them as supports by which their own position can be elevated. They are not threatened by people around them who have gifts which they do not possess, or who are more gifted than themselves. This point is dramatically illustrated by a business practice of David Ogilvy, of the world-renowned advertizing agency, Ogilvy and Mather. In his book *On Advertising* he recounts how he makes the point to his new branch managers of the need to be appointing and growing people of ability. When a new branch office is opened he sends a gift to the new manager. It is a wooden doll of the Russian *matrioshka* variety. Unscrew the outer doll, and a smaller doll is found inside. Around the smallest doll in the set David Ogilvy ties a paper with the following message: 'If each of us hires people who are smaller than we are, we shall become a company of *dwarfs*, but if each of us hires people who are bigger than we are, Ogilvy and Mather will become a company of *giants*.'[11] Likewise in the church we are in the people-growing business: helping people to achieve their full potential in Christ.[12]

A LIFE-ENHANCING WORSHIP EXPERIENCE

As a youngster I used to sing the chorus,

> Turn your eyes upon Jesus,
> Look full in his wonderful face,
> And the things of earth will grow strangely dim,
> In the light of his glory and grace.

While continuing to appreciate the important truth which these lines were seeking to express, namely the need to focus attention on the Lord without the distraction of worldly concerns, I think that the wording is misleading. Rather than the world becoming 'strangely dim' in the light of his glory and grace, I believe that the world takes on its true perspective and colour. We see all the more clearly as a result of experiencing the glory and grace of God. A similar misconception is expressed in a bumper sticker I noticed on a car parked at a Christian university. It announced that the owner was a 'visitor to this planet'! The biblical image of the pilgrim cannot be reduced to that of a tourist, for life's pilgrimage on this planet is long and arduous, entailing a commitment to this world in its present sorry state as well as a vision for its eventual transformation.

Life and truth

The worship of God's people lifts us above the multitude of mundane concerns which surround us in our daily lives. It restores true perspective and challenges us to reorder our priorities as we dwell corporately in God's presence and see the world from his vantage point. Churches which are attracting significant numbers of those who were formerly nominal Christians are characterized by worship which expresses a transcendent dimension. There is a life-enriching and life-transforming divine encounter. This divine dimension cannot be fabricated. Worship must not be reduced to entertainment, education, or even evangelism, because God himself is the focus of our worship. The entertainer, the educator and the evangelist will get in the way of the possibility of a divine encounter if they are not sensitive to the leading of the risen Lord through promptings of his Spirit. Without that sensitivity ministry becomes performance and worship is impoverished to the point where it loses its Godward awareness and focus.

In worship our focus is on God, and our singing, praying, teaching and liturgical responses are designed to lead us into his presence. Our generation is both an audience generation and one that is hungry for an authentic experience of God. People may gather in significant numbers to be entertained or edified, but they will only undergo significant transformation leading to incorporation into the body of Christ if they encounter the presence of the Lord. Where there is the realization of God's presence in our worship, the unconverted and lapsed will respond to the Lord's call as those who are fleeing to him for forgiveness and restoration, rather than as those who are calculatingly 'deciding for Christ'.

There are two vital elements in the communication process: truth and life. Sometimes the Holy Spirit exposes an individual to the truth first in order to experience the life. At other times it is involvement in a community displaying abundant life which stimulates a person's spiritual appetite to know the truth. Unfortunately, we seldom succeed in preserving this balance, especially in our worship. For instance, in some more cerebral traditions we confine ourselves to hymns which, although rich in doctrinal content, only speak *about* God. In traditions which are experience oriented, God is directly addressed through the hymns and songs which express personal devotion and a longing for the relationship to become more intimate, yet without any expression of the foundational truths on which such intimacy must be based. The danger of the first approach is an arid intellectualism, and of the second approach, a self-indulgent emotionalism. The only adequate response to nominality is a healthy balance of the truth as revealed in Jesus Christ with the abundant life imparted by the risen Lord through his Spirit.

The role of faith

Transcendence involves a conviction that God comes to inhabit the praises of his people and that there is significant evidence of his presence in the impact which the worship service makes upon the worshippers. Where there is a rising level of expectation within the community of believers much more is likely to happen. Jesus himself said that he could do no mighty work in Nazareth because of their unbelief and he chided his disciples for their lack of faith in failing to heal the epileptic. When individuals with the gift of faith in God's power to work miracles are supported by a community of faith of expectant believers, then God will minister through his church. People will be challenged and changed through the various elements of the worship experience, whether it be the singing of the hymns, listening to the Scriptures being read, a choral item, a testimony, the words of the liturgy, the preaching, partaking of the communion elements of bread and wine, or prayer groups formed to minister to one another in the context of corporate worship.

The whole person is ministered to: mind, body and spirit. Such Spirit-filled ministry has both personal and corporate aspects. It lifts the worshippers towards God and also sends them into a needy world to share something of what they have received. Individuals who have themselves met with God, and observed other people experience significant encounters, are those most likely to be advocates for their church among the needy people with whom they come into contact. It is not the attraction of esoteric experiences, but of God meeting us either in the mundane or in the overwhelming needs of our daily lives. As people experience the immediate and long term benefits for themselves, so they will overcome their inhibitions and commend the ministries of their church to others.

Take care in the preparation of public worship

The weekly worship service is the 'shop window' of the church. It is the time when the scattered community gathers to express its corporate identity and to be renewed in the presence of the Lord. It is the weekly occasion when the church goes 'public'. On that occasion, beyond all others, the committed attenders need to feel a sense of pride in the quality and relevance of what happens during the worship service. When they are reduced to boredom, or inflamed by embarrassment, they will cease to be advocates for their church. I sometimes ask congregations, 'Tell me frankly, what changes need to be made around here, in order for you to feel motivated to invite your unchurched family members, friends, neighbours and work colleagues?' It is a tough question, but one which needs to be faced if churches are to begin to address the nominality problem in their midst.

INCREASING THE COMMITMENT LEVEL OF THE CONGREGATION

As we have previously noted, there are a variety of reasons for low commitment level in the congregation. One which we have already addressed is lack of commitment among the leaders which the congregation simple mirrors by its own apathy. Lyle Schaller, with characteristic thoroughness, lists twenty-seven causes of passivity in the local church.[13] Without taking time to list all that he mentions, the following responses are identified with his list in mind.

Leaders' commitment to the church they serve

The senior pastor sets an example to the entire church of servant leadership and sacrificial long-term commitment to the local church he or she has been called by God to lead. Strong mutual commitment between pastor, paid staff and the membership of the church results in low staff turnover. A significant proportion of the paid staff is likely to be recruited from the ranks of the congregation. The larger the church, the more often this is the case. The leader has the courage to lead, is able to keep the big picture in focus and make proactive rather than reactive decisions. Leaders have an instinctive strategic grasp and sense of timing which enables them to be at the right place at the right time in order to provide motivation and serve as a rallying point. They are willing to be confrontational when the occasion demands, but take pastoral measures to ensure that their action does not result in people feeling alienated.

A congregation is motivated for service when the church has a clear sense of mission rather than being preoccupied with self-preservation issues. It is primarily concerned to shape the future rather than to restore the past. This commitment to mission is shown by the way it deploys its ministry resources. The most able and dedicated people are located at the frontiers of the church's life and witness. The gifts and leadership abilities of individuals who have recently joined the church are promptly recognized by inviting them to occupy positions of influence. A substantial proportion of the church's budget is also assigned for outreach ministries embracing both evangelism and service. Paid staff are in place to resource, coordinate and participate in ministry teams composed of unpaid volunteers, rather than to do ministry on behalf of the people.

Congregational participation in the decision-making process

The opinions of the congregation are regularly sought by the leaders, who then maintain ongoing communication concerning the issues which leads to the taking of appropriate action. In this regard, Schaller comments,

> A comparatively widespread cause of congregational pas-
> sivity is soliciting ideas, suggestions, complaints, recommen-
> dations and criticisms from all the members with great
> publicity—and then (a) ignoring all this material or (b)
> digesting it, but never reporting back to all the members on
> what happened or (c) vetoing all or nearly all proposals for
> innovative programming.[14]

The leaders ensure that it is not just the people on either end of the communication spectrum who are heard because they are the ones making the most noise, but they also schedule opportunities for the silent majority to voice their opinions. When it comes to carrying a vote and implementing the decisions, the most influential segment consists of the middle ground occupied by the progressive-conservatives and the conservative-progressives. They also provide the social cement which prevents polarization (see Fig 4.6).

As a congregation grows in size there is an inevitable tendency for the decision-making process to move from being participatory to being representative. 'In congregations with over three or four hundred mem-

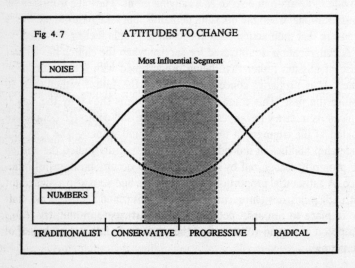

Fig 4.7   ATTITUDES TO CHANGE

bers it may not be possible to secure meaningful involvement in this process from more than one-fifth to one-half of the members.'[15] As issues become increasingly complex and the congregation increasingly diverse, people are often content to let their elected representatives deal with complicated matters on their behalf. They have voted them into their positions because they have confidence in their expertise and only wish to be consulted when a congregational decision is required after the intricacies have been worked through. The responsibility of the leaders is to be constantly asking the question, 'Who needs to know?' and to ensure that consultations with appropriate people are taking place at each stage of the planning process.

Effective leaders are in close and constant touch with their constituencies. They recognize that most significant ministry developments in the local church take place from the grass-roots up rather than the mountain-top down. It is their task to relate the ministry initiatives to the overall philosophy of ministry of the church and to ensure that new ministries are not diversionary.

The congregation's involvement in ministry

High levels of motivation depend on every ministry programme having a clearly defined purpose and on insistence that its effectiveness is periodically evaluated. The leadership team members responsible for each area of ministry have a strong sense of call from God and of being affirmed by the congregation and its pastors and elders. They realize the significance of their contribution to the ministry goals of the church and the wider concerns of God's kingdom. Such an awareness means that their motivation level matches their commitment level. People with high commitment but low motivation may continue to serve reliably, but they are apathetic or defeatist about the results of their labours. They are more protective than purposeful. On the other hand, people with high motivation for their ministry concerns but low commitment to the local church are likely to fragment operations by promoting their independent agendas and generating rival loyalties. Individuals with low motivation and low loyalty represent those who have usually been pressured into doing a job they did not really want to do but lacked the strength of character to say 'No'.

The significant churches of the 1990s will not be built around professionally led, centrally organized and church-based programmes. Their ministry focus will be on people rather than programmes, and the strategy will be to meet people where they are or on neutral territory. In other words, in a predominantly unchurched society ministry will need to be decentralized and dispersed. George Barna provides some wise guidelines in developing new programmes.

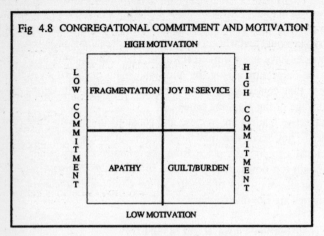

Fig 4.8 CONGREGATIONAL COMMITMENT AND MOTIVATION

HIGH MOTIVATION

LOW COMMITMENT		HIGH COMMITMENT
FRAGMENTATION	JOY IN SERVICE	
APATHY	GUILT/BURDEN	

LOW MOTIVATION

There were three dominant justifications for launching new programmes.

First, by offering a program, more people were likely to know about the existence of the type of support available through that ministry, and therefore greater numbers of people could be served. In some ways, having a program made the process of seeking help easier: there was a designated time or place at which people skilled in helping would be readily available.

A second justification was that establishing a program was a way of acknowledging the breadth of need for such outreach. This enabled the church to involve more people in that form of ministry, and allowed them to provide some consistency in methods of helping people in need.

The third reason for a new program was that some needs required special expertise in order to provide effective, healthy outreach.[16]

Voluntary organizations, including churches, do not function effectively if they are over-reliant on elected committees to implement programmes. The committee structure all too often creates an artificial division between the decision-makers and those who are supposed to implement the decisions. One central board or committee is needed to ensure coordination, continuity and accountability in the implementation of the purposes for which the organization exists. The majority of the initiatives and work deployment take place within the *Task Force*, which differs from the committee concept in the following aspects. The Task Force consists of a hand-picked team, all with a passion for the particular ministry and bringing experience and gifts to bear on the accomplishment of the task. They are not responsible to any particular interest group whose concerns they are intended to safeguard. New people can readily be fitted into these positions. Task forces also provide fruitful opportunities for service for those people who can only serve on a short-term basis due to other commitments, or are highly creative people whose energies evaporate as soon as the systems are in place and in good working order. Some people are project persons rather than long-term commitment types.

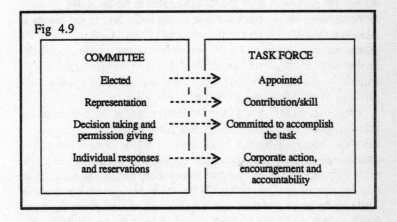

Fig 4.9

COMMITTEE		TASK FORCE
Elected	------>	Appointed
Representation	------>	Contribution/skill
Decision taking and permission giving	------>	Committed to accomplish the task
Individual responses and reservations	------>	Corporate action, encouragement and accountability

Expressing appreciation

While the church does not exist as a mutual admiration society, it must affirm each person in terms of who they are as persons made in the image of God and therefore of intrinsic worth, and also in response to their contribution to the life and ministry of the local church. Volunteers must neither be exploited nor taken for granted. People need to feel appreciated and we should make a special point of looking out for those persons who seldom if ever receive any public recognition. This does not necessarily entail having them stand in front of the congregation to receive applause. Some would be acutely embarrassed by such public visibility. The key is to thank each person in an appropriate manner, which may mean writing them a letter, sending flowers or treating them to a meal, etc.

EVANGELIZATION WITHIN THE WORSHIPPING CONGREGATION

The task of evangelization has suffered from a serious misconception in the minds of many people, especially within the evangelical tradition. The western emphasis on conversion as an individualized crisis experience has caused us to lose sight of the process element in the evangelizing task.

Realize the good news is for the church as well as for the world

Beyond every initial response made by an individual to the claims of Christ on their life, lie repeated challenges to hear afresh the call of the gospel message, leading to a deeper understanding of the atonement, further steps of obedience, or simply to being overwhelmed once again with the realization of the extent of God's love and forgiveness and the privilege of our adoption into the family of God.

These comments should not be interpreted as an argument for repeated conversion in the sense of a person stepping in and out of salvation. The Holy Spirit's initial work in regenerating a person is a once-for-all work of God. However, conversion, understood as a person's response to the Holy Spirit's operations within their life, is an ongoing process, and we continually have to be brought back to the basic truths of the gospel for those fresh realizations to take place. We never reach a stage where we no longer need to hear the saving truths proclaimed. The congregation is in continuing need of 'evangelization' if it is to serve as a 'gospelling' community in the world. When an evangelistic sermon is preached, the mature believer cannot simply sit back in the belief that the message is only for the unsaved who are present in the church on that occasion.

This also applies to the evangelistic preacher and one-to-one witness.

When the gospel message ceases to have an impact on the communicator, he or she is in danger of becoming nothing more than a religious salesperson. In sharing the gospel we ourselves are struck afresh by that message and often changed in the process of communication. I often ask my students, 'Tell me, when Peter was in the home of Cornelius, sharing the gospel with a Gentile audience, who was converted?' A careful reading of the text shows that Peter was as much struck by the experience as Cornelius and his household (see Acts 10 and 11).

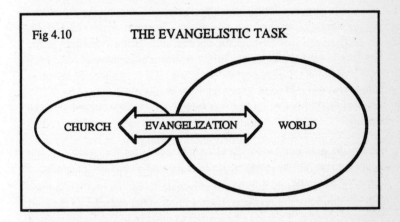

Fig 4.10   THE EVANGELISTIC TASK

CHURCH   EVANGELIZATION   WORLD

The church is renewed both as we ourselves respond afresh to the gospel message and as we see others making an initial response. It is in those churches which seldom see people coming to Christ through worship services and group activities where nominality is most likely to prevail.

Make the most of the occasions provided by the church's calendar of events

A further clarification may be in order at this point. The plea I am making is not that the ABCs of the gospel should be proclaimed from the pulpit every week. Such an approach to ministry would inevitably cause a hardening to the message through sheer repetition and would also mean that people who had made the initial act of commitment would not grow much beyond that point. Rather, the need is for the implications of the gospel to be recognized in the wide range of topics covered in the course of preaching the whole counsel of God. In my own ministry, I have discovered that, not infrequently, people have come to an initial or deeper realization of their need of the grace of God when the sermon was not primarily evangelistic in intention.

The challenge to engage in 'internal' evangelism differs from the challenge presented by the dechurched and unchurched nominals, and is different again from the challenge to evangelize those who have had no previous exposure to the message of the Bible and the life of the church. All three challenges require different approaches.

The themes covered during the course of the church's year provide ready-made opportunities for liturgical churches to focus on the gospel message. Great occasions such as Advent, Christmas, Easter and Pentecost all have obvious evangelistic applications. Other occasions in the church's life such as baptisms, infant dedications, confirmations, weddings and funerals also provide occasions for a pastorally sensitive challenge to those present to consider the claims of Christ.

Appropriate opportunities for response need to be coupled with the challenge. Some church traditions tend to overdo such responses, reducing them to a standardized format usually referred to as the 'altar call'. When the same format is used routinely it can easily become a ritual which loses its impact on the regular worshippers. There needs to be a variety in the forms of response appropriate to the theme of the message, the nature of the occasion, the tradition of the church and the kind of people present. They may be invited to meet in a designated area of the church, kneel at the communion rail, hand in a card, or request a booklet from the minister on the way out.

Sometimes the act is more symbolic, involving lighting a candle or hammering a nail into a cross. In discussing how to communicate the gospel effectively to the unchurched the point is often made that great care has to be taken over the language used. People unfamiliar with the Bible will not know the meaning of theological vocabulary and those outside our particular church tradition will be mystified by the religious jargon which we bandy around. The language issue is equally important when evangelizing nominal Christians. Often they are familiar with the terminology but have only the vaguest idea of what it means. Alternatively, they may have been turned off by the language, or by painful reminders of situations in which they were made uncomfortable under a barrage of such verbiage. Therefore, we have to find other ways of communicating those biblical concepts, utilizing carefully thought-out paraphrases and contemporary illustrations and giving definitions of technical terms.

These disciplines are required in both evangelical and non-evangelical contexts. In the former, people may have heard the 'buzz words' so often that they have become devalued, and in the latter, people may dismiss the message because they associate the language with discredited TV evangelists, or occasions when they were accosted by zealous but insensitive religious scalp-hunters who caused offence by the manner and timing of their approach. In communication terms, we have to become 'receptor oriented' in seeking ways to get across the message. The challenge facing us is to communicate the gospel in our very different twentieth century western setting with the same clarity that the church strove to achieve in the Mediterranean world of the first century.

Invite guest speakers gifted in challenging church attenders

It is often easier for pastors in their preaching to invite newcomers and visitors to consider the claims of Christ than to present the same challenge to members of the congregation. In such cases it may be helpful to invite a visiting minister with a special gift for evangelizing churched people. He or she provides a fresh voice or presents a new angle. Furthermore, some church members, and even longstanding leaders, will be prepared to talk confidently to such visitors precisely because they will be gone the next day. When individuals who have been holding out on the pastor respond to the preaching of the gospel by a visitor, the pastor must not feel jealous that the visitor succeeded where he or she had failed. Rather it is an occasion for rejoicing.

Another bonus in inviting a visiting minister to conduct an evangelistic mission directed at the congregation is that it provides the pastor with an opportunity for follow-up, asking selected individuals what they thought about the message they had heard. The fact that the gospel challenge was given by someone other than the pastor on that occasion allows for a 'distancing' which sometimes produces a more open discussion which may lead to significant personal ministry.

The focus of this chapter has been largely concerned with church renewal in terms of the internal dynamic, encompassing spiritual and structural issues. Revitalization of the existing members is a prerequisite for the church to engage the world. The upward and inward journey of restoration and renewal usually precedes the outward journey of mission.

The next three chapters explore three key contextual factors which have a significant relationship to nominality: urbanization, secularization, and religious pluralism. Then, in the final chapter we shall focus on the need for the church to develop a decentralized, mission-orientated structure and mode of operation, providing the support which the people of God need to help them survive spiritually in the market place and form 'communities of witness' to win back those frustrated and disillusioned by institutionalized religion.

NOTES

1. Lyle E. Schaller, *It's a Different World* (Abingdon Press; Nashville, 1989).
2. Kennon L. Callahan, *Effective Church Leadership* (Harper and Row; San Francisco, 1990).
3. Ibid, p 4.
4. George Barna, *User Friendly Churches* (Regal Books; Ventura, 1991) p 25.
5. Howard A. Snyder, *Liberating the Church* (InterVarsity Press; Downers Grove, 1983).
6. Lyle E. Schaller, *Activating the Passive Church*, p 12
7. George Barna describes a number of failed attempts to mimic one famous church with a weekly attendance of 14,000 in *User Friendly Churches*, pp 18–20.
8. Schaller, *Activating the Passive Church*, p 105.
9. Max De Pree, *Leadership is an Art* (Doubleday; New York, 1989) pp 119-120.
10. Barna, op cit, p 164.
11. David Ogilvy, *On Advertising* (Random House; New York, 1985), p 47.
12. For a fuller account of leadership in the local church see the author's *Followed or Pushed?—Understanding and Leading Your Church* (MARC Europe; 1987). Another book warmly recommended is Carl George and Bob Logan, *Leading and Managing Your Local Church* (Fleming H. Revell; Old Tappan, NJ, 1987).
13. Schaller, *Activating the Passive Church* pp 51-66.
14. Ibid, p 55.
15. Ibid, p 87.
16. Barna, op cit, pp 43-44.

CHAPTER FIVE

THE PROTESTANT MINDSET AND URBAN REALITY

I N RECENT YEARS missiologists have increasingly drawn attention to the significance of urbanization for world evangelization. If the church does not redeploy its human and material resources and develop strategies appropriate for the rapidly-growing and cosmopolitan populations of the urban world, then it will have failed to respond to the most significant demographic change of this century. Our concern, however, is with a related issue which has not been given so much attention, namely the *re*-evangelizing of the nominal urban Christian—ie, the winning back of those who still identify themselves as 'Christian'. In this chapter we will explore the significance of urbanization as a contributing cause of nominality, and then seek to develop strategies which relate to the dynamics of urban life. The goal is the reintegration of those who have distanced themselves from the church, and the incorporation of those who have never been members of the churchgoing community.

As we contemplate the urban challenge we are confronted with the contradictions that the very factors which assist churches in the evangelization of urban populations are the same as those which contribute to the loss of believers from the church when they relocate as migrants either from rural areas or small towns to large cities, or from one city to another. Urban relocation causes social disruption which opens up the possibility of fresh personal contacts and the forging of new allegiances; the crowded, cosmopolitan and mobile nature of urban life provides anonymity and freedom to make new choices, especially when individuals are released by virtue of their move, from peer-group pressure. It is readily apparent that such considerations have both a positive and a negative impact on the church's urban mission. The result of the Nominality Survey which the author conducted in cooperation with MARC Europe showed that mobility, on balance, was a positive rather than a negative influence. The more frequently people moved the more likely they were to be involved in church activities (see Appendix, p 279).

In countries experiencing rapid urbanization, in which there is a sizeable Christian presence, the church will have to face the challenge of retaining contact with its constituencies when they are on the move and often scattering in many different directions. Those people migrating from rural and small town communities to big cities are particularly vulnerable, because the churches in the city do not have the same community visibility and social strength as the churches from whence they come. They may be moving from an area of the country in which their denomination was particularly strong to an area where it only registers a token presence. In consequence these migrants may feel 'detribalized' or spiritually disenfranchised.

In urban societies secularization and pluralism are particularly pervasive. In the next two chapters we will explore the significance of these factors as further contributors to nominality. Some people become disoriented as the belief system which they experienced as normative in their former community is now relegated to counter-culture status in their new location. In their new urban settings they begin to face questions which were never raised while they were living in the secure confines of the environment in which they had been nurtured. So they become particularly vulnerable to the new alternative value systems which are now making their presence felt, and to which they have no adequate answers.

A further factor to be borne in mind in seeking to win back lapsed churchgoers, is that some of them may have relocated as a way out of their obligations to the churches where they were previously members. They may have been wanting to withdraw for some time, due to boredom or over-commitment, but were unable to do so on account of the social bonds which tied them to the church. Moving to another location provides the opportunity to break those ties. It is not unusual for persons who were pillars of the church to drop out of church life entirely once they move away. Some people, in fact, move house for precisely that reason. On the basis of 'once bitten, twice shy', they are particularly hard to win back. They need to be given the clear assurance that the new church will provide a significantly different kind of experience and that their willingness to get involved again will not be abused by overloading them.

In order to realize the extent and urgency of the urban challenge we need to review the progress of urbanization from the time of the Industrial Revolution. Prior to that monumental social upheaval there were, of course, many large cities around the world; but they were of a difference genre and accounted for only a small percentage of the population.

THE CHURCH'S INADEQUATE RESPONSE TO URBANIZATION IN BRITAIN DURING THE INDUSTRIAL REVOLUTION

As late as 1800 only 2.2 per cent of the population of Europe lived in cities, and that was the most urbanized of the continents.[1] Although 600,000 people lived in London in the early 1700s, Daniel Defoe could walk from St. Paul's Cathedral in the centre of London to the open fields in twenty minutes—a distance of half a mile![2] It was the development of new industry and the building of factories which provided the magnet to draw people from the countryside in vast numbers.

The social impact of the industrial revolution

The use of steam power and the development of mass production techniques spelled the gradual demise of cottage industries, although they continued for some time under a system known as 'putting out', by which the home-based artisans acted as subcontractors to supply mechanical parts for the new factories. The new industrial age also stimulated radical social changes by its marketing of human labour, its concentration of work in single enterprises, the emergence of the entrepreneur as a catalyst of change, and the generating and servicing of rapidly expanding markets by the development of more efficient transportation and communication systems. Before long, even the agricultural sector was profoundly affected by these social changes as industrial society provided markets, influenced demand and developed delivery systems until agriculture itself became another industry.[3]

It was during the first half of the nineteenth century that Britain became the birthplace of the Industrial Revolution. The first census of 1801 revealed that 20 per cent of the population lived in cities and towns with 10,000 or more inhabitants. By 1851, the urban population for the first time exceeded the rural population in size, with 38 per cent living in towns of more than 10,000. The overall population had doubled in size during that fifty year period. By 1931, 70 per cent were located in towns and cities. These new concentrations of population were not so much distribution centres, as the market towns had been, but centres of production.[4]

Another consequence of concentrating the work-force in factories was the need to develop transportation to ferry workers back and forth. As long as towns remained small, factory, shop and office workers could make the journey on foot, but as distances increased between the home and the work place so this became less practical. The development of transportation was also necessary to sustain the services of the rapidly growing cities and distribute the goods being produced there, as well as deliver the foodstuffs grown in the countryside.

The social disruption caused by rapid urbanization was severe and far-reaching. The work-force became dependent upon the fluctuating fortunes of the industries which provided employment, and the growing labour pool from which employers could hire meant little protection for the workers, who suffered grievous exploitation until they were able to organize themselves into trade unions. The break up of the rural community also led to the loss of established community leadership as people lost touch with one another in the process of relocating. Their arrival swelled the socially dislocated masses congregating in the densely populated areas to form communities which lacked supportive social structures.

The church's response to urbanization

In response to such major shifts in population the churches of England did too little too late. For instance, in the year 1736 the City of Sheffield consisted of one parish serving 10,000 souls. It was not until the 1830s that the Church of England began a programme of parochial reorganization, and fresh urgency was given to the task in the 1860s and 1870s following the national churchgoing survey of 1851. The same report also stimulated the Free Churches in their chapel building efforts.[5] Not only were there too few church buildings to house the burgeoning population, but the static parish structure did not relate to urban reality, which created high density communities and mobile populations. Prime Minister Disraeli replied in the 1870s to a bishop who confessed that 'the

Church would probably lose the city', 'Don't be mistaken, my Lord, the church has nothing to lose, for she has never had the city.'

Over two hundred years later the situation is most areas of the western world is no brighter with regard to the churchgoing habits of urban populations. In fact it has deteriorated significantly. The national churchgoing survey conducted by Robert Mann in 1851 revealed that 39 per cent of the population were in church on census Sunday, but that in the case of the seventy-three largest towns in England and Wales which had a population of over 10,000, only 25 per cent were in church.[6]

Church historian E. R. Wickham declares that 'From the eighteenth century and progressively through the nineteenth century, since the emergence of the industrial towns and the working classes, the labouring poor, the artisan class, as a class and as adults, have been outside the churches.'[7]

It is no accident of history that the nonconformist movement developed alongside urbanization. Initially, the majority of the Methodist and Baptist leaders in the chapels which sprang up in the towns and cities during the first half of the nineteenth century were rugged individuals who closely identified with the urban proletariat. However, with the passage of time the ministry vocation developed into a professional career. Educational requirements increased to the extent that professional leadership could no longer keep pace with demand, and the academic agenda so far distanced them from the community which had bred them that they could no longer identify with their roots and encountered rejection because they had betrayed their cultural identity. Not even Methodism, which in its earlier years had been the most significant religious movement among the labouring classes, could survive for long the challenge of industrialization.

By the early 1900s the middle classes were also beginning to stay away from church as the Bible lost its hold on cultural values. A census of 1902-3 in London revealed that under 20 per cent of the population were churchgoers, justifying the 'heathen' reputation of the capital in comparison with the rest of the country.

No further national censuses of church attendance were taken until Peter Brierley of MARC Europe (a division of World Vision) undertook a churchgoing census for England in 1979, for Scotland in 1984 and for Wales in 1982. His research revealed attendances of 11 per cent, 13 per cent and 17 per cent respectively.[8] This exercise was repeated for England in 1989, which indicated a further decline in the decade of 1 per cent overall.[9]

Brierley's data not only reveals the low attendance nationally in a country which is highly urbanized, it also shows that church membership and the churchgoing population is lowest in those counties with high concentrations of heavy industry: the shipbuilding and mining areas of Tyneside, the coal-mining and steel-making areas of Yorkshire and the mining and engineering areas of the East Midlands and the industrialized counties of South Wales (West Glamorgan, Mid Glamorgan, South Glamorgan and Gwent).[10] We also note low attendances in East Anglia where rural depopulation has caused the closure of many village churches or necessitated services being held less frequently due to the shortage of priests and ministers to officiate at poorly attended church services.

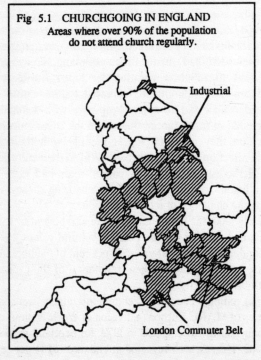

Fig 5.1 CHURCHGOING IN ENGLAND
Areas where over 90% of the population
do not attend church regularly.

Industrial

London Commuter Belt

(*'Christian England'*, MARC Europe)

URBANIZATION IN THE UNITED STATES FROM THE TIME OF THE CIVIL WAR

The Church's response to urbanization and industrialization in the USA followed a different pattern. Initially, the urban population grew more as a result of continuing waves of new immigrants drawn mainly from Europe. As strangers in a new land they struggled to retain the community support provided by ethnic identity. A basic component of this identity was expressed in their distinctive religious affiliations. Episcopalian, Presbyterian and Lutheran communities initially imported their ministers and priests from the home country.

The European parochial mindset versus the North American pioneering mentality

Until the great trek west began in earnest, the mainline denominations with imported histories accounted for the vast majority of churchgoers. The balance of power shifted rapidly as the pioneers moved across the Great Plains and over the Rockies. The church structures of the mainline denominations were too slow and cumbersome to keep pace with an expanding population base. It was the circuit-riding Methodist preachers and the Baptist farmer-preachers who kept in touch with the growing edge and established churches in the frontier towns, while the Presbyterians, Episcopalians and Lutherans waited until the construction of the railroads and schools before they ventured forth.[11] The Methodist and Baptist religious entrepreneurs facilitated the rapid growth of home meetings and small churches. Their rugged yet family-based religion responded to the needs of pioneers and the homesteaders who followed in their train.

Religious fervour and church growth had been spurred and shaped from early colonial times by the Great Awakening fostered by the ministries of Jonathan Edwards and George Whitefield. The significance of these great movements for the churching of urban populations is overlooked or played down by many church historians. As a consequence of the First and Second Awakenings, churches mushroomed in their thousands within a matter of a few years.[12]

Urbanization came more slowly in the United States than in Europe. In 1800 less than four per cent of the population lived in cities of 10,000 people or more; by 1890 that figure had reached 28 per cent.[13] It was the onset of the Civil War in 1861 which accelerated the trend to urbanization through the need to establish an industrial base to win the war. The

North had a head start on the South, so the longer the conflict continued the clearer became the outcome. Prior to the war, the few cities that existed served as marketing and trading centres rather than locations for industry and commerce.

Reaping the urban spiritual harvest through 'citywide crusades'

The first cities of any significant size were located in the north and east. These formed the industrial base of the Union. Dwight L. Moody began his ministry in Chicago just prior to the outbreak of the Civil War when the city's population was approximately 40,000. There he presented his forthright challenge to the rapidly expanding population, which consisted of people moving in from the farms and small rural communities of America in search of work in the newly developing industries which were expanding rapidly to meet the war demands. He was not inhibited by the European parochial model but had an extensive ministry, not only through the Tabernacle he constructed, but also through the Bible Institute which he founded to train evangelists and church planters. These students were to provide the evangelistic challenge and pastoral care for the many people who had become dislocated from their churches and churchgoing communities through migration to the city. The city-wide crusades conducted by Moody and Sankey appealed primarily to the urban middle class. 'He [Moody] apparently drew chiefly the previously converted or the half-converted displaced church people who reaffirmed their faith when he reclaimed them and sent them back to supportive churches.' [14]

Urban migration continued for the next hundred years, so that, by 1980, 75 per cent of the population was located in metropolitan centres. Between the years 1850 and 1950 internal migration was mainly from rural areas and small towns into the mushrooming metropolitan areas of the north-east. During that period migrants from outside the United States mainly came from Europe. After the Second World War the pace accelerated, with large numbers of people swelling the cities of the west and south: Seattle, San Francisco, Los Angeles, San Diego, Denver, Houston, Pheonix, etc. Within the twenty year period 1960-1980, the rural population dropped from 23 per cent to 9 per cent.

D. L. Moody's role in reclaiming for Christ new urban migrants from rural and small town America in the mid nineteenth century is paralleled by Billy Graham's ministry to the new waves of urban migrants in the aftermath of the Second World War. The population flow from the north and east to the west and south represents a significant redistribution. The national census of 1980 revealed that the bulk of the population was to be found west of the Mississippi. As in Europe during the eighteenth century, the church in the United States has likewise been hard pressed to keep pace with such large-scale and rapid demographic change. The mainline churches have suffered most, partly because of the 'pretensions to grandeur' mentality which they have carried with them from Europe.

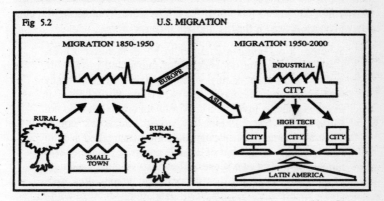

Fig 5.2 U.S. MIGRATION

From face-to-face communities to free associations

The older churches were established through colonization rather than by conversion. They represented the social structure of a pre-industrial European society. They are the churches people are born into because they permeate extended family networks. The German term *Gemeinschaft*, a family-based natural society, represents community as resting on the three pillars of blood, place (land) and mind, or kinship, neighbourhood and friendship. Ferdinand Tonnies saw the modern city as replacing the traditional *Gemeinschaft* structures with the mechanical society of the *Gesellschaft* which is based on individualized, contractual relationships. In 1887 he wrote,

> The more general the condition of *Gesellschaft* becomes in the nation or a group of nations, the more this entire 'country' or the entire 'world' begins to resemble one large city ... The city consists of free persons who stand in contact with each other, exchange with each other and cooperate without any *Gemeinschaft* of will there to develop among them except as such might develop sporadically or as a leftover from former conditions. On the contrary, these numerous

> external contacts, contracts, and contractual relations only
> cover up as many inner hostilities and antagonistic interests.[15]

The mainline churches imported from Europe, which retain their parochial mentality, are better suited to stable, homogeneous populations. They often lack the dynamism and flexibility of more independent churches which have grown through attracting new people from outside their religious community. Robert Bellah has recently applied the *Gesellschaft* concept to the North American scene, contrasting the concept of community with that of *lifestyle enclave*:

> Whereas a community attempts to be an inclusive whole,
> celebrating the interdependence of public and private life
> and of the different callings of all, lifestyle is fundamentally
> segmented and celebrates the narcissism of similarity. It
> usually explicitly involves a contrast with others who 'do not
> share one's lifestyle'. For this reason, we speak not of
> lifestyle communities, though they are often called such in
> contemporary usage, but of lifestyle enclaves. Such enclaves
> are segmented in two senses. They involve only a segment
> of each individual, for they concern only private life, especially leisure and consumption. And they are segmented
> socially in that they include only those with a common
> lifestyle.[16]

Statistics of church membership and church attendance broken down by region show that the least churched region of the United States is the Pacific region, and especially the north-west.[17] This is not because people there are less religious than in other regions and therefore more resistant to recruitment by the churches. The explanation rather lies in the failure of the majority of the churches to relate to a fast-growing, highly mobile and heterogeneous population. Unlike the mid-west where Lutheranism prevails, or the South which is the home of the Baptists and Methodists, there is no dominant denominational presence in the Pacific region, with the exception of Roman Catholicism which is particularly strong in Southern California due to the heavy migration of Latin Americans.

Mainline churches are at their most vulnerable when they are in a society which does not have a significant proportion of the population sharing their 'tribal' heritage. Their evangelistic concern focuses on the reclaiming of their own kind, rather than on intentional outreach to the dechurched and unchurched. Into the gap created by their inertia the

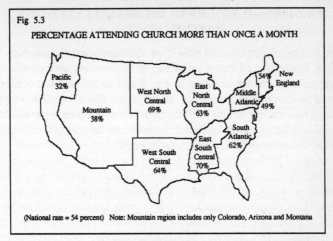

Fig 5.3

PERCENTAGE ATTENDING CHURCH MORE THAN ONCE A MONTH

Pacific
32%

Mountain
38%

West North
Central
69%

East
North
Central
63%

Middle
Atlantic
49%

54% New
England

South
Atlantic
62%

East
South
Central

West South
Central
64%

(National rate = 54 percent)   Note: Mountain region includes only Colorado, Arizona and Montana

(Stark and Bainbridge, *Future of Religion*, p 77)

independent churches have stepped with aggressive programmes of church planting in the burgeoning satellite communities. Significant numbers of high-visibility worship centres have been established, promoted by celebrity appearances, a reputation for signs and wonders, mass media exposure, and a high-octane mixture of transcendental worship experience and strong human relationships. For a transplanted and often transient population such churches provide a sense of belonging, significance and security. The downside is that the relationship of the individual to the local church is often fragile and short-lived. In a society with few abiding relationships, a high proportion of people move from church to church like choosy and critical customers taking their custom from one store to another. If the service is not to their satisfaction, or a competitor appears offering greater convenience or a more attractive range of products, then they abandon the store where they previously shopped without any sense of disloyalty or loss.

When long-standing allegiances are broken and replaced by a dazzling and baffling range of choices, people not only move from one church to another, they are also liable to drop out all together without anyone in the church feeling responsible for them or even noticing their absence. Churches, for their part, do not feel strongly committed to transient members and attenders when they terminate a relationship which was as casual as it was brief.

THE IMPACT OF URBAN LIVING ON RELIGIOUS COMMITMENT

A great deal of emphasis is placed on the significance of the city in modern missionary literature, and this is appropriate when one considers the pace of urbanization in the world today and the cultural, political and economic influence of the city. When we look at the evangelistic strategy of the early church as recorded in Acts and the Epistles, we also see how Paul and his associates targeted the cities and planned for extensive stays in such strategic centres as Corinth and Ephesus (Act 18,19). Corinth was the chief city of Greece, located on the crossroads for travellers and traders. It was also a centre for the trafficking of ideas. Alongside the wisdom and philosophy was also evidence of humankind's religious search shown by twelve temples dedicated to a variety of gods, including Aphrodite, the goddess of love, Asclepius, the god of healing, and Apollo, whose worship exalted male strength and beauty.

Ephesus was the largest and most famous city of Asia, a trade centre on the River Cayster noted for its many fine buildings, including the Temple of Artemis which ranked among the seven wonders of the world. Luke clearly attaches great importance to Paul's ministry in Ephesus, considering that of the 113 verses which record his entire fourth missionary journey, 84 are devoted to activities in that one strategic location.

Characteristics of pre-industrial society

In considering the evangelization of a pagan city, or the re-evangelizing of nominal Christians lost in the city, we cannot simply transpose strategies from the New Testament to the contemporary urban reality. Pre-industrial cities were very different in terms of their social anatomy. Until the Industrial Revolution, people still lived in community within the city. The majority of people worked from their own homes in pursuance of their craft or trade, or else worked as a slave or supplier to a more affluent family. The vineyard constituted the largest commercial enterprise. As long as people worked where they lived and were surrounded by people with whom they interacted on a daily basis there remained a strong sense of community.

The large cities of the ancient world functioned like a federation of merged villages. There were extensive networks of social relationships through which news passed with remarkable speed. Thus the churches of

New Testament times lived a goldfish bowl kind of existence. The believers were under constant scrutiny, so it was important that they lived lives consistent with the gospel if they were to make a significant positive impact on their neighbours. While, on the one hand, this exposed living placed high demands and expectations on the believers, it also made available a powerful social network for the progress of the gospel.

Social diversification and community fragmentation in the industrial city
The industrial and post-industrial cities have a very different social anatomy which makes it more difficult for the church to register a significant impact. With the sinking of mines and the building of factories, labour was removed from its home base. With the rapid growth of technology, a bewildering range of new skills had to be acquired. Factories had to be supplied and serviced by industries which expanded the size of the labour pool needed to work these new concentrations of industry. These industries also created the means of mass transportation to sustain the city with its unprecedented degree of population mobility and its need to export its industrial products and import the foodstuffs to feed its population. When people sleep in one location, work in a second and establish social relationships in distant areas of the city, community erodes. People may not relate to those who live around them, preferring to establish their friendships elsewhere. The residential community becomes reduced to a 'roosting area', otherwise known as a dormitory suburb. The resulting fragmentation leads to conflict in terms of people's self-identity, not knowing where they establish their primary sense of belonging. Is it within the family, at their place of work, or in some other setting? Those people who are unable to resolve this tension become disturbed by a sense of 'anomie' or absence of normal social standards.[18] Furthermore, the individual is no longer known so completely and intimately as is possible in a pre-industrial urban society, face-to-face rural village, or small town community.

Overcoming the parochial mindset
The complexity of urban society creates great problems for local churches, especially those which operate with a parochial mindset. The parish represents a geographical area within the city. From the perspective of church leaders operating with this model, the city is the sum of its parishes. The trouble that this conceptual framework, which was estab-

lished in a pre-industrial European society, does not match the urban social reality. The vast majority of the population does not think in terms of a 'parish' or residential community, but in terms of the city. Unlike many church ministers, who may live near their churches and regard the encircling residential communities as their primary sphere of contact with people, their congregations relate to the city in a complex variety of ways. Where there are domiciled is only one of a number of reference points, and may not be the most significant, especially in the case of singles, professional people, or those with leisure interests which assume great importance in terms of their self-identity and fulfilment as persons. The static, honeycomb parochial structure does not match the multi-directional free flow of urban populations.

Fortunately the parochial mindset is not as entrenched in North America as it is in Europe, which may contribute to the fact that churchgoing has remained at a much higher level in America, despite 150 years of rapid urbanization and large-scale population migration. However, many mainline church leaders still talk in terms of 'the parish' and plan their pastoral and evangelistic strategies utilizing a geographical, rather than a sociological, conceptual map. This outlook is fostered by the fact that mainline Protestantism is seldom really at home in the city. It is an alien environment which must be resisted by a fortress mentality or abandoned in favour of a more congenial suburban environment. Such lack of theological understanding of the city and pastoral inadequacy in relating to the needs of those who earn their livelihood in the city, contribute significantly to the nominality problem, due to people feeling abandoned there.

SUBURBIA IN TRANSITION

As we have already noted, the pre-industrial city was very different from the city which emerged in response to industrialization. Having begun in the home, businesses were transferred to factories and offices located close by. Vast numbers of people were attracted to the new commercial and manufacturing centres which made living conditions increasingly congested and unhealthy. Many wealthy families owned country homes which provided an escape from the tumult, smells and grime of the city.

Evangelical utopias

Robert Fishman maintains that the suburb as we have come to know it in the Anglo-American world was the direct product of the Evangelical Movement, and that it began in London, through the Clapham Sect. This group of prominent evangelical Anglicans included William Wilberforce; John Thornton, Director of the Bank of England; his son Henry Thornton (1760-1815), one of London's wealthiest bankers; John Venn, rector of Clapham from 1792 to 1813; Charles Grant (1746-1832); and John Shore (Lord Teignmouth, 1751-1834), founder of the Bible Society and a former Governor General of India. Their family values were challenged by the social conditions developing as a consequence of rapid industrialization.

> This contradiction between the city and the Evangelical ideal of the family provided the final impetus for the unprecedented separation of the citizen's home from the city that is the essence of the suburban idea. The city was not just crowded, dirty, and unhealthy; it was immoral. Salvation itself depended on separating the woman's sacred world of family and children from the profane metropolis. Yet this separation could not jeopardize a man's constant attendance at his business—for hard work and success were also Evangelical virtues—and business life required rapid personal access to that great beehive of information which was London. This was the problem, and suburbia was the ultimate solution.[19]

As Clapham Common suburbia developed between 1735 and 1790, so the conditions were ripening in America for the transference of the concept across the Atlantic. Catherine Beecher, daughter of Lyman Beecher, a leading Evangelical preacher, wrote her *Treatise on Domestic Economy* (1841) espousing the home-based piety and nuclear family concepts of the Clapham Sect in England, values which could best be preserved by geographical separation from the city. The primary architect of American suburbia was Andrew Jackson Downing, who contacted Calvert Vaux in Paris in 1850 as a professional colleague. Vaux was an Englishman who had been influenced by the suburban ideal of English evangelicals.[20] However, the development of suburbia which began in America at the end of the 1850s proceeded more slowly because the situation was less urgent due to the fact that American cities in the first half of the nineteenth century were much smaller than their English counterparts. While London had a population of over one million in 1800, New York had only grown to 60,000. It was the Civil War which gave the tremendous stimulus to urbanization which in turn triggered the suburban movement, with Chicago and Philadelphia leading the way.

The extensive geographical spread of the city resulting from suburbanization was only made possible by the development of adequate transportation systems to handle the twice daily tidal flow of increasing numbers of people. At first the commuters were ferried by horse drawn carriages and later by electric trams, steam trains, and then the omnibus. It comes as no surprise that the transportation barons were often the land speculators.

It is evident that the development of suburbia has profound implications for the urban mission of the church. No longer can parish-based ministers think in meaningful terms of their responsibility as 'the cure of souls' of the people resident within their parish boundaries. Most people in suburbia do not have such a strong sense of identity with their residential neighbourhood. That represents just part of their weekly life. They often have a wider circle of social contacts among their work colleagues or through their leisure pursuits than that prescribed by their parish boundary. Neighbourhoods which still retain a sense of community are most likely to consist of the retired, families with one parent at home with pre-school children, or communities formed around a major industry or with a particular ethnic identity. It is in such localities that the parish model can still function.

Suburbs becoming satellites

The suburban concept itself is in transition, which complicates the task of Christian mission still further. Initially, suburbs developed around a central area and the communication network developed like the spokes of a wheel. Chicago conforms to this pattern of development see Fig 5.4. Now we are seeing a decentralization as we move from the industrial to the high-tech and information age. Los Angeles was the first city to manifest this phenomenon on a large scale, beginning in the 1940s. It did not begin to develop as a city of any significance until the 1880s with the arrival of the railroad and the discovery of the technology to dig artesian wells, without which it would be impossible to sustain a large population in a desert region. At first the burgeoning city relied upon the 'Pacific Electric' railcar system to shuttle its quarter of a million commuters, but by the 1920s congestion had reached unacceptable proportions. The problem was basically a competition between public and private transportation, for even at that time Los Angeles has the largest per capita automobile ownership than any city in the world. Through the influence of the oil and automobile industry and the North American desire for independence, the automobile won over public transportation; the decision was made to develop a decentralized highway network throughout the Greater Los Angeles area, and so the decentralized city was born (see Fig 5.5). The demise of the public transportation system created even greater reliance on the automobile to the extent that it is not unusual today for a California family to have three or four cars to clog the highways. This concept is now the victim of its own success, for unlike the centralized system in which only the routes in and out of the city centre are clogged during the rush hours, the Greater Los Angeles area is creating a universal traffic jam which is forecast to get worse, threatening the need for double decker freeways as the next step. However, this solution is not popular among residents in an earthquake-prone region. The City Fathers are once again developing mass transportation consisting of underground metro and light rail systems.

Fig 5.4 | THE CHICAGO FREEWAY SYSTEM

The development of high-tech industries and the advent of the information age have also altered dramatically our concept of suburbia. The original suburban ideal was to remove the home from the hubbub of city life and industrial pollution. But now the new industries have moved out to the edges of suburbia to be located on 'industrial estates' or with neighbourhood office complexes. Migration was popular for older businesses seeking to modernize, such as warehousing, because there were often tax incentives to move to areas wanting to develop and attract a commercial base, and migration was also a way of overcoming union resistance to mechanization with its inevitable job losses (Milton Keynes, Swindon and Washington are UK examples). At the same time, we have seen the development of shopping malls and supermarkets to provide convenience shopping in an attractive environment, all under one roof with abundant parking. Restaurants and leisure facilities are often to be found there, which have helped turn mall shopping into a weekend recreational activity!

Ministry in a suburban setting

Such decentralization has further eroded the parish concept. No longer is there a one-directional tidal flow in and out of the community,

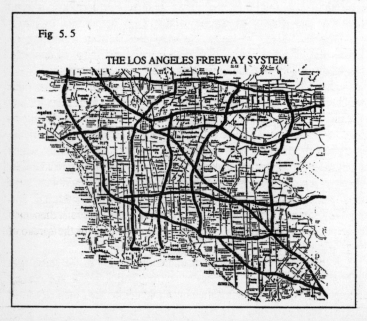

Fig 5.5

THE LOS ANGELES FREEWAY SYSTEM

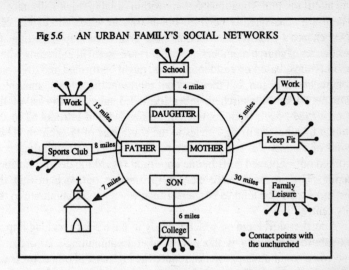

Fig 5.6 AN URBAN FAMILY'S SOCIAL NETWORKS

but people are continually heading off in all directions. As a result, those churches operating on a parish concept are saddled with a structure which does not relate to the urban reality. Furthermore, a rigid adherence to a ministry philosophy and strategy determined by parish boundaries effectively prevents the local church from a widespread ministry outreach made possible by their members' range of contacts, most of which will be made outside their residential community.

The church they are most like to introduce to their friends is their own church, and, provided that the ministry programme is relevant and valuable to the people they invite, they will not be deterred by having to travel back and forth in their cars. I estimate that a reasonable driving distance in the UK is about 7 miles, while in the United States, which represents an even more mobile culture, people will drive up to 25 miles. Whenever church leaders are locked into our parish mentality such mobility will inevitably be regarded as a problem to be endured. But once they come to terms with the sociology of the technopolis then such decentralization and mobility can provide opportunities for the spread of the gospel.[21]

A decentralized urbanization redefines community in the sense that the home now represents the hub or starting point. 'From that central starting point, the members of the household create their own city from the multitude of destinations that are within suitable driving distance'.[22] There are consequently no fixed boundaries in which the extent of a local church's ministry can be confined. Pins on a map depicting the residences of church members or attenders are useful in indicating where small groups, based on residential areas, might be formed and even new congregations begun, but they may not represent the actual communication networks. A church member located 5 miles north-east of the church might have been contracted, befriended and introduced to the church by a person living 7 miles to the south-east of the church. Their point of contact was the place where they worked or regularly dined, worked out or played golf! In one important regard the decentralization taking place in many large cities helps mission outreach in that the distances travelled tend to be shorter than when people commute to the city centre.

A further development which is likely to have a far-reaching impact on suburban ministry is the advent of 'telecommuting'. In order to overcome commuting problems, reduce the high cost of office space and retain employees in the face of family responsibilities (care of pre-school children or dependent elderly parents), an increasing number of workers are being encouraged to work at home using a computer and modem. The home location is especially appropriate for those employed in data input, insurance assessment and telemarketing. The Los Angeles County has an experimental telecommuting programme for 3,000 of its employees, and Naisbit calculates that by the year AD 2000, 30 per cent of the North American work force will be working in whole or part from their own homes.[23] When people have been in their home all day they may be more ready to go out to the midweek activities run by their local church than was the case in the days when they arrived home exhausted after spending up to three hours each day commuting.

A FUTURE FOR THE CHURCH IN THE INNER-CITY?

The decentralization resulting from the development of suburbia has resulted in the marginalizing of the city centre and the abandonment of the older residential areas and industrial sectors which surround that once thriving centre. The city centres most likely to survive are those which are centres for government, banking and investment houses, and for entertainment and tourism. Such development brings little benefit to the older nearby residential districts. The suburbanization of society has

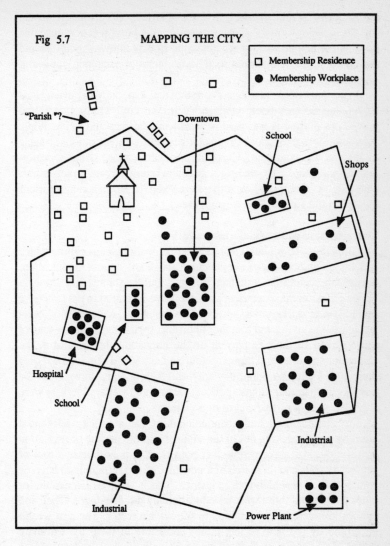

Fig 5.7   MAPPING THE CITY

□ Membership Residence
● Membership Workplace

"Parish "?

Downtown

School

Shops

Hospital

School

Industrial

Industrial

Power Plant

had serious detrimental effects in terms of eroding the tax-based income for the development of the community, the provision of affordable housing for people who were vulnerable to exploitative landlords, and the creation of homogenized societies in terms of economic status and ethnicity.

As we have seen, mainline Protestantism, especially the evangelical brand, has seldom been comfortable in the city. The segment that moved out of the city was predominantly middle class and white. While some old, once-prestigious Protestant city centre congregations struggle to survive, the continuing Christian presence is more strongly represented by Catholicism and the African-American and other ethnic churches. At the present time there are over 700 Korean congregations located in the Greater Los Angeles area.

Characteristics of a working-class culture

The Industrial Revolution created a distinct working-class culture which spreads across boundaries of ethnicity, though not without modification. Australian sociologist Vaughan Bowie helpfully summarizes these in *Green Shoots in the Concrete*.[24] He first draws attention to the collective orientation of working class society. This mutual dependency was generated by the need to band together to protect their interests in the face of the coercion of their employers or the alienation they felt from the centres of authority and power. Suburbanization had removed not only their bosses but also public servants who were mainly drawn from the middle class, so that judges, police, teachers and welfare workers were regarded as either irrelevant or oppressive.

The marginalizing and abandonment of the inner-city residential areas by people moving out to the suburbs and the decline or relocation of old industries make people feel powerless, it is no longer a case of getting on your bike in search of a new job, but of retraining to become employable in new high-tech industries. This is wellnigh impossible for older people and those who are educationally disadvantaged. Their job options are increasingly confined to the service sector. The new wealth generated by the new society is not accessible to them by legitimate means. As a consequence crime increases, with the drug trade providing the fastest, if most precarious, track to affluence.

In a world characterized by economic insecurity and severely restricted social mobility, people live a day at a time. If they have a job, their concern is to keep it rather than to progress to something better.

When salaries are minimal, recreational options are limited. People live according to an established routine relieved by occasional bursts of spontaneity, rather than according to a varied schedule.

Life is accepted, albeit grudgingly, without much reflection or analysis. If you cannot change anything, why take the trouble to try and understand it? People feel victims of happenstance, so most people take the path of least resistance and try and keep out of trouble. When trust begins to break down in a neighbourhood then families and individuals begin to withdraw into themselves. Thus the inner-city is a mixture of the gregariousness of those who find significance and companionship in the street scene and the isolationism of those who have cut themselves off for safety's sake.

Communication tends to be more animated with sudden mood swings. With a limited vocabulary the only way to emphasize a point is by repetition or turning up the volume. From a middle-class perspective the raised voices can sound like a continuous confrontation, whereas in their cultural setting more people have a range of vocabulary which allows them verbally to cut each other to pieces without so much as raising their voices!

The reasoning process is more likely to be inductive—from the particular to the general—than deductive. For this reason working-class people are not interested in policy papers and strategy documents; they focus on the specifics. They are not the kind of people who like to sit on committees either in the community or the church. Their thinking is more lateral than linear, not in the logical development of an argument, but a free association of ideas. They are more at home in the Hebrew and Aramaic cultural world than the Greek, and relate better to the stories and parables of the Bible than to the Epistles of Paul.

Among working-class people there is a reluctance to get involved in organizations, be they community or religious. The major exceptions are most likely sporting clubs, pubs and bars, which provide a supportive community not dependent on a high level of verbal skills.

In stable, close-knit communities and among gangs who occupy the streets there is a strong sense of territory which must be protected from intruders, be they rival gangs or the police. People who feel trapped are resentful of those who come and go at will, and especially of those who seek to render community service while living at a safe distance. Inner city ministry demands an incarnational approach by people who are prepared to identify long term with the community. It is a boss who goes and a brother or sister who stays. Lyle Schaller believes that the most effective years of a person's ministry do not begin until the fourth to seventh year. That figure is extended to ten years in the case of those pastoring in the inner city. And not infrequently it takes ten years in order to begin to make a significant impact. Many inner city congregations believe that the ministers they get are there because they couldn't get anything better, and that they will leave as soon as a more attractive opening is presented to them. Credibility has to be established by making it clear that the leader is there as a matter of calling and choice and is committed for 'the long haul'. Nominality tends to be less of an issue within churches located in and serving inner-city communities. Congregations are usually much smaller than in the suburbs, with a higher level of mutual commitment among members in their struggle to survive and maintain their Christian witness in tough circumstances.

Commitment to the city

It would be inaccurate and unfair to present the parochial structure in an entirely negative light. One of its great benefits has been to maintain a Christian witness and make available the ministries of the church in areas which would have been abandoned when insufficient church members gathered to make the church viable. In many North American cities, Protestant churches continue to exist in run-down residential areas as well as in the commercial centres. If it were not for ethnic churches filling the vacuum left by the white congregations who moved their church out to where their members were located or to accessible sites beside freeways, church buildings would have been bulldozed out of existence.

A new problem is created by the 'gentrification' of formerly run-down areas and the trend to build high-rise apartments adjacent to the commercial districts. How will these upwardly mobile new residents be contacted now that there are no churches able to relate to that socio-economic bracket left in the locality? The enormous cost of land and property in the commercial areas will make it economically prohibitive for churches to move back to re-establish themselves on the same basis as in the past. Different approaches will need to be devised to establish Christian communities in these highly influential and high-pressured segments of society which, for the most part, have adopted a 'yuppie' lifestyle which challenges the Christian value system. It is this segment of the population, which has become distanced from the churches to an alarming extent, which is attracted to alternative religions and philosophies.

ELEMENTS IN THE DEVELOPMENT OF NEW URBAN STRATEGIES TO RE-ACTIVATE NOMINAL CHRISTIANS

Urban societies are tremendously complex, so it is helpful to have a model which provides a range of lenses with which to analyse the city in order to develop appropriate strategies for winning back into the fellowship of the church the many people who have become nominal. One of the most helpful models is that developed by R. A. Murdie, which provides a residential and urban web based on socio-economic criteria.

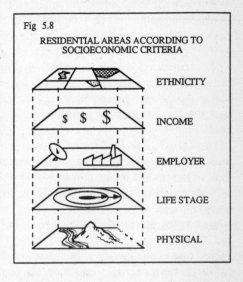

Fig 5.8

RESIDENTIAL AREAS ACCORDING TO SOCIOECONOMIC CRITERIA

ETHNICITY

INCOME

EMPLOYER

LIFE STAGE

PHYSICAL

Some areas are characterized by a particular ethnic composition; a range of ethnic groups might congregate in different segments of the city. The population in another area is determined by socio-economic criteria—areas of cheap housing, middle income, and exclusive, high-income communities. In other cases it is the physical characteristics of the area which are distinctive: smog free areas along the water-front or at a higher elevation.

Exegete the city

Effective urban mission and evangelism requires church leaders to be trained in urban sociology and to be able to 'exegete' the city. In other words, they need to know where to go to obtain information on their city and community and to acquire the skills to interpret what is going on around them. The people most likely to know the anatomy and significant trends in the community are to be found in the town hall, school authorities, the local chamber of commerce, estate agents' offices, university or community college sociology departments, job centres, major employers and the police.

In exegeting the city a number of key questions need to be posed:

—Who are the major employers?
—What are the most urgent and widespread community needs?
—What percentage of the community population is in the various income categories as compared to the city, county or nation as a whole?
—What proportion of the population are home owners?
—What percentages of the community population are in the various age categories, as compared to the city, county, or nation as a whole?
—Are the people moving into the community significantly different from those moving out, in terms of age, income level and ethnic identity?
—To what extent do local stores, cinemas, social and religious organizations reflect the presence of an ethnic community?
—What new industries are moving in and which are moving out?
—Are local shopping and recreational amenities improving or deteriorating in the locality?
—What is the projected growth or decline of the city in the next 5, 10, and 20 years?
—How many churches serve the community?
—What is the numerical strength of each congregation, and how extensive is its non-attending membership/community?
—Which of the churches are growing, which are static and which are in decline?
—To what factors can the growth in the thriving churches be attributed?

Sample surveys
The most obvious way of discovering needs and attitudes in a community is often overlooked: visiting homes and going where people congregate in the pub, at the school gate, in the shopping mall, and asking them! When Pastor Rick Warren began a new church in Saddleback Valley Community Church in Mission Viejo, a new upper-middle class community in Southern California, he visited five hundred homes asking the following five questions:

1. Are you an active member of a nearby church? (If the answer was yes, the interview ended).

2. What do you think is the greatest need in Saddleback Valley?
3. Why do you think most people do not attend church?
4. If you were looking for a church, what would you look for?
5. What advice can you give me as a pastor?

From the responses he received he discovered labels were more of a hindrance than a help in the yuppie culture in which he found himself. The key to unlock their hearts was to find ways to address their greatest felt needs. Most unchurched people did not have any theological hang-ups which kept them from attending church; it was simply that they had not thought seriously about it, or felt that they had better things to do. This was not surprising considering that most unchurched people thought that sermons were boring and irrelevant to life, ministers were always asking for money and church people were unfriendly to visitors. Before they were prepared to come, they wanted to be reassured that their children would be adequately cared for. The list may vary from area to area and country to country, so there is no substitute for doing one's own 'market' research.

Communication strategies

In facing the challenges urban society presents to the re-evangelizing of nominal Christians, the church will need to rethink its communication strategies. Traditionally it has relied upon its ability to gather the community in order to communicate its message. The challenge was regularly presented to existing members to go out into their community to bring more people along with them to benefit from the pulpit preaching and the groups meeting on the church premises in adult education programmes. Such a challenge continues to work to a limited extent as long as the congregation is representative of a broader society which is fairly static and homogeneous or, in the case of those few congregations which have achieved high community visibility, because of their numerical strength and the attractiveness of their programme. A growing percentage of local congregations find themselves reduced to a social enclave, existing on the margins of a society which ignores their existence.

The churches, like the town hall, face a serious communication problem, and for the same basic reason—the erosion of community. Within the majority of urban settings, communication is no longer primarily achieved through the community, but at the higher level of mass media and on a person-to-person basis. From its congregational base the church must reach up into the media level and reach down to generate a person-to-person communication network, if it is to communicate its message effectively.[25]

Deployment of church leaders
One unfortunate consequence of the parish concept has been the disproportionate distribution of leadership resources, with a much higher proportion of clergy per capita in the rural areas and small towns than in the densely populated urban areas. Furthermore, the rapid population shifts which have occurred through internal migration of people from the country into the cities in search of work and a higher standard of living, have outstripped the resources of mainline churches to provide adequately trained leaders in church planting. If the ministry of the church does not arrive as promptly as the other amenities and community services it becomes much more difficult to reach the new residents at a later date.

Beyond the denomination
Among highly mobile and heterogeneous populations, denominational labels are of little significance. New residents are more likely to join a church which has a compatible ethos and has developed a range of programmes to meet their needs, than to remain loyal to their own denomination at all costs.[26] This is especially the case in regions where no church has achieved a dominant position and where a variety of ecclesiastical traditions are to be found. Furthermore, if churches are going to have an impact on such areas they will need to establish a high public profile to attract people through their programmes, or be able to generate a word-of-mouth, person-to-person advocacy.

Re-establishing community
In western societies we have witnessed the steady erosion of family life. The extended family has been broken up with the creation of the suburban nuclear family. One generation becomes separated from the next due to increased mobility, the result of following work availability or career opportunities, or a better social environment in which to raise a family or enjoy retirement years. Changing social and sexual mores have resulted in cohabiting on a wide scale. In such a socially dysfunctional environment the church must work to re-establish community structures. The widely-felt need for support relationships and groups

explains the rapid growth of the small group movement on both sides of the Atlantic Ocean. But within the church setting this has not been without its problems. Some ministers are suspicious of such decentralization, fearing that it will result in the fragmentation of the ministry programme and their own loss of control. Other clergy, who have been enthusiastic about small groups, found the additional administrative and training burden too great for them to handle, so that the group network eventually collapsed. The vast majority of clergy who trained twenty or more years ago received no preparation to help them start, manage and facilitate a small group ministry. As a consequence, groups died for lack of training resources and through self-preoccupation to the neglect of a ministry beyond the existing small-group members.

Planting new churches, revitalizing existing churches
In a mission context characterized by rapid urban expansion, a two-pronged approach is required. One entails the rapid formation of new communities of witness, some of which will eventually become new congregations. This may occur either through one group rapidly growing, or through bringing together of a cluster of such communities of witness. In the second approach, the established churches located in the decaying inner city, in older sectors which are now being redeveloped, or in smaller outlying communities which are being absorbed in new suburban development projects, will need revitalization. Church leaders can no longer confine their thinking simply to the parish, but must learn to think in terms of an overall vision and strategy for the entire city.

A broader vision then needs to be translated into corporate action. Larger and more influential congregations must be prepared to evaluate honestly their impact upon the combined Christian witness of the churches serving the area. Are they acting as whirlpools, sucking more and more of the resources into their own vortex, or are they contributing to the multiplication and dispersal of ministry through the area? Does their presence result in a weakening of the ministries of smaller churches struggling to serve the community, or serve to affirm and reinforce their efforts?

The distinctive contributions of the megachurch and the small church
Over eighty per cent of all Protestant churches in the United Kingdom, North America and Australasia have less than 200 active members.[27] So the large church model should not be presented as the norm or ideal for

urban ministry. However, it must be recognized that a significant and growing percentage of churchgoers are to be found in the larger congregations. Large churches have the advantage of being able to stage celebratory worship, offer a wide range of specialized ministries to meet the diverse needs and high expectations of urban people and achieve a high public profile. In comparison, small churches must not be regarded simply as churches which failed to grow. The small church has the potential to offer greater intimacy and often has a much closer identity with the immediate community. Large and small churches must not regard their relationship as competitive, but as symbiotic—each needs the other and must endeavour to establish a mutually supportive working relationship.

Large churches can provide inspiring occasions for combined worship. They can host training opportunities for the benefit of leaders in smaller churches who do not have the specialist resources to develop the leaders of their various ministry departments. The large church can also help organize a coalition of churches to make representation to civic leaders regarding community issues.

Smaller churches together provide a range of worship options and some of them target a particular section of the community which has a distinct ethnic identity or appeal to a particular socio-economic bracket. Unlike the pre-industrial society which was heterogeneous in terms of rich and poor living in close proximity, the modern city tends to segregate people into homogeneous groupings: people employed in the same industry, singles living in apartment complexes, and area populated by a particular ethnic group, people living in areas according to the price of housing in that sector of the city, etc. This creates a certain inevitability about the homogeneous make-up of many congregations.

Homogeneity has both a positive and a negative side. On the plus side it is able to contextualize its ministry to a particular culture, which will enhance its evangelistic effectiveness. It speaks the language of the people it is seeking to reach and is addressing the issues which are significant for their lifestyle. On the debit side, contextualization can easily degenerate into enculturation, which means that the gospel becomes subservient to culture. This comes about either through a deliberate editing out of the more radical and demanding aspects of the gospel which pass judgement on the culture, or through an unconscious limiting of awareness. Therefore, alongside homogeneous structures, we also need heterogeneous structures so that we shall encounter people of other cultures, help one another remove cultural blinkers and come to a fuller understanding of the gospel. The Christian message presents an ongoing challenge, for the gospel is always bigger than our perceptions and is constantly calling us to move further than we want to go.

The large church must resist the tendency to dominate the scene and marginalize the smaller churches. In the United States the large church of the 1960s-1980s was characterized by extensive centralized pro- grammes operated by a large professional staff. For a number of reasons this has not been the European model: society is less mobile due to a strong local community identity; cross-city travel is not so convenient due to fewer urban freeways; church facilities are more limited through lack of space to build educational and recreational facilities and provide off-street parking; and there is a suspicion of specialization and pro- fessionalism. Europeans are less goal oriented and programme focused in their approach to life. Furthermore, the success of the centralized programming approach to attract the community into the life of the church depended on the continuing social strength of the churches. This is now being eroded in the USA as it was eroded in Europe following the First World War. Consequently, an increasing number of prestigious churches are now beginning to struggle to maintain their established programmes. Unless they change their philosophy of ministry they are in danger of sharing the fate of the dinosaur. As we will argue in the final chapter, the large church of the 1990s will be far more decentralized than the megachurches of the 1960s and 1970s.

The emergence of the metachurch model

In response to this changing scenario Carl George, of the Fuller Institute, California, has developed the concept of the 'metachurch'. By using this term he is seeking to establish a new organizational model which will both help remove growth-restricting obstacles and ensure the deployment of ministry throughout the complex mosaic of urban societies.[28] His concept entails the training of large numbers of leaders for small groups, with ongoing supervision and resourcing achieved by clustering the small groups in units of five. The centralized programming will have two primary aims: to provide a range of one-off and short term programmes to address specific needs; and to arrange support groups for those with ongoing deep-seated problems (chemical dependency; divorce recovery, abused spouses; etc.). Such a range of activities will provide entry points into the life of the church as well as supplement the ongoing pastoral care, service and evangelistic outreach of the small groups. Carl George's decentralized model is close to the ministry strategies adopted by growing churches in the United Kingdom, but with the addition of some important ministry management insights and more comprehensive conceptual modelling. The metachurch model will be explained in greater detail at the conclusion of the final chapter.

The changing role of theological education and leadership training

The considerations outlined in this chapter, coupled with the issues covered in the previous two chapters, have profound implications for the future of theological education. The social changes which have taken place as a consequence of the move from the industrial to the high tech and information age mean that those trained with the old assumptions which governed the practice of ministry will require a great deal of in-service training. Seminaries also will need to be sufficiently in touch with societal trends to ensure that they do not end up training potential leaders for yesterday rather than today and tomorrow. While the traditional theological disciplines remain foundational, they will need to be applied and supplemented by a focus on spiritual formation and competence in a wide range of ministerial skills. The widespread recognition of further training among many pastors is shown by the demand for continuous education and Doctor of Ministry programmes throughout North America.

A significant proportion of seminary students are now older and already have ministry experience. Many individuals who are concerned to prepare more adequately for church leadership do not regard the traditional theological education programme as a viable option because rising costs have put seminary education out of reach, especially for older students who are married, have a family to provide for and mortgage payments to meet. In addition, many do not want to leave the ministries in which they are already engaged in order to train for ministry! Consequently they are looking for intensive courses and seminars to provide the insights and skills they are seeking to acquire to upgrade their performance.

Operating out of a sense of frustration with the theological academic establishment, some larger churches are now training their own leadership through apprenticeship programmes in particular ministry specializations. These people have often proved their ability to perform effectively in their secular jobs, and are not interested in enrolling in a full theological degree programme. Others are excluded from seminary education in the USA because they are self-taught church planters establishing independent churches, or they are pastors belonging to denominations which do not require formal seminary education as an ordination requirement. There are now significant numbers of pastors of proven effectiveness who are looking to the seminaries to help them at various stages in their ministries. Seminaries will have to adopt more flexible course programming schedules and decide whether they want to extend their ministry to assist men and women demonstrating great competence in the practice of ministry who do not have the basic undergraduate requirements to study at the M.Div. level.

In response to this changing educational scene, seminaries will need to engage in some innovative planning in an effort to make theological education more affordable and available. Theological education needs to have a closer identification with the task of ministry and deploy its resources through 'distanced learning' programmes so that more people can study as they engage in ministry and thereby reinforce theory by immediate application. Any such schemes would need to preserve academic integrity by proper monitoring both within the academic institution and at the local church level. The great challenges arising from urban mission reinforce the need for more preparation, not less. The areas of competence must extend beyond improving leading and management skills to an ability to engage cultural context which are highly secular and pluralistic. These contexts are the themes of our next two chapters.

SUMMARY

In this chapter we have attempted to heighten awareness of the challenge presented by urban societies which are highly diversified and mobile. Churches which maintain their programmes and routines without regard to the different contexts and complex networks of relationship to which every individual member belongs are likely to be plagued with nominality. In the case of families, the social networks become even more complicated and extended, so that the church must work especially hard to hold together a divinely intended institution which society is endeavouring to tear apart.

The ministry challenge is to track these social networks, provide personal support for their church members and remain alert to the significant issues which are surfacing in each context. Ministers must see beyond their traditional role expectations. They must 'think city' rather than lower their line of vision to the point where they can no longer see beyond local church, parish and present membership. The church in the city needs to establish 'listening posts' throughout the area to be able to detect and respond rapidly to changing situations. On the one hand, the gospel needs to be related to the cultural distinctives of working-class people and various ethnic groups; on the other, it needs to be worked out in the context of the high-pressure high-performance milieu of professionals and executives.

Western cultures are struggling to rebuild a sense of community in urban societies. For there has been a widespread breakdown not only in the inner city and within the business community, but also in the suburban dormitory satellites. When people feel that they do not relate to or belong anywhere, they are heading for an identity crisis with profound repercussions not only for themselves, but for society at large. They become distrustful of other people and manipulative in their relationships. Some people turn in upon themselves, becoming selfish pleasure seekers preoccupied with their personal rights, or competitive workaholics. Others opt for a lively social life, flitting from one fleeting relationship to another. Social life is lived at a surface level of glib verbal exchanges, with value placed on style rather than on substance. Shallow social environments are breeding grounds for nominality, which is simply surface-level religion.

In the urban context, the church has to become a counter-culture movement; not in the sense of withdrawal, but of engagement with the wider society. The church must act prophetically by demonstrating authentic community based on networks of small groups. The small groups help to contextualize the kingdom of God in different working and living environments. Yet these groups do not exist in isolation, otherwise the church would simply reflect the atomized nature of society. Rather they are interlinked and brought together to celebrate the greatness of God and the riches of the gospel. At such times the church becomes an anticipation of the New Jerusalem—that inspiring urban vision which is descriptive of God's goal for history.

NOTES

1. *World Urbanization, 1800 to 2000* (Population Reference Bureau Information Sheet; Washington, 1971).

2. Quoted in Robert Fishman, *Bourgeois Utopias* (Basic Books Inc; New York, 1978) p 20. Rome at the height of its power in AD 274 covered just six square miles within the Aurelian walls.

3. Krishan Kumar, *Prophecy and Progress—The Sociology of Industrial and Post-industrial Society* (Penguin Books; Harmondsworth, 1978) p 65.

4. See Kumar, *Prophecy and Progress* and Roy Joslin, *Urban Harvest* (Evangelical Press; Welwyn, 1982) p 158.

5. Joslin, *Urban Harvest*, p 25.

6. John D. Gay, *The Geography of Religion in England* (Duckworth; London, 1971) p 74.

7. E. R. Wickham, *Church and People in an Industrial City* (Lutterworth Press; 1953) p 69.

8. *Prospects for the Eighties* (MARC Europe; 1979); *Prospects for Wales* (1983); *Prospects for Scotland* (1985).

9. *'Christian' England* (MARC Europe; 1991).

10. Scotland is an exception due to the strength of the Roman Catholic population in the industrial towns.

11. Martin Marty, *Pilgrims in Their Own Land* (Little Brown and Company; Boston, 1984) p 169.

12. J. Edwin Orr, *The Light of the Nations* (Paternoster Press; London, 1965) p 28.

13. Fishman, *Bourgeois Utopias*, p 39.

14. Marty, op cit, p 315.

15. Ferdinand Tonnies, *Community and Society* (Harper and Row; New York, 1963) p 232. Translated from the German original, *Gemeinschaft und Gesellschaft* (1887) and edited by Charles P Loomis.

16. Robert N Bellah et al, *Habits of the Heart* (Harper and Row; New York, 1985) p 72.

17. Rodney Stark and William Sims Bainbridge, *The Future of Religion: Secularization and Renewal and Cult Formation* (University of California Press; Berkeley, 1985) pp 76-77.

18. Emile Durkheim, *Socialism* (Collier Books; New York, 1962).

19. Fishman, op cit, p 36.

20. Fishman op cit, p 124.

21. Robert Fishman draws attention to the significance of this decentralization for the USA in the following comment:
In my view, the most important feature of post war American development has been the almost simultaneous decentralization of housing, industry, specialized services, and office jobs; the consequent breakaway of the urban periphery from a central city it no longer needs; and the creation of a decentralized environment that nevertheless possesses all the economic and technological dynamism we associate with the city (*op cit*, p 184).

22. Fishman, op cit, p 185.

23. 'John Naisbitt's Trendletter' (*JNTL*, Washington DC, 3 August 1989).

24. Peter Kaldor, Vaughan Bowie, Glenn Farquar-Nicols, ed, *Green Shoots in the Concrete* (Scaffolding; New South Wales, 1985) see chapter 11.

25. See Gavin Reid's *To Reach A Nation* (Hodder & Stoughton; London, 1987) chap 12.

26. See Lyle Schaller's *It's a Different World* (Abingdon Press; Nashville, 1987) chap 3.

27. Peter Brierley, *'Christian' England*, p 137

Of all the Anglican and Free Churches, 39% or two in five, have congregations of 50 or fewer, and of these 14% are 25 or under. That means that 13,500 churches have fewer than 50 people, and 4,900 under 25. No wonder many look to larger churches for resources for developments. A further 25% have between 100 and 200. Only 8%, or one in twelve, have above 200.

Lyle Schaller, *The Multiple Staff and the Larger Church* (Abingdon Press, Nashville, 1980) p 28, provides the following figures, reckoned as a percentage:

CLASSIFYING AMERICAN CHURCHES BY SIZE

Average Attendance at Worship	Percentage	Type
35	25%	Fellowship
75	50%	Small
140	75%	Middle-sized
200	85%	Awkward size
350	95%	Large
600	98%	Huge
700 or more	100%	Minidenomination

For comparison, Peter Brierley provides the following figures for England:

40	25%
85	50%
150	75%
200	85%
400	95%
600	98%
700 or more	100%

28. Carl F George, *Preparing Your Church for the Future* (Fleming H Revell; Tarrytown, New York, 1991).

CHAPTER SIX

THE INFLUENCE OF SECULARIZATION

T HE CONTEMPORARY WORLD-VIEW shaping and directing western
societies has become so permeated by secularization that we find
it almost impossible to extricate ourselves from its influence in
order to view it with any measure of objectivity. It is so all-persuasive
that we have become oblivious to its presence. In fact it is only as we
come into contact with societies which have been isolated from the
secularization process, as in the case of animistic tribal groups, or which
steadfastly resist its influence, as in some Muslim societies, that we are
made uncomfortably aware that we live in very different conceptual
worlds. In fact, it sometimes requires the critique of non-western
societies to make Christians aware of the extent to which secular thinking has not only marginalized the church from society, but has itself
permeated the belief system and institutional life of the church.

The Christian lives in an unavoidably ambivalent relationship to the
world. For the world is regarded in the Bible from two standpoints. In
terms of its creation and ultimate destiny, it is a world which belongs to
God, which depends upon him for its continuing existence and over
which he rules. In relation to the present order, it is still largely in the
hands of Satan, who continues to defy the authority of God. Christ's
victory on the cross has secured the ultimate outcome of the battle, the
defeat of Satan, but the conflict will continue until Christ's return.

The secular mindset represents a world view which considers this
world as a closed, self-sustaining system and regards humans as autonomous beings, answerable to no high authority. Consequently, people
who have faith in a Supreme Being find themselves having to live in two

worlds with incompatible world views. Those who try to compartmentalize their life find themselves tortured by contradictions and torn by living
with double standards and divided personal loyalties. To opt out of the
world is not a practical alternative, and many who lack the intellectual
resources, spiritual stamina and support groups to work through life's
challenges, yield their primary allegiance to the world. Thus secularization becomes a major contributing cause of nominality. It constitutes a
formidable force which must be understood both as an intellectual
system and as a social dynamic if its presuppositions and priorities are to
be effectively challenged.

THE HISTORICAL FACTORS CONTRIBUTING TO SECULARIZATION

Secularization has a long history and is a social process with a number of
strands. Until the end of the medieval period religion permeated the
whole of life, providing a 'sacred canopy'[1] to control, integrate and
provide a sense of purpose. It was a world in which 'natural phenomena'
were regarded as expressions of the will of God or malevolent beings. It
was a world of mystery, miracles, angelic visitations and omens. Thus
the acceptance within a culture of a 'sacred canopy' covering every
aspect of life had both positive and negative consequences.

On the positive side it provided a sense of security, corporate identity, mutual responsibility and purpose. Religion is successfully
socialized by 'the establishment of symmetry between the objective
world of society and the subjective world of the individual'.[2] Negatively,
religion was used from time to time to legitimize a ruling hierarchy as
divinely appointed to ensure cohesion and conformity, and thereby to
bring about the oppression of the mass of the population. Furthermore,
the whole world-view was permeated by superstition and a fear of
demonic interference or divine malevolence.

At the end of the Middle Ages there began to appear the first of a
series of social movements which contributed significantly to a radical
change of world-view. One fundamental consequence of these developments was the 'disenchantment' of the world,[3] to use Max Weber's
graphic term describing the distancing of the 'natural', everyday world
from the influence of the supernatural. These movements stretched from
the fourteenth century to the present time.

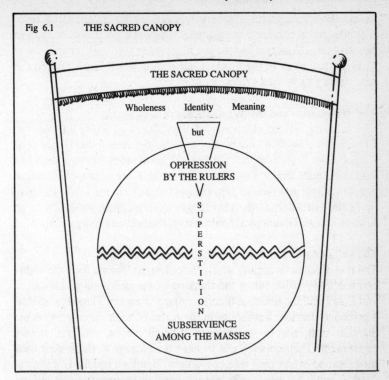

Fig 6.1   THE SACRED CANOPY

THE SACRED CANOPY

Wholeness   Identity   Meaning

but

OPPRESSION
BY THE RULERS

S
U
P
E
R
S
T
I
T
I
O
N

SUBSERVIENCE
AMONG THE MASSES

The Renaissance and the liberation of culture

This period of 'rebirth' in European history, covering the period from the fourteenth to the sixteenth centuries, began in Italy with a focus on humankind's relation to the material world, which was a significant change of focus from the medieval period's preoccupation with God and the world to come. This significant shift of emphasis provided the intellectual and cultural stimulus to create a conducive climate in which secularization could eventually flourish.

As Renaissance insights were carried north in the fifteenth and sixteenth centuries, a cultural revival ensued which directed attention to the Greek New Testament and the study of the early church Fathers. Erasmus (1466-1536) was one of the great theological thinkers, while Francis Bacon (1561-1626) emerged as a philosopher of science. The study of the ancient texts helped to generate a desire for the reformation of the church to conform to the simplicity and priorities of apostolic times. Also renaissance thinkers represented an independent voice which began to criticize clerical abuse. There is a great deal of truth in the adage that 'Erasmus laid the egg that Luther hatched'. It comes as no surprise that many of the younger generation which had espoused the new humanism, turned Protestant after 1571.

The Reformation and the fragmentation of the Church

The breaking of the monopoly of the Church of Rome in Western Europe had a twofold impact. Not only did the church divide into two, Catholic and Protestant, but a process of continuous fragmentation has continued until the present time. Today there are scores of Christian denominations and sects in Europe and hundreds in the USA. Furthermore, the attention of the church was diverted from society at large towards internal theological controversy, renewal and reorganization.

The Enlightenment and the autonomy of the individual

The rise of scientific inquiry which characterized Europe from the eighteenth century arose out of the thinking of the philosophers Descartes and Locke and the scientific theories of Isaac Newton. They represented a profound distrust of authority in the realm of scientific enquiry, arguing that truth was to be obtained through reason, observation and experiment. Their concern was to have the courage to think their own thoughts and live by their own convictions. Bentham and the Utilitarians tried to apply the Newtonian 'natural laws' to government and human relationships. While some thinkers of the Enlightenment were atheists and hostile to the church, many who held a deistic position continued within the church. Relationships tended to be more positive in Protestant areas of Europe, where rationalistic theologies were developing, than in Catholic regions.

Enlightenment thinkers were confident that the morals and values of society could be based on reason alone without recourse to divine revelation. They placed their confidence in education and the development of science and technology to bring about the 'inevitable progress' of humankind. Karl Barth described the Enlightenment as 'a system founded upon the presupposition of faith in the omnipotence of human ability'. Concern for 'human dignity' and 'human rights' was based on the autonomy of the individual, rather than on Christian values of the individual made in the image of God and called to a life of service to society.

Science and its alternative explanations

The scientific explanations of the origin of the universe, the nature of life, the factors influencing human personality, the progress and goal of human history and the basis of religious experience have served to challenge traditional Christian understandings formulated in a pre-scientific age.

The reliance of the modern western world on scientific reasoning and the spectacular results of its research has led to a dependence on the scientific approach applied to every area of life. Peter Berger commented in 1969 that, 'What people actually find credible as views of reality depends upon the social support these receive.'[4] Belief has a powerful social dimension as well as a logical basis and this presents a considerable challenge to the Christian advocate when plausibility of contemporary structures is antagonistic to Christianity. In Peter Berger's view,

> secularization has posited an altogether novel situation for
> modern people. Probably for the first time in history, the
> religious legitimations of the world have lost their plau-
> sibility not only for a few intellectuals and other marginal
> individuals but for broad masses of entire societies.[5]

Urbanization and the freedom to choose

Urbanization, which escalated with the industrial revolution, caused the break-up of many traditional, face-to-face communities. Five factors influenced the rise of secularism in this context. The people who swarmed into the burgeoning cities were separated from the family networks and peer groups which exerted social pressure to maintain traditional beliefs. Their new location provided the anonymity and novel social context in which to establish new allegiances and embrace new ideas. Their distancing from the soil, freedom from dependence on the cycles of nature for their livelihood and entry into a world which was the product of human creativity gave support to the slogan that 'man is the measure of all things'. William Blake, the English poet and mystic, observed of the Industrial Revolution that,

> Great things happen when men and mountains meet.
> But these things do not happen when men jostle in the street.

It was the convergence of the above five factors which provided the intellectual climate and social context which enabled the philosophy of secularism to permeate the assumptions and social structures of western society so that society became profoundly secularized.[6] The resultant loss of God-consciousness provides a seductive intellectual climate in which to build an alternative belief system, buttressed by powerful social affirmation, which marginalizes religious convictions. Such marginalization drives the Christians in the direction of increasing nominality.

THE IMPACT OF SECULARIZATION ON SOCIAL STRUCTURES

Os Guinness in *The Gravedigger File* perceptively distinguishes secularism the philosophy from secularization the social process. Secularism, the philosophy, has a limited following whereas secularization, the process, has an all-embracing influence. He defines the process of secularization in the following terms: 'The process through which, starting from the centre and moving outward, successive sectors of society and culture have been freed from the decisive influence of religious ideas and institutions.' He writes that secularization is contagious in a way that secularism never was. Secularization, the process, goes deeper in that it provides the perfect setting for secularism (the philosophy). Its influence goes further, in that it affects religious people too.[7] This social process has the four main components.

1. The separation of domains
Instead of the one unified world which prevailed in the West until the end of the medieval times, we have to straddle two worlds: the public domain and the private.

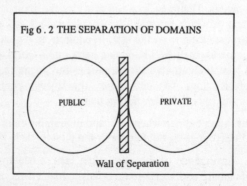

Fig 6 . 2 THE SEPARATION OF DOMAINS

PUBLIC   PRIVATE

Wall of Separation

The public domain is a macroworld of powerful public institutions and private business. It is a world of politics, commerce, industry, banking, education, the military and the mass media (print and electronic). This is a highly pragmatic world governed by empiricism and 'Wall of Separation' expediency. Religion is only permitted into this domain when its presence can be used to bolster institutions, preserve cohesion and heighten morale in times of national crisis. The two benign, socially approved forms are either a quaint or pompous ceremonial state religion, as in Europe, or a sentimentalized, deistic, civil religion as in the United States.

This development leads to the nation-state presuming to take the place of God as the source to which citizens look for happiness, health and social welfare. Its political institutions find themselves making promises which they are unable to deliver, because the bureaucracies which are developed absorb disproportionate amounts of the available resources. The wily learn how to cheat the system and the genuinely needy fail to receive the benefits.

Furthermore, with flagging economies, the system lacks adequate financial resources, and the situation is further exacerbated by the breakdown of the family and the neighbour networks which formerly functioned as the first line of care providers.

The private domain is the world of the family and leisure pursuits, among which religion may vie with hobbies and sports. Because the influence of religion is severely restricted in the public sphere, its influence tends to be played down and its residual strength in the private sphere almost totally ignored.

2. The compartmentalizing of life
Life is no longer regarded holistically, that is, lived within a community of people who hold the same world-view and with whom we share every aspect of life. Rather, even among people within the same family, life may be divided into numerous autonomous spheres. One sphere may be private and common to all, while other more public spheres will either include or exclude other family members. This gives rise to soul-searching questions of identity and competing allegiances. Each of the two spheres take on different characteristics. The public sphere is a world of giant institutions over which the individual feels he or she has little or no control. It is an impersonal world, often manifesting itself as uncaring and ruthless. In this 'real world' as it sometimes presumptuously refers

to itself, personal faith and moral absolutes are scarcely tolerated. The 'religion' of the market-place is that of secularism, despite the fact that religious people my be thick on the ground in many working locations. In other words, the public sphere represents a 'no-go' area where the rule and relevance of religion is strictly excluded even for the most religious people. Each sphere represents different ranges of activities, individuals involved and languages used. The knowledge specializations which are developed within the confines of each sphere cause increasing difficulty when people try to communicate with one another from one sphere to another.

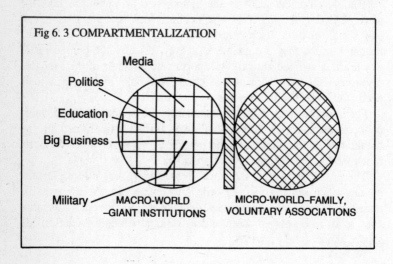

Fig 6. 3 COMPARTMENTALIZATION

Media
Politics
Education
Big Business
Military
MACRO-WORLD
–GIANT INSTITUTIONS
MICRO-WORLD–FAMILY,
VOLUNTARY ASSOCIATIONS

Religion is relegated to the status of a department of sociology and religious people become a minority special-interest group. People who are interested in the Bible, church attendance and a religious world-view largely confine their conversations to one another, and develop a specialized vocabulary which means that their communications are restricted to those already initiated into the lingo.

3. The impact of the public on the private sphere

The public sphere makes a tremendous impact on the private sphere by virtue of the fact that it dominates the wider social context: the majority of the population is educated by, earns its living in, seeks health care from, and is governed by, secular institutions. In such environments, secular values go largely unchallenged, and when voices of concern and protest are raised those institutions can wield weighty economic and social sanctions against religiously motivated nonconformists.

Time magazine's cover story for December 9, 1991, entitled 'America's Holy War', raised the question whether the separation of church and state had gone too far. It conceded that for the past generation the courts had fenced God out of the country's public life. It highlighted the conflicting viewpoints of the 'separationists' versus the 'accommodationists'. The former argue that with nearly 1,200 different religious bodies, the only way to keep the peace is to keep them all out of the shared public sphere. The latter reply that by isolating God from public life, the courts have replaced freedom *of* religion with freedom *from* religion, which raised the question as to what alternative basis for morality and values will be substituted. This is a pressing issue which is highlighted by anomalies and moral contradictions. The *Time* article provides the following graphic example:

> In this nation of spiritual paradoxes, it is legal to hang a picture in a public exhibit of a crucifix submerged in urine, or to utter virtually any conceivable blasphemy in a public place; it is not legal, the federal courts have ruled, to mention God reverently in a classroom, on a football field or at a commencement ceremony as part of a public prayer.

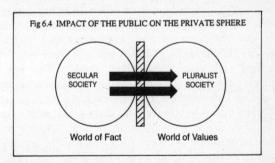

Fig 6.4 IMPACT OF THE PUBLIC ON THE PRIVATE SPHERE

SECULAR SOCIETY — PLURALIST SOCIETY

World of Fact — World of Values

In addition, the mass media, both print and electronic, bombard our senses and invade our homes. The question bounces back and forth as to whether the TV programmers are simply reflecting social values or whether they are shaping these values by portraying as normal that which is deviant or exceptional.

Interview programmes which probe into the lives of those who have been through harrowing experiences or who brazenly advocate promiscuous behaviour under the euphemistic label 'alternative life styles', are more geared to titillate than inform the audience, and thereby deserve the descriptive classification 'sleaze TV'.

David Frost has commented that through TV we allow people into our living rooms that we would not allow through the front door. The year 1991 also saw the advent of the TV phenomenon of 'porno-news', as senate hearings and trial proceedings reported in graphic detail the alleged sexual activities of political figures and social celebrities.

Traditionally, ethical values have been rooted in religious convictions. This position has been challenged in recent years by secular humanists who argue that humanism also expresses an ethical philosophy by basing ethical standards on the consequences of actions taken, rather than on divine sanctions. Paul Kurtz, for many years editor of *The Humanist* magazine, writes:

> While life has no meaning *per se*, it does provide us with opportunities to enjoy, discover, and create. The great challenge for the humanist is to lead the good life on his own terms and to take destiny in his own hands. Of the many values that the humanist defends, individual freedom is basic: the right of the individual to make up his own mind, to develop his own conscience, and to lead his own life without undue interference from others. Another humanist view is the commitment to creative growth and development. But the humanist does not believe that 'anything goes', as critics have charged. He does not believe that there is a right and wrong. That is an absolute libel against humanist philosophy and ethics. I submit that there are built within each individual tendencies toward growth. The great challenge of life is to actualize one's talents and satisfy one's needs, while also developing moral awareness and a sense of moral responsibility to others. Other values that humanists emphasize are those of democracy and shared experiences, which entail the belief that a democratic community and cooperative efforts in negotiating differences are the best means of achieving a peaceful and prosperous community.[8]

The basic elements contained in the above quotation are further elaborated in other sections of Kurtz's book. They represent a confidence in the basic goodness of human nature and in human potential and the scientific method; an emphasis on the individual as the central point of reference; and a commitment to the belief that ethics are autonomous and situational, so that the rightness of any action is determined by its consequences. As a basis for ethical understanding this view is weak in coming to terms with the darker side of human nature, in establishing a basis on which conflicts between individual and communal rights may be resolved, and in the balancing of rights and responsibilities.

Kurtz moves on to the offensive in his attack on the repressive nature of religiously based ethical norms and his advocacy of the 'new morality':

> The basic assumption of the new morality is the conviction
> that the good life is achieved when we realize human poten-
> tial. This means that we ought to reject all those creeds and
> dogmas that impede human fulfillment or impose external
> authoritarian rules on human beings. The traditional super-
> naturalistic moral commandments are especially repressive
> of our human needs. They are immoral insofar as they foster
> illusions about human destiny and suppress vital inclinations.[9]

The specifics of the 'moral libertarianism' advocated by Kurtz include the repeal of laws against abortion, birth control and voluntary steriliza-tion, a more liberal attitude towards sexual freedom, pornography and obscenity, the acceptance of nudity on stage and in the cinema—espe-cially where artistic values are involved, and the placing of sexual relations between consenting adults beyond the range of the law (p 35). Moral maturity is interpreted as ethical relativism. 'A mature person recognizes that he can tolerate divergent life styles without necessarily approving of them. In so doing, the horizons of his own personality may be broadened and enriched' (p 35). At the same time, Kurtz maintains that he is not advocating the flaunting of standards of decency and propriety. But where, in the live-and-let-live society envisaged by Kurtz, is the line to be drawn, and what is to stop it continually being redrawn as social acceptance is gained by careful promotion? The problem is what is deemed legal becomes regarded as moral.

Such viewpoints pervade the public sphere and invade the private domain through the entertainment industry and the public school sys-tem. This is not to imply that these influential areas of life are dominated by 'card carrying' secular humanists, but that the separation of domains and the relegation of religion to the private sphere has predetermined the rules of the game. This separation has created a clash of systems between the ethical reasoning of secular humanists and theists. Robert E. Webber, professor of theology at Wheaton College, expresses the concern of Christians:

> If man himself is the final arbiter of moral rules by which society is governed, then men can change the rules as they see fit. But if it is true that our moral nature is fallen, as Christian humanism argues, then man's collective moral life will move toward the lowest common denominator. Is this not what Paul is saying in Romans I when he states that 'God gave them over'? The implication is that when man removes the restraint of law, God allows the race to pursue their inclinations to the full. The danger of secular humanism is that, in its insistence on human autonomy and freedom, it may lead society over the brink. Were it not for God's common grace, society would affirm a moral chaos that would be its own ruination.[10]

Ten years later there is mounting evidence that Webber's prognostication has proved accurate.

The permeation of the private into the public sphere

Society, so far, has been spared many of the dire consequences of the undermining of ethical standards in the public sphere because the 'wall of separation' between private and public domains is porous. In the previous section we commented on the impact of the public on the private. But the influence is not all one way. Despite the fact that the familial structure of the private domain has been under strong attack,

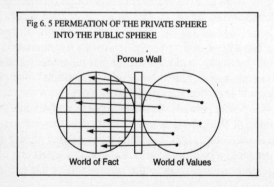

Fig 6. 5 PERMEATION OF THE PRIVATE SPHERE INTO THE PUBLIC SPHERE

Porous Wall

World of Fact   World of Values

there is still a residual strength and religious convictions continue to be nurtured in the family and the church. These values are lived out, more or less, by countless numbers of believers. In an earlier chapter we noted, sadly, that with nine-tenths of the churchgoing population there was no perceptible difference between them and non-churchgoers in relation to a range of social attitudes. This is an indication of the power of the downdrag exerted by society. Yet the one-tenth remains to exercise considerable influence as yeast, salt and light in the world.

The sharpness of the conflict of values in the public sphere highlights the need for church leaders to train the people of God to exercise moral and spiritual discernment in the market-place and daily life by open discussion of the current issues and the formulating of biblically informed Christian responses. Individuals in the 'firing line' also need the support of fellow-believers who are involved in the same issues and subject to similar pressures. We shall give further consideration as to how such support groups can be formed in the final chapter. In the second half of this chapter we shall consider how Christians might respond to the social trends arising from secularization.

INFLUENCE ON RELIGIOUS THINKING

Secularization has more profound implications than simply the marginalizing of the church from the institutional base of society: it has also relegated those who think 'theistically' to what Peter Berger describes as a 'cognitive minority',—a group formed around a body of deviant 'knowledge'. He observes that:

> Whatever the situation may have been in the past, *today* the supernatural as a meaningful reality is absent or remote from the horizons of everyday life of large numbers, very probably of the majority, of people in modern societies, who seem to manage to get along without it quite well. This means that those to whom the supernatural is still, or again, a meaningful reality find themselves in the status of a minority, more precisely, a *cognitive minority*—a very important consequence with very far-reaching implications.[11]

By what process have Christians become a 'cognitive minority' as a consequence of secularization? The steps may be traced according to the following sequence:

Relativization. While religion may retain a legitimate place as an integral part of the cultural heritage of peoples and groups, it is of purely psychological or sociological significance. For persons who regard religion as making a beneficial contribution in these areas, its presence may be tolerated or even encouraged. But the support given has nothing to do with the *validity* of religious explanations. Religious convictions represent no more than personal preferences. They may have value in providing myths to enshrine values and give a sense of purpose and a unifying principle to life, but their truth claims are dismissed as irrelevant. Most secular humanists clash head-on with the church in their conviction that, throughout history, religion has proved oppressive, divisive and exploitative.

Privatization. Os Guinness defines 'privatization' as 'the process by which modernization produces a cleavage between the public and private sphere of life and focuses the private sphere as the special arena for the expansion of individual freedom and fulfillment'.[12] As we have already noted, the establishment of the two domains—public and private—and the relegating of religion to the private sphere result in religion becoming 'closet religion'. It becomes largely a matter of personal piety nourished by corporate worship with like-minded individuals who congregate and then disperse to pursue their lives as usual.

Marginalization. This point is closely related to the previous one. A privatized religion is marginalized from the public arena. Consequently, when the moral ills of society are addressed religion must be excluded from an educational perspective based on a philosophy of situational ethics. For example, with the current concern to stop the spread of AIDS, the main plank of the strategy is to advocate 'safe sex'. Promiscuity is socially acceptable so long as it is between 'mutually consenting adults'. Therefore, an educational programme showing the various methods of 'safe sex', including anal and oral intercourse, is prescribed and the use of condoms promoted. The counter argument is that such 'education' is based on a permissive philosophy which will further encourage promiscuity and lead to a false sense of security as there is no such thing as 'safe sex'. The procedures advocated simply minimize the risks of immediate transmission of the disease. But what are the longer term consequences in terms of respect for persons, the building of a subsequent marriage on the basis of mutual trust, reinforcing family solidarity and the provision of a secure and protected environment for children? The issue is not 'safe sex', but the teaching of sex according to a clearly articulated and comprehensive set of moral values.

Trivialization. When religion makes an appearance in the public domain it does so in the trivialized form of ceremonial religion or the vacuous form of civil religion. In either case religion is rendered so innocuous that the mass media can largely ignore the religious dimensions of life. The print media provide more space than the electronic media. In the popular press prominent publicity is given to moral scandals among church leaders, bizarre incidents and, in the US press, to boundary conflicts between church and state. Then, what newspaper or popular magazine would be complete without a page or column devoted to astrological predictions? Very little time is allocated in TV programming to discussing religious issues or reporting religious news. In the USA, as distinct from Western Europe, the major TV and broadcasting networks do not have religious departments and consequently are devoid of reporting expertise when handling religious affairs. This is in marked contrast to other areas such as politics, fashion, health and sports. etc, each of which are handled by departments staffed by specialists. On the other hand, newspapers in North America do better than those of other English-speaking countries of the western world in that more regional dailies have religious affairs reporters who are theologically trained and sensitive to national and local church politics and pastoral issues.

Commercialization. Given the pluralistic nature of North American society, civil religion has to be defined in the broadest and vaguest of terms if it is to provide the 'sociological cement' to help bond society. But with increasing religious diversity prompting the reinterpretation of Thomas Jefferson's wall of separation between church and state as demanding the exclusion of religion from the public domain, society is becoming increasingly fragmented and destabilized. Originally intended to safeguard pluralism, in recent years the doctrine of the separation of church and state has been used to promote secularism in the public sphere. As long as the bulk of immigrants to the US came from Europe, there was a widely accepted Judeo-Christian ethic. In the years since World War II immigrants have increasingly come from non-Christian areas of the world, predominantly Asia. Notwithstanding the arrival of eastern religions to add further complexity to an already fragmented religious scene, and the encroachments of secularism, the Christian churches still retain great social strength, especially in the South and Mid-West. They are a force which politicians, educators and business people cannot afford to ignore.

The fact that American Protestantism is fragmented into hundreds of groups means that they have to compete against one another to achieve a larger slice of the 'market share'. Furthermore, American evangelicalism tends to be ahistorical in nature, with groups defining themselves in terms of their boundaries of distinctive doctrines rather than their historical roots. It is the religion of the camp meeting where people gather for a new experience, rather than the church of the community in which one is born and raised.[13] It is not surprising that, given the pluralism and consumerism of American society, churches here have to be 'seeker sensitive' and 'user friendly' in order to compete with other churches also seeking the allegiance of religious 'shoppers'. The social dynamics in North America in regard to the promotion of religion are very different from Europe. Europeans regard religious entrepreneurs with suspicion and prove to be much more sales-resistant. In Europe, *clan religion* has been the predominant basis of church allegiance. In North America, this has been eroded due to the mobility and heterogeneity of society, so that *consumer religion* and *celebrity religion* have made considerable inroads.[14]

Sanitization. The tendency in North America to commercialize religion arises from a failure to distinguish the need to *contextualize* the message so that it speaks to the issues of the day and is presented in concepts and language with which people can relate, from the danger of *enculturating* the message and editing it so that only those elements which affirm culture and meet people's aspirations are emphasized. The

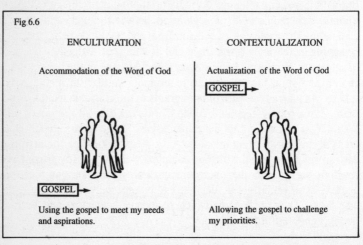

Fig 6.6

ENCULTURATION

Accommodation of the Word of God

CONTEXTUALIZATION

Actualization of the Word of God

GOSPEL ▶

GOSPEL ▶

Using the gospel to meet my needs and aspirations.

Allowing the gospel to challenge my priorities.

latter represents a marketing of religion which may popularize culturally acceptable religiosity whilst denying vital elements of the gospel message.

The renowned German theologian/preacher Helmut Thielicke made the distinction between contexualization and enculturation by describing the former as the 'actualization of the word', whereas the latter was the 'accommodation of the word'. In *actualizing* the word, 'the truth remains intact. The hearer is summoned and called 'under the truth' in his own name and situation'. In contrast, *accommodating* the word signifies calling 'the truth "under me" and letting me be its norm. It is pragmatic to the extent that it assigns truth the function of being the means whereby I master life'.[15]

The relationship between gospel and culture is complex. Some aspects of most cultures the gospel affirms. It may also serve to meet unmet aspirations. But the gospel also passes judgement on certain elements of every culture, because the consequences of the Fall of humanity from grace is evidenced in every area of life. In other words, the gospel acts redemptively in all cultures; it speaks in terms of judgement as well as grace.

RESPONDING TO SOCIETAL TRENDS

Secularization's bifurcation of life into two separate spheres, with secularism monopolizing the public domain and pluralism relegated to the private domain, results in people having to live in two conceptual worlds. For Christians those two worlds exist in constant tension and, at times, open conflict. This should not come as a surprise as our Lord made it clear that the Enemy still exercises considerable power in this world and that believers cannot serve two masters (God and materialism) without having to face the issue of where they give their primary allegiance. Because of their mutual incompatibility, both cannot be served without one or the other gaining the ascendancy. Thus the key areas need to be identified where there is likely to be a conflict of worldview, and biblical responses discussed. In addition to forums in which specific issues can be addressed, there will also be the need for support groups to help individuals make a corporate response to specific situations. The structural aspect will be explored in some detail in the final chapter. At this point we will confine our attention to possible conceptual Christian responses towards trends in society.

Lesslie Newbigin faces head-on the difficulty of the challenge presented by secularization. Quoting the great English statesman W.E. Gladstone's remark that 'Should the Christian faith ever become but one among many co-equal pensioners of a government, it will be a proof that subjective religion has again lost its God-given hold upon objective reality', Newbigin observes:

> The result is not, as we once imagined, a secular society. It is a pagan society, and its paganism, having been born out of the rejection of Christianity, is far more resistant to the gospel than the pre-Christian paganism with which cross-cultural missions have been familiar. Here, surely, is the most challenging missionary frontier of our time.[16]

The following represent some of the principle features of the neo-pagan society.

Individualism

In Western secular societies individuals are preoccupied with personal rights often to the neglect of corporate responsibilities. The Bible underlines two complementary and equally important truths in this area. On the one hand, it emphasizes the intrinsic worth of the individual, as made in the image of God. Furthermore, Christ came to give life, not simply for the salvation of the world in a comprehensive sense, but for the making whole of countless numbers of individuals who have to respond personally in order to receive the benefits of his reconciling work on the cross. On the other hand, the Bible places great emphasis on the importance of community. The church is described in organic rather than institutional terms, as 'the body of Christ'. The believer is commanded to live not for himself but for Christ. The fact that Christ voluntarily laid down his life becomes a principle of discipleship. Paul writes, 'He (Christ) died for all, that those who live should no longer live for themselves but for him who died for them and was raised to again' (2 Cor 5:15, see also Jn 15:12,13; Rom 4:7-9; 1 Jn 3:16). Although for many the laying down of life will not entail literal martyrdom, the principle of unselfish living is an inescapable requirement, 'Each of you should look not only to your own interests, but also to the interests of others' (Phil 2:4). There is no true giving of the gospel without at the same time giving away something of ourselves (1 Thess 2:8).

The gospel affirms that we only discover our true identity and purpose in life within the context of community—a community which provides support, requires accountability, helps people grow in character, assists them to discover in what ways God has uniquely gifted them and provides them with opportunities for Christian service. The church is in the people-*growing* business, which needs to be distinguished from people-*processing*. People-growing entails respect for the individual and a recognition of each person's distinct personality, gifts and calling. Discipleship signifies commitment to Christ as teacher, learning from him in relationship with other followers, obeying his commands and availing ourselves of the resources which he provides for the accomplishment of his purposes in the world.

Consumerism

As Lesslie Newbigin has observed, all human activity tends to be regarded as an unending cycle of production for the sake of consumption. Standard of living has been equated with quality of life, or to put it in bleak, bumper-sticker terms, 'He who has the most toys wins'. Materialistic philosophies have so permeated western societies that they have been incorporated by some segments of the church and translated into a theology of affluence with the so-called 'prosperity gospel'. Striving to accumulate becomes a seductive goal in life, generating selfishness, ruthlessness and shallowness. It is no wonder when the seed of the gospel is sown among thorns that before long the wheat is overwhelmed by the thorns, which Jesus explained represented 'the worries of this life, the deceitfulness of wealth and the desires for other things'. They do more than divert attention; ultimately they choke spiritual life (Mk 4:7,18,19).

The church must stand against the tyranny of materialism by advocating a simpler life-style and demonstrating in its corporate life, as well as in the individual lives of its members, an alternative value system in which joy and fulfilment are experienced through interpersonal activities and in bringing joy to others, rather than in the insatiable pursuit of possessions.

Centralism

Once again we turn to Newbigin for insights into the reasons for the emergence of bureaucracy in modern society and is dehumanizing consequences:

> The division of labour and the consequent pluralization and complexification of society require the development of tech-

niques for large-scale control. Bureaucracy applies the mechanical model to this task. It provides machinery in which there is a high degree of division of labour, of specialization, of predictability and of anonymity. It is of the essence of bureaucracy that it sets out to achieve a kind of justice by treating each individual as an anonymous and replaceable unit. In its ultimate development bureaucracy is the rule of nobody and is therefore experienced as tyranny.[17]

The individualism which we discussed under a previous heading represents an over-reaction to the depersonalizing influences of our society. As a defence against being treated as an ID number rather than given a name and respected as a person, people exert their autonomy as individuals. They demand their rights. But an over-reaction based on self-interest merely serves to undermine trust and erode community.

The suspicion of impersonal bureaucracies and centres of power remote from the grass roots, which is a characteristic of western societies, translates into a suspicion of denominationalism in the church scene. While the mainline churches decline, the independent congregations and community churches thrive. People are reluctant to commit themselves, so that church attendance does not translate into church membership. For the Baby Boomer generation (born between 1946 and 1964) the key word is *involvement*. They are prepared to become involved as they are known and appreciated as individuals and as they are encouraged to participate in programmes which recognize their gifts and concerns, have significance and provide growth potential. To hand out job lists or make blanket appeals for volunteers often elicits little response from 'baby boomers' because such approaches are perceived as evidence that the leadership is out of touch with the people who make up the congregation. The significant churches of the nineties will be those congregations which have learned that the secret of growing big is growing small. This concept will be further explained when we consider the 'metachurch' model.

Hedonism

The problem for a hedonistic society is the elusive nature of pleasure and happiness. It arises from a failure to recognize that pleasure and happiness are experienced as the by-products of an underlying purpose, the accomplishment of which leads to a sense of fulfilment. It is precisely this possibility which has been undermined by the secular mindset. Many people bravely try to inject a logic-defying sense of purpose into a world-view which regards 'reality' as the product of myriads of chance and random occurrences. Others have given up on that search and opted to live for pleasure as an end in itself. The quest is addictive, in that each 'pleasurable' experience fails to provide any satisfaction which has either depth or permanence, so other ambitious, tantalizing experiences need to be sought after. Living for the enjoyment of experiential high moments results in the deadening of the senses due to over-stimulation, or to the inescapable awareness that every emotional high-point is followed by a crushing anti-climax. The pursuit of a hedonistic life-style which regards experience as an end in itself leads ultimately to self-destruction. In contrast the gospel offers a life inspired by a sense of purpose and expressed in a commitment to serve the Lord by reverential worship and responsiveness to the needs and opportunities which he presents to us.

Pragmatism

This entails living life according to what works, or what you can get away with. The key consideration is not to miscalculate and get caught. It is the conducting of one's affairs according to expediency rather than according to moral principles arising from a personally appropriated value system. Societies based on pragmatism inevitably find that trust levels are eroded. Israel went through such a period in its history after the conquest of Canaan and during the subsequent moral confusion occasioned by daily contact with the pagan inhabitants of the land. During these turbulent years the people turned from God's law and resorted to 'doing what was right in their own eyes'.

In his perceptive book, *The Seven Habits of Highly Effective People*, Stephen Covey argues the need for the adoption of 'a principle-centred paradigm'. Instead of depending on personality (popularly misnamed 'charisma') or the acquisition of techniques as the primary means of influencing people around us, we should rather revert to an older value, that of 'character ethic as the foundation of success' in influencing and motivating people. Covey provides the following astute observation:

> If I try to use human influence strategies and tactics of how to get other people to do what I want, to work better, to be more motivated, to like me and each other—while my character is fundamentally flawed, marked by duplicity and insincerity—then, in the long run I cannot be successful.

> My duplicity will breed distrust, and everything I do—even
> using so-called good human relations techniques—will be
> perceived as manipulative.... Only basic goodness gives life
> to technique.[18]

Covey calls for 'primary greatness' in response to a society which, lacking moral values in the public sphere, has promoted 'secondary greatness' by granting social recognition to people for their *talents*, whilst ignoring the need for primary greatness or goodness in their *character* (p 22). Covey advocates an inside-out approach.

The inside-out approach says that private victories precede public victories, that making and keeping promises to ourselves precedes making and keeping promises to others. It says it is futile to put personality ahead of character, to try to improve relationships with others before improving ourselves.[19]

Covey distinguishes between a *practice* which is situationally specific and a *principle* which is of universal application. Among the essential ingredients of this principle-centred paradigm he lists: fairness, integrity and honesty, human dignity, service, quality and excellence, a belief in human potential and growth and the need for patience, nurture and encouragement. It is encouraging to note that, in the wake of an avalanche of scandals involving people in public life, Covey is gaining a wide hearing for his philosophy of life which seeks to help people replace their paradigm of pragmatism with one founded on principle. In order to resist relentless social pressures to jettison moral principles in the interest of expediency, Christians in the workplace need a community to provide a forum where issues can be raised, strategies developed and support provided, to help them retain their integrity and inject effective counter-measures.

RESPONDING TO THE INTELLECTUAL CHALLENGE OF SECULARIZATION

Martin Marty distinguishes three forms of secularity: (a) *Utter Secularity*, typified by Voltaire and Marx, which constitutes a frontal attack on Christianity; (b) *Mere Secularity*, where God and the church are bypassed and ignored; and (c) *Controlled Secularity*, consisting of a folk or civil religion which deifies traditional values.[20] Whatever form of secularization is encountered, it must be engaged at the conceptual level. The following points represent some of the key areas where intellectual engagement will be necessary.

Recognize the continuing social strength of religion

While religious sociologists until the 1960s almost universally prophesied the demise of religion in the face of the unrelenting challenge of secularization, by the 1980s a different note began to be sounded. The older view is being challenged not only by sociologists with a strong commitment to the church, such as the Roman Catholic Andrew Greeley, but also by Rodney Stark and William Sims Bainbridge. In their joint work *The Future of Religion*, published in 1985, they make the following statement:

> We acknowledge that secularization is a major trend in modern times, but argue that this is not a modern development and does not presage the demise of religion. Rather as we attempt to demonstrate throughout this book, secularization is a process found in all religious economies; it is something that is always going on in all societies. While secularization progresses in some parts of society, a countervailing intensification of religion goes on in other parts. Sometimes the pace of secularization speeds or slows, but the dominant religious organizations in any society are always becoming progressively more worldly, which is to say more secularized. The result of this trend has never been the end of religion, but merely a shift in fortunes among religions as faiths that have become too worldly are supplanted by more vigorous and less worldly religions.[21]

The authors argue that where the churches retain social strength in society they produce '*sects*' or renewal movements as expressions of unfulfilled religious aspirations. From a sociological standpoint, 'sect' simply means 'a religious group that is relatively small, in tension with the larger society (one might say 'balled up' against it), and that makes very strong claims on the loyalty and solidarity of its members'.[22] In areas where the church is socially weak, as in England, Germany and the Pacific Coast states of the USA, the tendency is for *cults* to be imported. Whereas the sect represents a schismatic movement, the cult is deviant. Fig 6.7. represents the likelihood of sect emergence or cult importation, depending on the extent of the influence of the church in any given society.

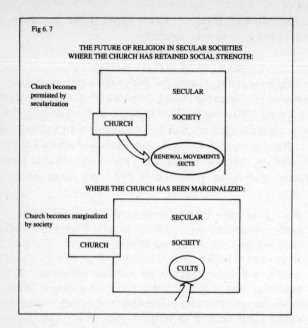

Fig 6.7

THE FUTURE OF RELIGION IN SECULAR SOCIETIES
WHERE THE CHURCH HAS RETAINED SOCIAL STRENGTH:

Church becomes
permiated by
secularization

SECULAR

SOCIETY

CHURCH

RENEWAL MOVEMENTS
SECTS

WHERE THE CHURCH HAS BEEN MARGINALIZED:

Church becomes marginalized
by society

SECULAR

SOCIETY

CHURCH

CULTS

The conclusion that Stark and Bainbridge come to as a result of applying their model in North American and European contexts is as follows:

> Our theory of religion forces the conclusion that religion is not in its last days. We think that the most modern scholars have misread the future because they have mistakenly identified the dominant religious traditions in modern society with the phenomenon of religion in general. Most observers have noted correctly that major Christian-Judaic organizations are failing, but they have not seen or appreciated the vigor of religion in less 'respectable' quarters.[23]

Expose the mythological basis of the secularization model

In writing *A Rumour of Angels*, a sequel to *The Sacred Canopy*, Peter Berger wished to correct the overstatement of power and irreversibility in his original thoroughgoing secularization model. The prediction of the sociologists of the 1960s that secularization would bring about the demise of religion have so far proved to be unfounded. On the contrary, the evidence mounts that people are incurably religious. Andrew Greeley observed that, 'however much the context has been changed, the basic functions religion plays in human life are essentially the same, as they always have been throughout human history'.[24]

The positive influence of secularization has been to de-demonize society in the sense of releasing people from the tyranny of belief that the significant events which affected their lives were extensively caused by capricious supernatural forces. However, it accomplished this through a reductionist approach to the nature of reality, and simply to deny the existence of these forces has proved both inadequate and illusory. While the plausibility structures of society were determined by left brain (strictly rational) thinking, demonic activity remained camouflaged. Now that due emphasis is being placed on the significance of right brain activity in human endeavour, contributing intuitive creativity and imagination and stimulating a longing to experience the transcendent, the demonic begins to shed its camouflage. Thus there is growing societal acceptance of the practice of seeking spirit guidance through the meditation of New Age psychic 'channelers', and a disturbing resurgence of satanic rituals involving curses and ritual sacrifices.

A Christian response to secularization is inevitably ambiguous. From the negative standpoint it represents human rebellion against God by regarding the world order as an autonomous and self-sustained sphere. On the other hand, secularization was made possible by the gospel, which subjected the 'powers' to God, thereby freeing the universe from demons and laying open the universe to the Word of God—the Logos, who enlightens reason. The biblical doctrine of creation also implies that God has conferred on the created order a limited independence of being, so that its intricacies can be explored and explained from an independent standpoint.[25] Problems arise when the secularization model becomes absolutized and intolerant towards other perspectives on reality, at which point it becomes vulnerable to demonic influence.

Identify the key areas of scientific inquiry

There are not as many areas of direct conflict between scientific theories and religiously based convictions as is popularly believed. The following headings indicate some of the major issues.

The origin of the universe. In point of fact the Bible has little to say about the process of creation. The first two chapters of Genesis are designed not to answer the question '*How* was the world created?', but '*Through whom* was the world created and for what purpose?' Theists believe that behind the Big Bang (if that is in fact how the universe began) was the person of God, for whom the creation of the universe was a purposeful activity. Without a person as prime mover we could not speak of the universe as being good, or establish within that created order a basis by which to ascribe meaning or purpose. When Christian fundamentalists anachronistically read the Bible as a scientific textbook and give literal interpretations to poetic language, they become needlessly dogmatic concerning issues where the Bible allows for a variety of interpretations. The issue of whether or not there is a Prime Mover behind the creation process is a matter for philosophical rather than scientific debate.

The evolutionary process. While scientific opinion was based on Darwinian mechanistic evolutionism, there were irreconcilable differences of viewpoint between theistic and atheistic scientists. If 'life' is to be explained exclusively in terms of mechanistic categories then the biblical usage of that word is rendered meaningless. But now that the weak points in Darwinian theory have been widely acknowledged and the mechanistic base replaced by an appreciation of organic wholeness, many of the difficulties begin to dissolve.[26]

1. Fossils do not show the change from one species to another by small gradations (variations); they show the sudden appearance of a new species by an abrupt transition.

2. Change is so prominent a feature of the theory that it is hard to understand how relatively stable species can occur. If everything remains in a state of constant modification it must be impossible to pick out species with relatively fixed characteristics.

3. The number of possible variations, starting from a given individual is very large.... The number of possible combinations of variations, starting from the varying individuals of the same species, is greater still... modifications to any one species would stream out in a million different directions.

4. It is inconceivable that a complicated organ such as the human eye could develop through an accumulation of variations. Until it has a complicated appropriate structure it does not function as an eye, is therefore not yet a factor in selection and consequently does not come into existence.

5. The premise that variations are inheritable is essential to the theory. This premise has proved false as a general rule.

Explore the relationship between mind and meaning

Christians must enter more fully into the debate about the relationship between the brain and the mind. Is a person's mental life to be totally explained in terms of the function of approximately ten billion electrical circuits in the cerebral cortex? On what basis can a brain, which is the product of evolution resulting from chance mutations, discern meaning? How does the brain discern patterns, thereby constructing wholes from the constituent parts?[27]

Conflict with the secular scientific community generally arises at the philosophical rather than the empirical level. Secular scientists tend to be reductionist in their approach, insisting that their explanations of phenomena in terms of causality represent a total explanation of reality. Their presuppositions thereby masquerade as proofs. The inductive method, which entails observation of phenomena and the massing of converging probable proof, leads to the development of sustainable hypotheses. Knowledge thus derived provides valid understanding which can then be more widely applied, but such knowledge is limited and partial in that it does not move from the *how* to the *why* questions.

If our understanding of reality cannot relate the parts to the whole, if it has no organizing principle, the causality eventually gives way to chaos.

> The limits of rationality are set at the point where thought is no longer capable of giving conclusive explanations and vindications. This is the case when it ceases to be able to give cogent reasons. Thought is unable to give cogent reasons:
> 1. for the validity of its own reasoning powers,
> 2. for the presupposition that the datum is knowable,
> 3. for the direction which thought must take.[28]

The search for an organizing principle for reality is logically impossible without adopting either a theistic or pantheistic position. The work of Einstein, Planck and Heisenberg have given rise to a New Physics which grapples with this issue. If the sub-atomic particles which constitute the building blocks of the physical order act randomly, how are we, the products of that process, to speak meaningfully about them? It is not surprising that significant thinkers within the New Physics are drawn towards eastern religions to provide the philosophical underpinning for their scientific enquiries. For instance, Fritjof Capra, the Nobel Prize winning Austrian physicist, sees the cosmic dance as the clue to the nature of the physical world.[29]

Others have given up the search for any organizing principle or 'theoretical centre'. Such are the post-modernists who strive to live in a world of partiality and flux, with experiences which defy explanation and in situations which are so unstable that they cannot become the object of sustained reflection. John Rajchman describes the post-modernist as living in a 'world market of ideas' which in its elasticity and lack of theoretical centre 'is like the Toyota of thought: produced and assembled in several different places and sold everywhere'.[30]

There is irony in the fact that many twentieth century Christians, who have too readily accepted the mechanistic explanation of the universe, are now unable to offer an attractive and convincing alternative world-view to compete with the pantheistic philosophies of eastern religions. By adopting a 'god of the gaps' approach which squeezed divine involvement in the created order into those sections which defy human explanation, God was progressively excluded from the human arena as scientific research filled in the picture. This mistaken line of argument stemmed from a weak understanding of the role of the Trinity in creation, especially of the Holy Spirit's ongoing relationship with the created order, as well as an acceptance of the basic premise which they were attempting to refute.

Demonstrate that Christianity relates to the big issues and the whole of life

The New Testament does not confine the benefits of Christ's reconciling death at Calvary to individuals in their relationship with God. That such personal reconciliation is foundational is beyond question, but it is intended as the starting point which makes possible the extension of Christ's reign on earth, culminating in the gathering of all creation at his feet. The picture of cosmic redemption presented in the New Testament ultimately embraces the whole created order. This being so, the Christian faith cannot be confined to the home or cordoned off within the sanctuary without a denial of its essential nature.

According to the apostle Paul, the gospel enters on the world scene at every point to challenge and dethrone the principalities and powers. These demonic influences infiltrate every human institution—law, custom and tradition—so that they begin to exert an inordinate and eventually tyrannical influence. Such institutions may be good in and of themselves, but their purpose is diverted so that they no long serve their God-intended purposes but become an end in themselves. Lesslie Newbigin identifies three examples in the New Testament of elemental powers which have become demonic through being absolutized.

The *power ordained by God of Romans 13* becomes the Beast of Revelation. The *Torah*, that loving instruction which God gives his people, the beauty of which is celebrated in Psalm 119, becomes a tyrant from which Christ has to deliver us. *Tradition*, the handing on of good practice from parent to child as is so beautifully described in Deuteronomy, becomes an evil power which comes between human beings and the living God.[31]

In addition to these New Testament examples Newbigin identifies other principles from contemporary society. *Numbering*, which enables us to measure and quantify, becomes a tyrant when, as in modern reductionist thinking, it is absolutized and nothing is valued except what can be measured and quantified. *Chance*, which is a fundamental element in this contingent universe, becomes the sovereign power governing the emergence of life and determines personal fortunes and the economic health of a nation. Thus, those who have become rich shake off their responsibility for the plight of the poor.

The Christian believes that only in Christ can the *structures of society* be rescued from demonic control. 'God still upholds the structures; without them the world would collapse and human life would be unthinkable. But the structures lose their pretended absoluteness. Nothing now is absolute except God as he is known in Jesus Christ; everything else is relativized'.[32]

Every endeavour must be made to ensure that the gospel is not relativized and privatized. The New Testament makes it unmistakably clear that the gospel is Good News from God which relates to every area of life in every age (Eph 1:21; Col 1:15-17; 2:14,15).

Root the Christian faith in history and absolutes

The secular mindset is most likely to clash with those religions which purport to be based on historical events rather than mythical stories. It is not surprising that, in order to head off the conflict, some biblical theologians have retreated from attempting to argue the historical reliability of the stories concerning God's saving interventions in the history of Israel and through the coming of the Messiah. Biblical accounts recording the incarnation of Christ, his virgin birth and angelic announcements, the miracles he performed demonstrating his power over nature, human sickness and death, his resurrection from the dead and his bodily ascension into heaven, are recast as subjective symbols of faith. To divorce the Christ of experience from the Jesus of history is to relativize Christianity and emaciate the gospel. Once the truth claims of the faith have been undermined, Christianity can safely be relegated to the private domain because it has been reduced to a religious option which may be of help to those persons in psychological need of a crutch to help them hobble through life, but has little to do with truth claims and the big issues of life. In response it must be emphasized that the focal point of Christianity is not a *crutch* but a *cross*, and there is all the difference in the world between these two symbols. The purpose of a crutch is to enable people to hobble through life, whereas the cross empowers people to face and conquer the domination of evil within themselves as well as resist its onslaught from the surrounding world order. The cross deals with evil in the most radical manner by insistently providing the means for us to die to our self-centredness as a prerequisite to living a victorious and abundant life by means of Christ's resurrection power.

To those people who are tempted to get diverted into this tortuous and slippery road which eventually peters out in the marshlands of subjectivity, the apostle Paul offers this urgent counsel:

> Now I would remind you, brothers and sisters, of the good news that I proclaimed to you, which you in turn received, in which also you stand, through which also you are being saved, if you hold firm to the message that I proclaimed to you—unless you have come to believe in vain.
>
> For I handed on to you as of first importance what I in turn received: that Christ died for our sins in accordance with the scriptures, that he was buried, and that he was raised on the third day in accordance with the scriptures, and that he appeared to Cephas, then to the twelve. Then he appeared to more than five hundred brothers and sisters at one time, most of whom are still alive, though some have died. Then he appeared to James, then to all the apostles. Last of all, as to one untimely born, he appeared also to me (1 Cor 15:1-8, NRSV).

Becoming infectious Christians communicating a gospel message which challenges the presuppositions of secularization

In this chapter we have argued that the march of secularization is not unstoppable and that there is increasing evidence that the army of secularizers beginning to break rank. If western society is on the brink of the disintegration of the world-view which has undergirded it for the past 250 years, the pressing question is, 'What will replace it?' There are other contenders in the field apart from Christianity. Which will gain the formulative influence in our generation, and for how long will its view prevail?

The Christian faith has much to say in response to the unanswered questions raised by secularism. The loss of a sense of purpose and self-identity has created a desire for self-transcendence, once it is recognized that hedonism is not more than a palliative yielding diminishing returns. An appreciation of the truth that humankind is made in the image of God underlines humanity's uniqueness and remarkable potential. The biblical witness to the fall from grace of humankind explains why people not only fail to live up to their potential, but live in direct contradiction to the divine intention for the human race. The gospel of God's forgiveness through the mediatorial death of Christ provides the key for people to be released from the 'script' which would otherwise determine their continued alienation and enslavement to self-destructive behaviour. Paul declares that if anyone is 'in Christ' they are thereby released from the old pattern of life by entering God's 'new creation'. Such a step entails more than a new start or a refurbishing; it describes an adoptive process which is sealed by the bestowing of a new nature (2 Cor 5:17; Jn 1:13).

In the service of Christ one can discover a new direction and sense of fulfilment in life. As noted previously, those who are 'in Christ' are intended to become the channels through which God can express his very character and accomplish many of his purposes. There is a divine aspect to every enriching and liberating human relationship.

SUMMARY

In this chapter we have noted that secularization has become so all-pervasive that we lose sight of its profound influence in Western societies. It has succeeded in penetrating the thought processes and value systems of the institutional church with the result that the gospel is accommodated to cultural norms rather than the Word of God being actualized to demonstrate a challenging alternative.

At the same time, we have appreciated that the process of secularization is not irreversible. It does not bring about the demise of religion, but rather becomes ultimately self-defeating by generating a hunger for that transcendent dimension of life which it has worked so persistently to deny.

The impact of secularization on life is to compartmentalize existence and undermine any logical possibility for meaning and purpose; as a consequence, contradictions arise as one area competes against another. Expedience rather than principle becomes the governing factor in decision-making. The way of life that Jesus taught is of a different order. At the heart of the gospel is an emphasis on a divinely intended wholeness, integration and sense of fulfilment. Those people who become spiritual casualties to secularization lose that vision of personal and cosmic purpose. Spiritual vitality ebbs away until they are reduced to the nominal state, retaining the name Christian maybe out of a concern for appearances or a sense of nostalgia.

NOTES

1. See Peter L. Berger, *The Sacred Canopy—Elements of a Social Theory of Religion*, published in England as *The Social Reality of Religion* (Faber and Faber; London, 1969; Penguin Books; Harmondsworth, 1973).
2. Berger, op cit, p 15.
3. Berger provides illustrations of antecedents going back to the prophetic movement of the Old Testatment, which emphasized the transcendence of God and thereby provided a space for human rationality. See *The Sacred Canopy*, chap 5.
4. Berger, op cit, pp 45-47.
5. Berger, op cit, p 125.
6. I am grateful to George G. Hunter III for indentifying these five elements, which he has described in his excellent treatment of secularism from an evangelistic standpoint in *How to Reach Secular People* (Abingdon Press; Nashville, 1992), see pp 5-29.
7. Os Guinness, *The Gravedigger File* (InterVarsity Press; Downers Grove, 1983) pp 51-53.
8. Paul Kurtz, *In Defense of Secular Humanism* (Prometheus Books; Buffalo, New York, 1983) pp 8-9.
9. Kurtz, op cit, p 34.
10. Robert E. Webber, *Secular Humanism: Threat and Challenge* (Zondervan; Grand Rapids, 1982) p 52.

11. Peter L. Berger, *A Rumour of Angels* (Doubleday and Co, Inc; New York, 1969) p 18.
12. Guinness, op cit, p 74.
13. See David Luecke, *Evangelical Style and Lutheran Substance* (Concordia; St Louis, 1988) pp 52-59.
14. I am grateful to Os Guinness for these terms; see *The Gravedigger File*, pp 130, 151.
15. Helmut Thielicke, *The Evangelical Faith* (Eerdmans; Grand Rapids, 1974, 1977), Vol I, p 27.
16. Lesslie Newbigin, *Foolishness to Greeks* (Eerdmans; Grand Rapids, 1986), p 20.
17. Newbigin, op cit, p 33.
18. Stephen R. Covey, *The Seven Habits of Highly Effective People* (Simon & Schuster; New York, 1989. 1990), p 21.
19. Covey, op cit, p 43.
20. Martin Marty, *The Modern Schism: Three Paths to the Secular* (SCM Press; London, 1969)
21. Rodney Stark and William Sims Bainbridge, *The Future of Religion: Secularization and Renewal and Cult Formation* (University of California Press; Berkeley, 1985)
22. Peter L. Berger, *A Rumour of Angels*, pp 32-33.
23. Stark and Bainbridge, op cit, pp 430-431.
24. Andrew Greeley, *The Persistence of Religion* (1973), p 16.
25. See Arnold E. Leon, *Secularization—Science Without God?* (Westminster Press; Philadelphia, 1967), p 15.
26. In *Secularization—Science Without God?*, pp 23-24, Leon lists some of the weak points in the Darwinian theory of evolution.
27. See Donald MacKay, *The Clockwork Image: A Christian Perspective of Science* (InterVarsity Press; Downers Grove, 1979) and Richard J. Connell, *Substance and Modern Science* (Center for Thomistic Studies and University of Notre Dame Press; Houston, 1988) for an in-depth discussion of these issues.
28. Leon, op cit, pp 36-37.
29. Fritjof Capra, *Tao of Physics* (Shambhala; Berkeley, California, 1975).
30. Quoted by Stephen Connor in *Postmodernist Culture* (Blackwell; Oxford, 1989), pp 18-19.
31. Lesslie Newbigin, *The Gospel in a Pluralist Society* (Eerdmans; Grand Rapids, 1989), p 206, emphasis mine.
32. Newbigin, op cit, p 208.

CHAPTER SEVEN

THE CHALLENGE OF RELIGIOUS PLURALISM

I N THE TWO PREVIOUS CHAPTERS we examined the impact of urbanization and secularization on local church commitment, denominational allegiance and religious convictions. We also noted in passing that since most western urban societies are cosmopolitan in nature, ethnic diversity must be allowed for and celebrated by the acceptance of cultural and religious pluralism. Problems arise when pluralism is accepted not simply as a *fact* of life, describing the context in which one lives out one's daily life, but also becomes a *philosophy* of life for the majority of people. When pluralism flourishes in a secularized urban setting, an environment is created in which relativism prevails. At this point it is necessary to define both 'pluralism' and 'relativism' before proceeding with our discussion.

Pluralism is defined by *Webster's Dictionary* as 'a theory that there are more than one or more than two kinds of ultimate reality... a state of society in which members of diverse ethnic, racial, religious, or social groups maintain an autonomous participation in and development of their traditional culture or special interest within the confines of a common civilization'.

Relativism is defined as 'a theory that knowledge is relative to the limited nature of the mind and conditions of knowing. When applied to religion it regards all religions as potentially able to contribute insights leading to the one truth, and that no one religion can claim to reveal the truth about God in a comprehensive and pure form'.

Our concern is to explore the relationship between nominality and pluralism. When people live within a monocultural society there is a tendency for them simply to accept uncritically the social norms and religious beliefs of their community. Their religious beliefs are powerfully reinforced by social affirmation. However, when those persons move into an urban environment, in which they are surrounded by a multiplicity of faith positions which may range from atheism through polytheism to pantheism, then they become just one distinctive piece within a cultural mosaic. Religious pluralism is represented not only by the perplexing multiplicity of Christian denominations and independent churches, but also by the presence of the conflicting truth claims of cults and non-Christian religions.

Faced with such confusion and contradictions, different people opt for any one of a number of coping strategies. Some will confine themselves to their own 'community of faith' by minimizing social interaction with the world beyond their belief parameters. Others maintain social contact with those of other faiths while, at the same time, studiously avoiding any serious dialogue concerning religious beliefs. This is especially the case when individuals realize that their knowledge of their own faith, or their low level of commitment to their beliefs and religious community, makes them particularly vulnerable to dedicated advocates of other faiths who are more committed and persuasive!

A further response to pluralism consists of relativizing one's own position to the level of personal preference, which may be motivated by expediency to maintain a 'politically correct' stance in the public sphere, or because exposure to other religions has resulted in a genuine appreciation of the spiritual insights which they convey. Sometimes, Christianity in the West appears so secularized that it no longer has the spiritual resources to offer which religions less affected by secularization seem to enshrine.

The challenge of attempting to live out one's faith in a pluralistic society is felt more by the laity than by most pastors and church workers. Churches in urban settings struggling to maintain their witness and serve the needs of the multicultural inner-city community are more aware of the challenge of pluralism, while full-time church staff in large, predominantly monocultural, suburban churches are typically so immersed in running their church programmes as to have minimal contact with the wider, unchurched community.

THE IMPACT OF RELIGIOUS PLURALISM IN THE WESTERN WORLD

There is an urgent need for the churches to equip church members to live out their faith within a pluralist society. Church leaders must face honestly the variety of responses evidenced by the membership, and help them move from defensive coping stances to culturally sensitive, Christ-honouring strategies for the advancement of the gospel of the kingdom in both secular and religiously pluralist social contexts. Those who withdraw into their religious or cultural enclaves to minimize contact with those of other cultures and religious persuasions need support and training to regain confidence and poise.

Those who have taken up a confrontational stance, seeking to convert unbelievers by overly aggressive evangelism, may need to have their zeal tempered by attempting to understand the cultural values, religious dogmas, spiritual insights and rituals of those they are seeking to win over. Evangelization among the sincere adherents of other religions requires a sensitive approach, endeavouring to open up genuine dialogue to discover how God has already been at work among those persons in terms of their religious aspirations and spiritual insights. In a climate of mutual respect, ways must be explored to present the person and work of Christ, which are, as far as possible, free from western cultural distortions.

It must be recognized that many non-Christian religions which have appeared in the western world since World War II are being promoted, with varying degrees of success, among those who have become dissatisfied with their westernized and secularized versions of Christianity.

For instance, significant numbers of African-Americans have been converted to Islam because of its claims to be free from racial prejudice, its emphasis on community ('ummah') and its insistence that religion embraces every aspect of life—politics, education, law, art, etc. Hindu meditation techniques for stress relief and self-realization have permeated the professional strata of society through yoga classes, management seminars, transcendental meditation techniques and New Age bookstores, expositions and support groups.[1] While Buddhism has never made a popular appeal in the West, because its intellectually demanding philosophical base does not fit well with western pragmatism, it does have a following among an intellectual elite. As we saw in the previous chapter, whereas the majority of sociologists of religion were prophesying until recently the progressive weakening of religion through the influence of secularism, now there is a growing body of opinion which believes that secularism has in fact sown seeds of its own demise.

The collapse of traditional Marxist-Leninist societies in Eastern Europe in 1989 and 1990 also throws some light on the issue of the human drive for values which has traditionally found its roots in religiously based convictions. Whereas the western news media have emphasized the economic and human rights dimensions of the populist movements which have brought totalitarian regimes to accountability, the spiritual dynamic at work has been played down by most western news reporters and social commentators.

The resistance in Poland found its spiritual inspiration in the Roman Catholic Church; in the German Democratic Republic it was within the Lutheran Church; and in Hungary within the Reformed Church. In the former Soviet Union there was a widespread feeling that Marxist-Leninism had created a self-seeking society which had undermined trust and eroded civility. In the midst of scepticism regarding the benefits of *perestroika* there was a search for cultural roots which has been demonstrated in part by a popular turning to religion, be it the Russian Orthodox Church, Protestant faiths or Islam.

While former eastern bloc nations may look with envy at the material prosperity of western societies and their open forms of government, they are concerned about the casualties of unbridled capitalism. The spiritually discerning among them are aware also of the inadequacies of exchanging one form of materialism for another. It may be that Christians from Eastern Europe will contribute most significantly to the re-evangelizing of Western Europe, because they have travelled further down the road of radical secularism in its Marxist guise and are more alert to the vital role played by religiously based values and moral absolutes in undergirding democratic societies. The warnings of Solzhenitsyn to the West, about the destructiveness of materialism and permissiveness within its own borders, still remains largely unheeded.

The isolation of the church in the west

From a historical perspective the church in the western world finds itself ill-prepared to meet the challenge of a philosophical and religiously pluralist environment. From the conversion of the Roman Emperor Constantine in AD 312 until the nineteenth century, Christianity enjoyed a monopolistic position and was not seriously challenged from within the borders of 'Christendom'. Its main preoccupations during the

Middles Ages were to castigate Judaism for its rejection of Christ as Messiah and to hold back the Islamic invaders in Southern Europe following the defeat of the Crusaders in their attempts to secure the Holy Land for Christianity.

The decline of the Muslim threat with their retreat from Granada in southern Spain in 1492 (when 200,000 Jews were also expelled from the country) allowed Christianity to return to its internal debates occasioned by the Renaissance (1453 onwards) and the Reformation (1517 onwards). If the Islamic nations provided an impenetrable barrier separating Christendom from non-Christian nations to the south and east, the vast expanse of the Atlantic isolated Europe from whatever unexplored lands and unknown civilizations may have existed in the west.

The desire on the part of European nations to extend contact with the East was motivated by trade, not by religion. The search for a westward sea passage to India, in order to avoid the arduous, hazardous and expensive overland route through the Middle East, began in earnest with the exploration of the west coast of Africa by Bartolomeu Dias which eventually led to his rounding the Cape of Good Hope in his voyage of 1487-1488. Four years later Columbus crossed the Atlantic (1492) and the Portuguese navigator Ferdinand Magellan inspired the first voyage to circumnavigate the globe in 1519, though he himself lost his life in a skirmish with natives in the Philippines in 1521.

The Reformation created a religious pluralism in Europe which absorbed the energies of both religious and secular authorities as they worked through their theological disagreements and ecclesiastical and political powerplays. When the modern missionary era arrived in the nineteenth century, it came on the heals of European colonial expansion with its attendant beliefs in the economic power and cultural superiority of the European nations. Although the early missionaries had an ambivalent relationship with the colonial administrators, many were inevitably influenced by the pervasive climate of cultural superiority and therefore often disdainful of other cultures and religions. They saw their task as converting and civilizing. A long history of isolation had illprepared these pioneer missionaries for their missionary task.

Whatever their faults in terms of lack of appreciation for other cultures, their record is better than most of their compatriots who administered and traded in the colonies and beyond. For the missionaries as a whole demonstrated greater cultural sensitivity and took most trouble to master indigenous languages and provide education and health care. But the majority were not scholars and often acted out of inadequate knowledge, outright misunderstanding and culturally distorted perspectives. Charles Davis highlights the widespread nature of the West's ignorance of the spiritual perceptions and religious beliefs of non-western peoples.

> On the scholarly level an accurate, detailed knowledge of religions other than Christianity, of their sacred texts, customs, beliefs, rites and history, was first achieved by the West in the nineteenth century. Before that time knowledge was fragmentary and unreliable.[2]

The pluralistic environment experienced by the early church

In contrast to the churches of western Protestantism, the early church was born into a pluralistic world. Within fifteen years the followers of Jesus began to take their message outside the Jewish cultural enclave and into the Graeco-Roman world. This extension of their ministry was not without internal traumas as Gentile converts were added to the church in increasing numbers, until eventually whole congregations began to emerge whose members did not have a background in the Jewish scriptures and a cultural formation based on rabbinic teaching. Some Jewish believers became alarmed by the rapidly increasing numerical strength of the non-Jewish disciples of Jesus. Their defensiveness can be detected in James' response to Paul's enthusiastic report on his return from his Third Missionary Journey, 'You observe, brother, how many thousands of converts we have among the Jews, all of them staunch upholders of the law' (Acts 21:21, *Revised English Bible*). Those concerned for the spread of the gospel among Jews were determined not to be outshone by Paul's spectacular results among the Gentiles! James boasts that the quantity was not at the expense of quality!

The emergence of the modern western pluralistic society

Western societies are becoming increasingly cosmopolitan. This is a consequence of a number of significant factors: the internationalization of trading networks, pursuit of higher education, ease and declining cost of air travel, large scale migration of people from former colonial territories and 'guest' workers willing to do manual labour at lower wages. There are now large North African communities in many urban areas of France, Turkish workers in West Germany, and even a

Pakistani community in Oslo, Norway, which came into existence when immigration restrictions were tightened in the United Kingdom.

A further factor with which western secular societies are having to come to terms, is that most of these adherents of other faiths take their religion very seriously. This became clear with the storm which arose in Britain over the publication of *The Satanic Verses* by Salman Rushdie.

The problem is heightened by the fact that the religious views of other faiths are not only strongly held, but religion pervades the entire culture, affecting every area of life including education, politics, the judicial system and the arts. Both Hindu and Muslim communities fiercely resist the restricting of religion to the private sphere of life, which is a characteristic of the secularization process. Furthermore, resurgent forms of these religions have emerged in eastern nations and are now appearing in the West as missionary movements. Charles Davis observes that 'Hinduism has indeed acquired a new understanding of itself as a universal religion with a universal mission, a self-understanding it did not have before'.[3] The stance of Islam is more confrontational than that of Hinduism and Buddhism, which are more accommodating and inclusive in their initial approaches to westerners. The emergence of these ancient religions with missionary enthusiasm coincides with the loss of confidence by the West in its own cultural values. The diminishing place of Christianity in western society and culture has in some western nations reached the point of outright contempt for the church on the part of the majority of the population.

In a pluralistic society a high value is placed on tolerance and open-mindness. When it comes to religion this response does not carry a high price-tag due to the widespread indifference to religious issues. Such liberal-mindedness does not engender much respect among adherents of other religions, who are more likely to interpret the 'tolerance' they encounter as but more evidence of western cultural decadence epitomized by secularism's rejection of the transcendent and the sacred and the marginalizing of religion. A more healthy brand of tolerance is demonstrated by an attitude of profound respect for others without abandoning a strong commitment to one's own religious beliefs. Secularization so emphasizes the ephemeral aspects of life that religious attitudes become more the product of an empty head than an open mind.

If society at large has failed to respond adequately to religious pluralism, the Christian churches also have a poor track record. Most congregations largely ignore the existence of other religious groups. There is very little continuing dialogue outside the ranks of those who take a special interest in comparative religion and participate in inter-faith discussions.

THE IMPACT OF THE EAST ON THE WEST

Times have changed since the Edinburgh Missionary Conference of 1910, which adopted as its slogan 'the evangelization of the world in this generation'. While the Christian faith has advanced remarkably during this century, it has done so primarily among people of animist religions in Africa and parts of Asia and Latin America, rather than by winning significant numbers of adherents from the major religions. K. M. Panik-kar maintains that the missionary attempt to convert Asia has 'definitely failed'; more than that, he contends that it has left Hinduism, Buddhism and Islam 'stronger and more vigorous as a result of the adjustments they were called upon to effect' in order to resist the challenge of Christian missionaries and mount a counter-offensive.[4]

However, this is but one side of the story. While there may be a loss of missionary momentum on the part of western old-line denominations which have become increasingly preoccupied with their demise in their own countries, there are at the same time vigorous indigenous Christian churches emerging which are making a far greater impact than most western mission efforts. This is because they are more readily able to operate within the cultural context. The members of indigenous churches are more likely to be deeply aware of the issues which need to be addressed, being themselves converts from the religions whose adherents they are now seeking to evangelize.

Furthermore, they cannot be dismissed as western cultural aggressors due to the fact that they are nationals and are able to demonstrate Christian life-styles which are clearly non-western, as they incarnate the values of the gospel within their cultural settings. The emergence of vital and innovative forms of indigenous Christian community are more likely to arouse curiosity among the population at large, causing a reappraisal of long-standing negative attitudes or indifference to the message as presented to them by westerners. In some places conversions are taking place and churches are being established in areas which have previously proved most resistant to missionary effort.

However, our concern at this point is not with the impact which Christian mission has made on the major religions, but on the fact that revitalized versions of ancient Eastern religions are now being promoted in the western world using methods adopted from Christian missions and often with heavy financial backing and support of their embassies. Mosque construction and Islamic study centres are financed by Muslim governments. The Ahamadiyya Movement, which is aggressively missionary in its orientation, now numbers 12,000 in Britain. As yet there is little evidence of a significant impact being made, due in part to the westerner's perception of Islam's close ties with political intrigue, revolutionary violence and terrorist atrocities. Many Muslim leaders living outside the Middle East would dissociate themselves from extremist groups, committed to violence in the name of Allah, and emphasize the noble ideals of Islam. Westerners also like to compartmentalize their religion and are nervous about giving their allegiance to a religion making absolute claims embracing politics and law as well as 'spiritual issues'.

Some westerners have been attracted to the Muslim commitment to community ('ummah'). We have already noted that Islam's most significant advance in the United States has been among those members of the African-American community who have become disillusioned with segregationist Christianity and are looking for an alternative expression of their inherent spirituality. Islam provides an attractive alternative with its non-European roots in Arabia and North Africa and its professed record of commitment to racial harmony.

The fascination of the West with Hinduism has a long history. The philosopher Schopenhauer (1789-1860) praised the wisdom of the *Upanishads* and used it as a standard by which to judge Christianity. Then in 1893, at the World Parliament of Religions held in connection with Chicago World Fair, the young Vivekananda created a tremendous impression by his presentation of Hinduism as a universal faith for humankind. In 1897 he founded the Ramakrishna Mission, named after the guru who had inspired his own religious pilgrimage.

Hinduism is by nature inclusive, but its form of relativism should not be confused with western relativism. It is based not on empiricism but on monism. For the Hindu, relativism arises out of firmly held religious convictions which are identified by Charles Davis as:

1. the One manifests itself to men in different ways
2. the One is in the last analysis inexpressible
3. since religion reflects man as well as the divine, and men are at different stages of religious development, there are bound to be different apprehensions of the divine and different ways of religious life, each having its value for men at a particular level.[5]

For the Hindu, ultimate reality is encouraged through mystical experience, an emphasis which made a strong appeal to the hippie culture which arose in the 1960s. It is significant that this movement was spawned on the secular university campuses where it signalled as much a reaction against the secularism and rationalism of the academic environment as a rejection of the Christian church. To the extent that western forms of Christianity are permeated by secularization so the churches also create a hunger for transcendent experience which their human-performance worship focus is unable to satisfy.

It is also significant that the Jesus People and charismatic movements emerged as popular movements within and alongside the church. The latter has proved more enduring than the former, and has diversified with the spread of independent charismatic churches and federations of churches under the umbrella of such networks as Calvary Chapel, Abundant Life and the Vineyard. Within the Catholic and mainline Protestant churches, the charismatic movement seems to have lost many of its divisive tendencies through being 'killed with kindness' and at the same time to have lost some of its earlier vitality by failing to live up to the expectations it generated. Where the church retains its social strength, the charismatic movement is the most likely alternative, and where the church is weak in influence due to fragmentation or loss of credibility, then non-Christian 'spiritualities' are more likely to prevail.

The continuing and growing appeal of Hindu spirituality and interpretation of reality beyond the Hippie movement of the decade of the sixties we may attribute to the ongoing and widespread concern for inner growth and meditation techniques as ways to achieving self-realization, stress-management and a sense of connectedness with universal life-forces. This last mentioned compensates for the excessive individualism and self-reliance characteristic of western societies and the North American culture in particular. According to Russell Chandler, religious writer for the *Los Angeles Times*, thirty-four million Americans are concerned with inner growth, and 67 per cent claim to have had psychic experiences. They constitute a ready market for Hindu inspired spiritual insights and meditation techniques, which are packaged to enhance their appeal to westerners. In the 1960s and 70s this packaging took the form of Transcendental Meditation. In the 1980s and 90s the New Age Movement has emerged to provide a broader philosophical world-view. New Age publishing has become a billion-dollar phenomenon. At least 2,500 bookstores specialize in New Age Books and 25,000 titles are in print.

One only has to check out the footage given to New Age and psychic material in the high street bookstores in comparison with the religious section to appreciate the commercial significance of New Age oriented publishing. Local public libraries in the US are more likely to carry New Age than Christian magazines. One of the major airlines has a New Age channel among its audio programmes.

In all probability more than half the middle managers employed by major corporations have been on management training seminars developed by New Age inspired agencies. They include EST (Erhard Seminars Training), Sportsmind, Innovation Associates, Lifespring, Energy Unlimited and Transformational Technologies, and MindMaker 6 programmes. Russell Chandler reports that:

> in 1986, representatives of some of the nation's largest corporations, including IBM, AT&T and General Motors, met to discuss how metaphysics, the occult and Hindu mysticism, might help executives compete in the world market. In addition to management training New Age concepts are also permeating society through educational and health programs.[6]

At the philosophical level, the western world is searching for a new world-view to replace the Newtonian explanation of an ordered universe governed by rational principles and predictability, which has been assumed for the past two hundred years as a product of the Enlightenment. That cohesive world-view began to fall apart with Einstein's theory of relativity, followed by research into the randomness found in the behaviour of sub-atomic particles. Among physicists and theoretical mathematicians there is a search for a unifying theory to explain the physical world.

From the brief account given above it can be seen that New Age thinking is not confined to an esoteric group on the fringe of society; its influence is widespread, if patchy. The existence of a confusing variety of non-Christian religions and philosophies presents a pressing challenge to the churches. If they are going to minister effectively in a pluralistic society they must equip their members to make them aware of the tenets of Christianity in relation to other faiths, as well as speak with knowledge and empathy to those who are seeking significance and enlightenment through other faith explorations and commitments.

Many church leaders and ministers of local congregations are acutely aware of their lack of preparation to minister in today's multicultural environment. Most received little or no training in how to communicate the gospel among those of other faiths or to secularists. The assumption during theological training was that their ministry context would be among the faithful or trying to win back those who had become inactive. Theological academe's primary reference was to a classical theological discourse which was largely conducted as an internal debate between the various theological and ecclesiastical traditions rather than by interfacing with the unbelieving world. Kenneth Cragg extends this observation beyond Christianity when he writes:

> For all their ancient interplay, the major faiths have frequently privatized their diagnoses and their remedies, conducting their societies only by in-discussion with themselves. The sanctions of culture, issues of authority, a congenial idiom, have all contributed to this posture of inclusive self-reference. They have a firm preference for their own criteria, a will to suppose that their only loyal future is their past. Classic Christian theology has, for the most part, been a strictly domestic affair, pursued in respect of its own major concerns, by reference to its own canons and the interests of its own cultures dictated. It has only feebly responded to the intellectual and spiritual bearings given to it, for example, out of Asia. Today its cast of mind can no longer properly be only patristic, or Thomist, or reformed, or neo-orthodox.[7]

Stanley Samartha provides an Indian Christian perspective. In seeking to redress the situation, he challenges the seminaries to address the issue of responsible mission in a pluralist world. The following quotation reveals his own solution to the problem, which is to affirm adherents of other religions as pursuing valid alternative paths to the one truth. Although we may disagree with his approach, the challenge he presents is one which must be taken more seriously:

> To ask theological questions about this matter is to go to the very roots of our pluralistic existence today. To truly confront these questions, the study of religions has to be shifted from a *missiological* to a *theological* framework, particularly in our theological colleges and seminaries. The question is not *what* to do with so many religions that claim the loyalty and devotion of millions of followers in the world, but *why* are they so persistently present providing meaning and dir-

ection to the lives of millions of our neighbors. What does
this mean theologically—that is, for our understanding of
God and God's relationship to the whole created
oikoumene, of which Christians are not the only citizens. Or
can it be that it is the will of God that many religions should
continue in the world?[8]

The study of other religions, and the relationship between Christianity
and other faith positions must not be confined to mission oriented
programmes but must be included in the main M Div curriculum and
other ministerial training courses. The pluralistic nature of most ministry
situations, especially in the urban context, requires such an emphasis if
ministers are to be more adequately prepared as mission leaders and
trainers of the laity. The workaday world of many lay people means
close and frequent contact with people of other cultures and faiths who
may directly challenge the church member regarding the spiritual poverty of much of western Christian religiosity, as well as bear witness to
their own religious experiences and interpretations of reality.

Opinions differ regarding the impact that eastern and western world-
views will have on each other. Many western thinkers, together with
some from the East, have assumed that western secularism will eventually become a world-embracing philosophy which will dominate the
intellectual climate. Others believe that eastern spirituality and world-
views have sufficient inherent strength to resist any such ideological
invasion. Ninian Smart argues for this latter position in the following
comment:

> Further afield, Islam, Hinduism and Buddhism retain vast
> energies. It is nonsense to think of the world as essentially
> alienated from religion and ideology; and it is doubtful, to
> say the least, that non-Western cultures will have a Western
> future... There is no strong rational basis for supposing
> that the world-view ripples of technology will turn men
> away from their traditional religious and ideological
> beliefs.[9]

For many religious sociologists the issue is not the extent to which
western secularism will impact the East, but how eastern spirituality will
impact Western cultures. They point to the rapid growth of the New Age
Movement and its attractiveness to certain prominent individuals in the
scientific community; the proliferation of business and sports perfor-

mance, self-awareness and actualization programmes; and the extra-terrestrial and psychic themes in the movie industry, as evidence that eastern religions will become increasingly influential in the West. David Edwards, however, is not convinced. He points to the contrast between the static character of the East and the dynamic energy of the West.

> The spiritual legacy of Christianity, Judaism and Islam did much to inspire the scientific civilization; and it is difficult to imagine that this dynamism will be inspired in the future by the religion of the East.[10]

Emotional responses when religious positions are challenged

The strongest reactions are likely to be among committed adherents of those religions which claim exclusivity, namely Islam, Judaism and evangelical Christianity. Of the three, Christianity has demonstrated the greatest missionary zeal. As the least culture-bound, it has made the widest global appeal, to the point where its numerical strength is no longer weighted towards the West. The rapid growth of the church during this century in the non-western world has now tilted the balance. When the walls of separation are threatened by efforts to convert, then emotions run high, although an increased commitment to dialogue is a hopeful sign in terms of greater mutual understanding.

In contrast to the exclusivism of Judaism, Christianity and Islam, Hinduism and Buddhism maintain an inclusive stance. Their philosophical position can provide a surface veneer of generous toleration which is welcome in societies torn by sectarian mistrust and violence. However, it must be recognized that the toleration is dependent upon accepting an inclusive philosophy. As Charles Davis observes, it is offered on their terms:

> We are, in effect, being asked to surrender to a particular Hindu view of religion under the cloak of an anti-dogmatic comprehensiveness. I am afraid that the problem of the plurality and conflict of religions is not solved so easily. The religions of prophetic monotheism resist reduction to contemplative experience of the Absolute.[11]

This tolerance must be distinguished from the ideological openness manifested within western secular societies, which is not based on a monistic inclusiveness but on a philosophical centreless relativism. Charles Davis affirms the point discussed in chapter 6:

For many today religious belief falls into the class of personal preferences, where a tenuous assent may be given to a particular opinion for a variety of reasons, but where it is out of place to challenge another's opinion in the name of truth.[12]

Sometimes both the intolerant dogmatism displayed by those who are endeavouring to impose their faith on others and the over-reactive defensiveness of those seeking to defend their traditional religious allegiance, may arise out of insecurity. With the former it is a case of '*fight*-fright' and with the latter it is a case of '*flight*-fright'. Kenneth Cragg captures the complexity of the psychological aspects of adherence to belief systems, and the defence mechanisms which are activated as soon as anyone dares to challenge long held absolutist views regarded as divinely revealed:

The timid or the assertive will see the very fact of other belief-systems alternative to their own as disturbing. For it suggests a certain optionality, once it is realized how far an accident of birth may have determined the convictions in one's sincerity. Let us hasten to add that for vast numbers this optionality is never present in practice. There are relatively few who can take private initiatives of changed belief. Illiteracy, cultural determinism, poverty, and much else, preclude them. Nevertheless, once the idea interposes itself that circumstance has entered far into allegiance, that faith may be fortuitous, what of their finality? Will they still seem absolute? Living with pluralism implies the paradox that tenacity of adherence proves only the intensity of conditioning.[13]

In plainer language, the problem which arises as people step outside their religious friendship-networks into a world of ideological pluralism and relativism, is that the old, uncritically accepted, certainties begin to sprout question marks as they are challenged and alternative interpretations of life are advocated. How many 'culture-Christians' have spiritual roots which are deep enough, and provide a religious knowledge-base strong enough, to support their beliefs, enable them to retain emotional poise, intellectual integrity, and cultural sensitivity, and maintain a mission commitment as a 'cognitive minority' within a pluralist society?

We now proceed to consider the variety of ways in which Christian thinkers have attempted to relate Christianity to other religions.

THEOLOGICAL RESPONSES TO RELIGIOUS PLURALISM

It is important to recognize that the debate of theological issues cannot be confined to the specialists in the field of comparative religion. The issue has to be faced by any individual with a personal faith commitment who is endeavouring to live out that faith by maintaining an appropriate life-style and offering a declarative and explanatory witness in a pluralistic society. One of the best defences to prevent the spread of nominality is to ensure that believers have an intellectually robust faith because they have thought about the issues which arise when believers live in close proximity to people of other faiths. For it is nominal Christians who are most vulnerable when approached by committed and articulate believers representing non-Christian religions. Alternative responses which Christians adopt must be explored and evaluated in order to arrive at a position which the person feels is consistent with the uniqueness of Christianity and yet respectful of other religious commitments. The following describe the various approaches which are made in response to the problem.

All religions are equally valid paths to the one truth

This position maintains the relativity of all religions, including Christianity. Some argue that all religions represent quests by humans for spiritual enlightenment and therefore suffer the limitations and distortions of historical and cultural conditioning as well as the spiritual limitations of the seers, prophets and philosophers who have passed on their insights. Thus all religions are a record of the human quest for God, and the conclusion is drawn that we get the most comprehensive and supra-cultural understanding of the nature of God by drawing from these many traditions. The same outcome results if we represent all religions as authentic manifestations of God's self-revelation in ways appropriate to particular cultures and historical conditions.

Ernst Troeltsch (1865-1923) adopted this line of reasoning, arguing against Christianity's claims to absoluteness on account of its historical particularity which, to his mind, relativized the revelation it claimed to impart. In his later writings he came to doubt whether a person of one culture and religion could ever really understand and authentically appropriate an alien culture and religion.[14] In the face of the dehumanizing influence and anti-religious stance of secularism, some have proposed that adherents of different religions, rather than expending their energies trying to convert one another, should combine forces to combat the common enemy. John MacQuarrie advocates a 'global ecumenism' in which sister faiths recognize each other as responding to the same God, but under different symbols. In his view, proselytism must be replaced by dialogue, intended not as a trysting ground but as an opportunity for mutual enrichment as each benefits from the spiritual treasures of the other.

Indian theologian Raimundo Panikkar argues from a similar standpoint. He develops the image of the church crossing three rivers during the course of its history, each representing a new mission frontier. The first crossing was the Jordan, as the followers of Jesus sought to witness to Jesus as Messiah within their cultural setting. Baptism in the Jordan represented separation and a new beginning. It was the way of *exclusivism*. The second river was the Tiber, signifying the expansion of the Christian church in the Graeco-Roman world. In response to the intellectual challenge posed by pagan philosophies and mystery religions, the Christians adopted a crusading stance which has characterized the Christian community until modern times. However, prolonged exposure to other faith positions eventually leads to a mutual appreciation and an attempted conceptual integration. This search for *inclusivism* proves illusory and shallow, due to conflicting underlying presuppositions and perceptions. Now, Panikkar maintains, the challenge facing the Christian church is represented by the Ganges which must be crossed by the church preparing to engage in dialogue designed to bring about mutual affirmation by the recognition of irreconcilable differences. This is the approach of *pluralism*, in which each party comes with confidence because all contribute from their strengths to discover areas of common interest.

Panikkar's position entails a frank recognition that every religion is a product of cultural milieu and historical process. Each exists in its own right and must be understood from within, according to its own categories of interpretation.

> The rivers of the earth do not actually meet each other, not even in the oceans, nor do they need to meet in order to be truly life-giving rivers. But 'they' do meet; they meet in the skies—that is, in heaven. The rivers do not meet, not even as water. 'They' meet in the form of clouds, once they have suffered a transformation into vapor, which eventually will pour down again into the valleys of mortals to feed the rivers of the earth. Religions do not coalesce, certainly not

as organized religions. They meet once transformed into vapor, once metamorphosized into Spirit, which then is poured down in innumerable tongues.[15]

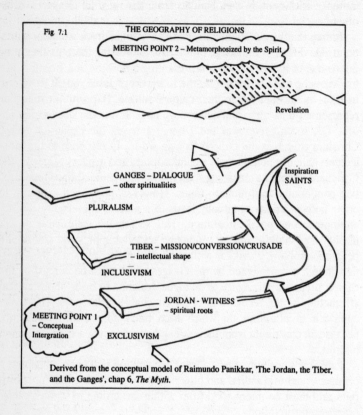

Fig. 7.1

THE GEOGRAPHY OF RELIGIONS

MEETING POINT 2 – Metamorphosized by the Spirit

Revelation

GANGES – DIALOGUE
– other spiritualities

PLURALISM

Inspiration
SAINTS

TIBER – MISSION/CONVERSION/CRUSADE
– intellectual shape

INCLUSIVISM

JORDAN - WITNESS
– spiritual roots

MEETING POINT 1
– Conceptual
Intergration

EXCLUSIVISM

Derived from the conceptual model of Raimundo Panikkar, 'The Jordan, the Tiber, and the Ganges', chap 6, *The Myth*.

Some Christians have taken the position that each religion brings its distinctive contribution to the global ecumenical mix. The mystical element is contributed by Hinduism, philosophical insights are derived from Buddhism and the ethical component by Judaism, Islam and Christianity.

The path of inclusivism is blocked by two major obstacles. It is incompatible with faith in Christ as this has been traditionally understood from the New Testament onwards, and it is at variance with the fact of the other world religions. Where religious traditions have intertwined, as in the case of Christianity, Judaism and Islam in the West, Taoism, Confucianism and Buddhism in China and Shinto and Buddhism in Japan, the result has not been so much mutual enrichment as polarization. The basic difficulty in relating religions is not simply that they give different answers to the same questions, but that they pose different questions. .

Wilfred Cantwell Smith pricks the 'naivety bubble' which surrounds many people who embark upon inter-religious debate with the following observation:

> One of the facile fallacies that students of comparative religion must early learn to outgrow is, we have felt, the supposition that the different religions give differing answers to essentially the same questions. We would hold that rather their distinctiveness lies in considerable part in a tendency to ask different questions.[16]

Not that all religions are the path to one truth, but each in its own right contains truth which cannot simply be transposed into another system without something vital being lost in the process of absorption. Each religion bears a distinctive witness and is the product of revelation in a particular cultural and historical context. As such it must stand in its own right and be interpreted in accordance with its own categories of interpretation.

Panikkar himself recognizes that the relationship of one religion to another cannot simply be established on the principle of complementarity, due to the existence of deep areas of incompatibility and conflict. One cannot simply bring together elements drawn from a range of world faiths, as attempted by the Ba'Hai movement. No faith can partake in genuine dialogue and remain intact. Panikkar believes that Christianity functions as a catalyst by applying the more radical principle of conversion through death and resurrection. However, he does not use this term in the traditional sense of conversion from Hinduism to Christianity. Rather the converting dynamic is contained within Hinduism:

> The process of conversion implies a death and resurrection, but just as the risen Christ, or the baptized person is the same as previously and yet is a new being, likewise con-

verted Hinduism is the true risen Hinduism, the same and yet renewed, transformed. In one world, the Church brings every true and authentic religion to its fulfilment through a process of death and resurrection, which is the true meaning of conversion.[17]

The impact of pluralism is to relativize all religions in the belief that no religion has the spiritual insight or historical and cultural inclusiveness to provide a comprehensive understanding of the Ultimate. This line of argument is expressed in the following quotations from Langdon Gilkey:

> Thus each particular religion is *true* and yet *relative*, a true revelation for the community, relative to other revelations to other communities, and relative to the Absolute that each only partially and so somewhat distortedly manifests.
>
> The interplay of absolute and relative—of being a Christian, Jew, or Buddhist, and *affirming* that stance, and yet at the same time relativizing that mode of existence—both stuns and silences the mind, at least mine.
>
> To understand God in relation both to a mystery that transcends God and to the nonbeing that seems to contradict God; to understand revelation in relation to other revelations that relativize our revelation; to view christology and gospel in relation to other manifestations of grace; anthropology in relation to *anatta* (no-self) and identity— this is the heart of our present baffling but very exciting theological task.[18]

The issues will remain baffling because the underlying premise is flawed. The argument that all religions represent valid alternative paths to the one truth fails because they not only have different starting points, but as the pilgrim explores each path, the discovery is made that the paths do not converge but diverge to the point that they are leading up very different mountains. John Hick is prepared to make this admission:

> Pluralism does not consider unity an indispensable ideal, even if allowance is made for variations within that unity. Pluralism accepts the irreconcilable aspects of religions without being blind to their common aspects. Pluralism is not the eschatological expectation that in the end all shall be one.[19]

Indeed, some pathways which seem promising at the outset lead into a quagmire of subjectivism, jungles of esoteric jargon, or on to a precarious ledge where one is faced with the choice of either attempting to retrace one's steps or make a suicidal jump. Christians who have committed themselves to a pluralistic religious pilgrimage go through predictable phases. Their christology becomes less and less centred on the historic person described in the New Testament and more vaguely expressed in terms of the Cosmic Christ or the Divine Word who inspires all religions. Their trinitarian understanding of God is replaced by one which may range from deism to polytheism. Some advocates of pluralism eventually abandon theism in favour of a concept of Ultimate Reality expressed as an undifferentiated life force.

Paul Knitter's pilgrimage into pluralism has led him to the point where he advocates giving up the search for a common understanding of God. Pluralism means the frank acceptance of irreconcilable differences, and that theological agendas should be set aside in the interests of facing the pressing human problems of injustice and poverty. Thus salvation is translated into a socio-political agenda summarized in the following quotations:

> instead of searching for 'one God' or 'one Ultimate' or a 'common essence' or a 'mystical center' within all religions, we can recognize a *shared locus of religious experience* available to all the religions of the world. Within the struggle for liberation and justice with and for the many different groups of oppressed persons, believers from different traditions can experience together, and yet from different perspectives, that which grounds their resolves, inspires their hopes, and guides their actions to overcome injustice and to promote unity...

> This understanding of the central role of the preferential option for the poor and nonpersons within interreligious dialogue means that the evolution within Christian attitudes toward other faiths that I described in my book *No Other Name?* is incomplete. The evolution, I suggest, is being called to a further stage. If Christian attitudes have evolved from ecclesiocentrism to christocentrism to theocentrism, they must now move on to what in Christian symbols might be called 'kingdom-centrism,' or more universally, 'soteriocentrism.' For Christians, that which constitutes the basis and the goal for interreligious dialogue, is that which makes mutual understanding and cooperation between the reli-

gions possible (the 'condition of the possibility'), that which unites the religions in common discourse and praxis, is *not* how they are related to the church (invisibly through 'baptism of desire'), or how they are related to Christ (anonymously [Rahner] or normatively [Küng], nor even how they respond to and conceive of God, but rather, to what extent they are promoting *soteria* (in Christian images, the *basileia*)—to what extent they are engaged in promoting human welfare and bringing about liberation with and for the poor and nonpersons...

But what makes the soteriocentric approach different from christocentrism or theocentrism is its explicit recognition that before the mystery of *soteria*, no mediator or symbol system is absolute. The perspective on *soteria* given by any one mediator is always open to clarification, completion, perhaps correction by the viewpoints of other mediators.[20]

Whereas adherents of different religions can pursue a common cause in identifying and seeking answers to the injustices in society, the biblical concepts of the 'kingdom of God' and 'salvation' cannot be relativized and emptied of their theistic content in such a cavalier fashion. The salvation described in the Bible is the result of the sovereign interventions of God and the kingdom comes as the surprising gift of God. Both salvation and kingdom have personal, corporate and cosmic dimensions. They are only realized in the person of the Messiah, who is identified as Jesus in the New Testament. There is all the difference in the world between the 'kingdom' concepts of Islam, with its legally enforced absolutes, and the kingdom of Jesus Christ, which exists here on earth in an interim state as a counter-culture minority community with the consequent ambiguities of the 'now' and 'not yet' of the kingdom. The Sermon on the Mount is not another version of the '*shirah*' of Islamic law.

All religions are preparations for the gospel as revealed fully and finally in Christ

This line of argument begins by recognizing that God has revealed aspects of his person and moral law in other religions. But it goes on to argue that the revelation they contain is fragmented and distorted and can therefore only serve in a preparatory role. Rather like the Jewish Mosaic law, other religions raise moral and spiritual aspirations which can only be fully met in Jesus Christ as made known in the New

Testament record of his person, manifold ministry and saving death and resurrection.

The Alexandrian School of Clement and Origen adopted this approach, as did Justin Martyr, who in dialogue with the Platonists spoke of Christ as the *logos spermatikos* who was seeding ideas into their philosophical reasoning. In this century the Edinburgh Missionary Conference of 1910 and the Second Vatican Council both regarded non-Christian religions as 'preparations for the gospel'. Some have carried this line of argument further to maintain that as Christ is united with each person so every person, whether they realize it or not, has been redeemed by Christ. The Roman Catholic theologian Karl Rahner has spoken of those adherents of other religions who have embraced the Christ-spirit without identifying themselves or naming the Name, as 'anonymous Christians'. Evangelization then becomes the task of leading each person to that realization. However, not everyone who argues for a universal revelation couples that with the universality of salvation.

The positive aspect of this second approach is that it refuses to accommodate the person and the work of Christ to other religions. Rather, it makes the revelation in Christ the norm by which all other religions are judged. However, there is a naivety regarding the outcome. It cannot be assumed that once the revelation in Christ is made known to sincere, informed and spiritually discerning adherents of other religions, they will then acknowledge the superiority of that revelation. On the contrary, experience shows that they are more likely to insist on the superiority of their own religious tradition.

This approach is based on an evolutionist premise, not of chronological sequence but of progressive revelation. Thus for Thomas Aquinas the development of natural theology was the evolutionary path to grace. At least that was the position he expounded at length in his *Summa Theologica*, but at the age of forty-eight he repudiated his life work with the statement, 'I can write no more; for everything that I have written seems like straw, by comparison with the things I now see and which have been revealed to me'.[21] Modern Roman Catholic theology continues to place a great emphasis on natural theology as the preparatory foundation for God's work of saving grace. In Karl Rahner's view, other religions embody not only the elements of that natural theology, but also elements of God's grace which only find their full expression in Christianity. Hans Küng takes a similar line of argument, although he expresses it differently, describing non-Christian religions as the ordinary paths to salvation, whilst the Christian religion is the extraordinary. The Second Vatican Council assesses other religions in the following terms:

> The Catholic Church rejects nothing which is true and holy in these religions. She looks with sincere respect upon those ways of conduct and of life, those rules and teachings which, though differing in many particulars from what she holds and sets forth, nevertheless often reflect a ray of that Truth which enlightens all men. Indeed, she proclaims and must ever proclaim Christ, 'the way, the truth, and the life' (John 14:6), in whom men find the fullness of religious life, and in whom God has reconciled all things to Himself (cf. 2 Cor 5:18-19).
>
> The Church therefore, has this exhortation for her sons: prudently and lovingly, through dialogue and collaboration with the followers of other religions, and in witness of Christian faith and life, acknowledge, preserve, and promote the spiritual and moral good found among these men, as well as the values in their society and culture.[22]

Acceptance of this understanding of other religions leads to a missionary approach which seeks to Christianize those religions from within rather than attempt to convert their adherents to abandon their faith in favour of Christianity. Indeed, such an approach would be dismissed as proselytism. This was the basis of the dialogue conducted by D.T. Niles and E. Stanley Jones with Hindus, and by Kenneth Cragg with Muslims.

A serious problem with this line of approach is the plain fact that other religions are not posing the questions which find their fullest answer in Christianity. The religions of the world cannot be placed within a pyramid which has Christianity as its apex. Rather the religions of the world represent a range of mountains, each with its own summit. Hans Küng observes that there is no evidence of a 'dynamic orientation' among Buddhists or Hindus towards Christianity; they are happy to remain where they are. From the standpoint of those persons of other religions, engaging in such an approach appears very ethnocentric and threatens the integrity of their own religion by subversion. Charles Davis argues that, 'If the Western synthesis, which Christians have endeavoured to impose upon the East, is repudiated as a synthesis, there is little point in advocating a synthesis between the Gospel and Hinduism, for example'.[23]

All religions are demonic distortions of the truth found only in the biblical witness to Jesus Christ

This position reflects the most negative and pessimistic assessment of religious systems. Tertullian (AD 160-215) expresses the confrontational stance that this position takes in his famous statements, 'What has Athens to do with Jerusalem?' He could find no fruitful point of contact between Christianity and the perversity of the pagan practices and Greek philosophy of his day. The leaders of the Reformation some twelve hundred years later took a similar stance in relation to the corrupt practices and erroneous doctrine of contemporary Catholicism. For them the differences seemed irreconcilable between a religion based on works and one based on grace. Catholicism was relegated to another form of paganism by both Luther and Calvin. It was the proof of human apostasy.

Such degeneracy of religion was not confined to other religions or Catholicism, but could also be applied to Protestantism. Karl Barth, appalled by the subservience of the Lutheran *volk kirke* of Germany to Nazism, joined the Confessing Church in protesting against the under-mining of the Christian faith in the interests of a German nationalism based on an insidious philosophy. He declared:

> Religion is never true in itself and as such. The revelation of God denies that any religion is true, i.e. that it is in truth the knowledge and worship of God and the reconciliation of man with God ... in short our Christianity, to the extent that it is our Christianity, [is] the human work which we under-take and adjust to all kinds of near and remote aims and which as such is seen to be on the same level as the human work in other religions.[24]

For Barth, only God can make God known. Religion 'is the attempted replacement of the divine work by a human manufacture. The divine reality offered and manifested to us in revelation is replaced by a concept of God arbitrarily and wilfully evolved in man.'[25] Barth thus affirms the negative assessment of general revelation as expounded by the apostle Paul in the first two chapters of his letter to the Romans. He acknowledges that all people have a knowledge of God's nature and power through his creation, but that they have used this knowledge to suppress the truth:

> for though they know God, they did not honour him as God or give thanks to him, but they became futile in their think-

ing, and their senseless minds were darkened. Claiming to be wise, they became fools; and they exchanged the glory of the immortal God for images resembling a mortal human being or birds or four-footed animals or reptiles (Rom 1:21-23 NRSV).

At the 1932 Brandenburg Missionary Conference, at which he was a main speaker, Barth described Christian mission as a journey into a void, with no point of contact. His negativism arose out of his christology. Truth in the religious realm is that which comes from Christ and leads to an acknowledgement of him as Lord and Saviour. In his later years Barth softened his earlier harsh appraisal of the religious aspect of human life. He concluded that religion, while sinful, still represented the vestiges of the covenant relationship of 'humanitas' with its creator, although in a degenerative and distorted form.

Many missionaries have supported this very negative evaluation of other religions. Their exposure has generally been to the folk forms of these religions, with the superstition, fear of evil spirits and rituals associated with immoral conduct. Sometimes their aversion was also influenced by the fact that their western world-view and lack of anthropological insights prevented them from understanding the significance of strange beliefs and practices. If they could have put aside their ethnocentrism they might have come to a more empathetic understanding. Furthermore, they were prone to compare the worst in other religions with an idealized form of Christianity. In their zeal to present the gospel they had not taken time to study the scriptures, devotional writing and traditions of other religions in order to recognize the spiritual insights and moral aspirations to be found in the highest forms of those religions. This is not to imply that all missionaries were negligent in their study of the culture of the people among whom they worked, but simply to point out that many missionaries were not of a studious disposition and embarked on their missionary careers with inadequate preparation in the cross-cultural communication of the gospel.

All religions contain elements both of fulfilment and antithesis

The fundamental issue which divided Karl Barth and Emil Brunner was the question of whether or not a true knowledge of God was possible outside biblical revelation. Barth was negative towards religion in general, and non-Christian religions in particular, precisely because he denied the possibility of such knowledge. Brunner, on the other hand, believed that God could in some measure be known apart from the biblical revelation. Consequently his assessment of the value of non-Christian religions is more positive. He sees elements which he can affirm as well as aspects which he must negate. For him the relationship between Christianity and other religions is more dialogical than confrontational. Humans are both sinners and yet made in the image of God; thus religions represent both a search for God and a flight from God. The spiritual truths and insights to be found in other religions are derived from general revelation. All empirical religions are, therefore, the 'product' of a combination of divine revelation and human sin which obscures and distorts the original revelation.[26]

This fourth position would seem to be the most tenable in terms of an appreciation of God's universal concern. Those who have been denied the opportunity to receive the Law of Moses have the law of conscience. In other words, they do not fall outside the sphere of God's loving concern and desire for their ultimate salvation. However, in arguing this position two concerns must be upheld.

The first is that the recognition of elements of divine revelation in other religions cannot be used as a basis for a 'mix-and-match'. No combination of elements can be fitted together to form an interlocking and meaningful jigsaw puzzle picture. No accurate picture of the nature of God or the means by which sinful humankind can be reconciled to him can be built from below on the basis of philosophical explanation. In other words, the insights of Christianity can neither be used to construct a larger whole nor can elements from other religions be combined to present what is to be found most comprehensively revealed in Christianity. Each religion is an indivisible whole whose integrity must be respected. For each not only provides different answers, but poses distinct questions relating to the nature of God, the human condition and salvation. Furthermore, religions are intertwined with cultures and represent an integral part of the self-identity of a people. This means that Christians must be prepared to enter into sensitive dialogue to uncover the spiritual roots, value system and cultural expression of a particular religious heritage. This stance is determined by a profound respect for the person as made in the image of God and the recognition that God is working out his saving purposes throughout the complex cultural network.

On the other hand, such openness does not imply a relativizing of religious insights and convictions. For those committed to the credal statements of the early church councils, Jesus is a historical fact and there is nothing in other religions to correspond with his incarnation as the Son of God or his atoning death on the cross for the sins of the whole world. The sharper the focus on the person and work of Christ, the greater become the dissimilarities between Christianity and other religions. It is Christ alone who secures our salvation. No one can find salvation by reliance on their own religious insights or moral performance.

It is this scandal of particularity which is such a stumbling block for people like Paul Knitter, who try to avoid the problem by advocating a religious pluralism which emphasizes a God-centred, as distinct from a Christ-centred, approach. Clark Pinnock has observed that the very notion of a God who loves all humankind is directly derived from the person of Christ who came to reveal the Father's love for the world and implement his saving plan. What happens is that liberals climb up the ladder of christology to arrive at a God defined as a loving personality and then think they can kick the ladder away, hoping no one will notice and nothing will be affected.[27]

Pinnock goes on to quote the question posed by Gavin D'Costa, 'How credibly can Hick expound a doctrine of God's universal salvific will if he does not ground this crucial truth in the revelation of God in Christ, thereby bringing Christology back onto centerstage?'[28] The pluralist approach to religion is based on a post-modern philosophy of relativism and centrelessness. Once embarked upon, it leads down the slippery slope of subjectivism; there is no longer the possibility of solid ground for religious convictions because truth claims have become relativized in terms of cultural context or as expressions of existential devotional commitment, rather than upheld as ontological statements.

REACTIVATING THE FAITH OF NOMINAL CHRISTIANS IN A PLURALIST SOCIETY

Laypeople living in a pluralist environment of religious and philosophical beliefs representing world-views and value systems, need training in terms both of knowledge and wisdom. They need adequate knowledge to provide a basic understanding of the religions which they are encountering in the course of daily life, coupled with an understanding of their own Christian faith in relation to other religions; and wisdom to know how to process and apply that knowledge in dialogue with sincere devotees of other faiths.

The universal scope of salvation

It is essential that the lay witness has a grasp of the universal scope of salvation and the role played in its outworking by the Trinity. Fundamental to this understanding is an unshakable conviction of the uniqueness of Jesus Christ as Son of God and Saviour of the world. In both Old and New Testaments it is clear that God's saving purpose is not restricted to the people of Israel. Before ever the special relationship was established by God with Abram, there was a universal covenant laid down with the entire human race. Genesis chapters 1-11 provide the global context, emphasizing God's concern for the whole world. There are frequent references in the Psalms to the fact that all the peoples of the world belong to God. There are over 150 references to God's universal reign (see for example Pss 22:27,28; 47:8,67; 72:8; 82:8; 100:117). The Psalms establish the authority of God in the affairs of people, insisting that his salvation should be dispersed to the nations, that at some time in the future there will be world-wide reverence for the Lord (the worship of the nations occurs fifteen times) and that Israel is responsible for declaring the glory of God to the nations (Ps 96:3,10). These references in the Psalms are highlighting and making more specific the promises originally given to Abram, that the nation brought into being through his offspring had a divinely appointed role to channel God's blessing to the nations of the world (Gen 12:2,3).

The prophets look forward to a time when Israel will be so filled with the glory of God's presence that the nations will be drawn to her (see Is 2:2-3; Mic 4:1-2; Hab 2:14; Mal 1:11; Zech 8:20-23). Such statements do not constitute missionary preaching in the New Testament sense. Their emphasis is on magnetism rather than mission: not on Israel going to the nations, but on the nations being spontaneously drawn to her. This global attraction will only occur at some future date, when the presence of the Messiah brings light to Israel.

> Arise, shine, for your light has come,
>   and the glory of the Lord rises upon you.
> See, darkness covers the earth
>   and thick darkness is over the peoples,
> but the Lord rises upon you
>   and his glory appears over you.
> Nations will come to your light,
>   and kings to the brightness of your dawn
>   (Is 60:1-3).

First, the Servant of the Lord will come to restore Israel, and then he will reveal himself through them to the world. Israel will herself become the servant of the Lord and then, God informs her, 'I will also make you a light for the Gentiles, that you may bring my salvation to the ends of the earth (Is 49:6).

The theme of universalism is taken over by Christ who comes in fulfilment of the prophecies concerning the Servant of the Lord in Isaiah. Jesus came not only as a light to Israel, but as the light of the world (Jn 8:12). He cleanses the Temple Court of the Gentiles in order to make it a fit place for the nations to come and pray (Jn 2:13-16; Mk 11:15-17). He shakes the exclusivism and complacency of the religious establishment by of speaking a day when non-Jews will come from east and west, from north and south, and sit down in the kingdom of God. And indeed there are those who are last who will be first, and first who will be last (Mt 8:11; Lk 13:29,30).

It is in the account of the events leading to Christ's crucifixion and his subsequent appearances to the disciples that we find the most references concerning the subsequent world-wide spread of the gospel. In the context of warning his disciples of the global calamities and personal trials they and subsequent generations of his followers must face, Jesus tells them that 'this gospel of the kingdom will be preached in the whole world as a testimony to all nations, and then the end will come' (Mt 24:14). As Jesus withdraws to a home in Bethany, a woman anoints his head with expensive perfume. Jesus defends the extravagance of her act by explaining that she is preparing his body beforehand for burial. Then he adds, 'I tell you the truth, wherever the gospel is preached throughout the world, what she has done will also be told, in memory of her' (Mk 14:9). While in the upper room with his disciples, Jesus speaks in graphic detail of the significance of his forthcoming crucifixion. His death will be like a grain of wheat falling into the ground. It is the 'death' of the seed which produces many grains (Jn 12:24). His being lifted up from the earth on the cross will result in 'all peoples' being drawn to him (Jn 12:32,33).

During his post-resurrection appearances to his disciples Jesus gave them repeated commands concerning their responsibility for the global communication of the gospel. Each of the gospel writers gives a slightly different emphasis. John draws attention to the continuity between the ministry of Jesus and that of the church (Jn 17:18; 20:21-23). Matthew emphasizes the objective of the task, which is to go into all the world in order to make disciples (Mt 28:18-20). The so-called 'longer ending' of Mark, which is not found in the earlier manuscripts but which reflects the experience of the church in Acts, stresses the principal method to be used—the preaching of the good news to all creation (Mk 16:15,16). Finally Luke, at both the conclusion of his Gospel and the opening of his account of the exploits of the early church, draws attention to the indispensable power of the Holy Spirit, without which it would be futile to attempt to undertake ministry in the name of Christ (Lk 24:49; Acts 1:8). Luke also fills out the content of the communication:

> 'That is what is written: The Christ will suffer and rise from the dead on the third day, and repentance and forgiveness of sins will be preached in his name to all nations, beginning at Jerusalem. You are witnesses of these things' (Lk 24:45,46).

There are two basic areas where wisdom is particularly required. The first is in regard to discerning the truth content in other religions. The Scriptures give abundant evidence of the operation of the Logos, who was not only active in creation but continues to give light to every person who comes into the world (Jn 1:9).

The second area is in regard to the unpredictable and unrestricted moving of the Spirit. The early church, for its part, embarked upon its divinely appointed mission to take the gospel into all the world. Its motivation for doing so was not so much a sense of obligation in response to the command of Christ, but rather the inner drive of the Holy Spirit.[29] The message of forgiveness of sins and the life abundant which was available in Christ was too good for the disciples to keep to themselves and the life which they experienced could not be contained within the ranks of the existing fellowship of believers. Their major struggle was in coming to terms with the communicating of the gospel cross-culturally. It took approximately fifteen years for the church to break out of its Jewish cultural confines and make the gospel available and intelligible to gentile audiences.

Peter's reluctant response to the dramatic leading of the Holy Spirit to take the gospel to the Roman centurian Cornelius, a gentile god-fearer, created the precedent for the far reaching ministry of Paul who was called as an apostle to the Gentiles. Acts chapters twelve to twenty-one record the breathtaking story of the spread of Christianity from Jerusalem to Rome. Thus the Great Commission recorded by Matthew becomes the Great Doxology at the conclusion of Paul's letter to the Romans (Rom 16:26). What Jesus had commanded was now coming to pass. Paul could say of the believers in Thessalonica that the Lord's message rang out from them throughout the provinces of Macedonia and Achaia (1 Thess 1:8). In his second letter he asks for their prayers that 'the message of the Lord may spread rapidly and be honoured just as it was with you' (2 Thess 3:1). With forgivable hyperbole Paul assures the Colossian believers that, 'All over the world this gospel is producing fruit and growing, just as it has been doing among you since the day you heard it and understood God's grace in all it's truth' (Col 1:6). He rejoices with the Corinthians that God 'always leads us in triumphal procession in Christ and through us spreads everywhere the fragrance of the knowledge of him' (2 Cor 2:14). Clearly the early Christians were neither inhibited or intimidated by the pluralistic culture of their day. They believed that Jesus was uniquely divine and that his death was for the sins of the whole world.

What about those who have never had an opportunity to hear the gospel?

What then should be the Christian's attitude to sincere adherents of other faiths? If in other religions there are found revelatory insights regarding the omnipotence and holiness of God, the fallen state of humankind and the fear of the Lord engendered by the realization of human culpability, do these insights constitute saving knowledge? Or is salvation only available to those who have heard and responded to the gospel by an explicit act of faith in Christ as Son of God and Saviour of the world?

Christians are divided on this issue. Some solve the problem by resorting to universalism, arguing that Jesus died for the sins of the whole world and therefore every person, whether they recognize it or not, are forgiven and assured of eternal salvation. The tragedy is that most people are ignorant of the fact or, for one reason or another, unable to accept it. The task of Christian mission is to inform people of the grounds of their salvation and to live out the benefits of Christ's saving work by demonstrating his love for the needy of the world. This position has a long history going back to Origen who argued against the heretic Celsus that all would be saved in the end. For Origen the purpose of hell was purgative rather than terminally punitive.

While this is an attractive possibility, it runs into two serious obstacles. In the first place the Scriptures contain many warnings about impending divine judgement which do not sound like idle treats (Mk 3:28-30; Mt 10:15; 12:36; Lk 13:5; Rom 14:10; Heb 9:27; 10:27; 2 Pet 2:4-9; Jude 6). The book of Revelation speaks of divine judgement as the 'second death' (Rev 2:11; 20:11-15). Secondly, as Clark Pinnock notes, 'the theory does not allow for humans in their freedom to say no to God'. For love to operate, freedom has to be given to the individual to accept or reject that offer. Pinnock continues his argument, 'Our relation with God, as well as our final destiny, are chosen by ourselves and not thrust upon us. God does not purpose to condemn anyone, but anyone can choose rejection'.[30]

The second response is the restrictive one, which confines the possibility of salvation to those who have heard and responded to the message of salvation. Those who have not heard the message are thereby outside the sphere of God's saving purpose both in this life and the next. All those who are numbered among God's elect, like Cornelius (Acts chapters 10, 11), will be given the opportunity to hear the gospel, either through a human messenger, or through a divine visitation. Others believe in the possibility of a second chance being granted after death, on the basis of 1 Pet 3:19-20 which speaks of Christ, after his death, preaching to the spirits in prison. However, this passage speaks in terms of a once only announcement to past generations of the disobedient. There is no hint that such a proclamation constituted a second chance for those who had rejected the way of righteousness.

This leads us to a third option, which is to recognize that the Logos (Word) of God was operative before being incarnated in Jesus, and that the word speaks to humanity beyond the confines of Israel. God bears witness to himself in every culture and to every individual heart. Salvation may then depend not on some minimal knowledge of Jesus and his atoning death, but on the individual's faith response to as much as God has revealed to that individual. In Old Testament terminology, the basis of salvation is the reverential fear of the Lord and submission to his person to live a life of loving obedience and righteousness. Religions *per se* cannot supply the means to reach such a position. It is only brought about by the grace of God, and that position of grace is only made possible by the work of Christ, whether applied retroactively to those born before his sacrificial death, or applied extensively to include those who are responding to God's gracious presence in their lives but who cannot identify their experience of divine intervention with the work of Christ.

Ideally, the test of whether those persons are genuine recipients of grace would be their positive response to hearing the gospel and realizing that the person and work of Christ represent the fulfilment of their deepest spiritual longings. In reality, such a potentially positive response may be obstructed by cultural and historical barriers erected by 'Christians' who, through inability to explain the message in understandable terms, failure to live by the message, or on account of atrocities committed against those of other faiths, have become hindrances to evangelization. It will require a great deal of patience, confession of past sins, careful dialogue (including listening, affirmation and explanation) and the living out of the message, for many of these formidable and long-standing barriers to begin to crumble.

CONCLUSION

In this chapter we have drawn attention to the vulnerability of the Christian churches in the West to the encroachment of religious pluralism. Among the indigenous population there is a pre-existent nominality born out of cultural conformity and spiritual apathy. To this is added an additional strain of nominality introduced by the adoption of a relativist approach to religion in response to an increasingly religiously pluralist social environment. Such a *laissez-faire* attitude results in naivety, confusion and vulnerability.

The devotees of other religions bring a forthright challenge to the nominal Christians who live alongside them, through their serious study and dedication in living out their faith. They may cause the nominal Christian to examine critically the extent and depth of their own faith commitment and to have an increased awareness of their compromises and blind spots which arise from an uncritical adoption of their cultural heritage.

Every religious institution, devotee, and conceptual framework is likely not only to embody elements which are of divine origin, but also those which are of a human or demonic nature. Peter Beyerhaus refers to these three elements as a *tripolar theology of religions*.[31] There is, firstly, humankind's religious awareness and concern for God; secondly, there is God's involvement with humankind, by way of revelation; and, thirdly, there is the demonic influence in the process. Discernment is required to sift out (and exorcise) the demonic, identify with the religious awareness and concern for God and explore what true insights regarding the nature of God adherents of other religions have become aware of and responded to in faith.

The second basic area where wisdom needs to be exercised is to discern that religion is not analysed and responded to in the abstract but it is embodied in actual persons. It is one thing to examine critically the tenets of another religion by studying its scared literature and theological commentaries. It is quite another to sit down with individuals who have been nurtured in spiritual and cultural contexts very different from our own. Those who are devoted followers of other religions cannot be stereotyped, any more than Christians can be made to fit a common mould. Each person responds differently to the claims of their religion, with varying depths of spiritual perception and consistency of life. In the course of open dialogue one comes to appreciate where each person is to be found on their spiritual journey.

In the concluding chapter we shall suggest appropriate structures for mission by which local churches can more effectively provide training and support to enable lay persons to respond to the challenges of religious pluralism and secularization. Such structures are urgently required to enable people to think through their own religious beliefs and relate them to the views expressed by those whose beliefs are shaped by alternative and often conflicting world-views. Such support groups will also enable them to minister more effectively to formerly committed Christians who are now uncertain and confused by the pluralist environment in which most of their social interaction takes place.

NOTES

1. For an informative account of the New Age Movement coupled with a discerning evaluation, see Russell Chandler, *Understanding the New Age* (Word Books; Dallas 1988).
2. Charles Davis, *Christ and the World Religions* (Hodder & Stoughton; London, 1970), p 15.
3. Ibid, p 16.
4. K.M. Pannikkar, *Asia and Western Dominance* (Collier Books; New York, 1969), pp 297, 331.
5. Davis, *op cit*, p 38.
6. See Chandler, *Understanding the New Age*, chaps 15-22.
7. Kenneth Cragg, *The Christ and the Faiths* (SPCK; London, 1986), pp 5-6.
8. Stanley J Samartha, 'The Cross and the Rainbow', in John Hick and Paul F.

Knitter (eds), *The Myth of Christian Uniqueness* (Orbis Books; Maryknoll, 1987), p 72.

9. Ninian Smart, *The Yogi and the Devotee* (Allen Unwin; London, 1968), pp 14-15.

10. David Edwards, *Religion and Change* (Hodder & Stoughton; London, 1969,), p 235.

11. Davis, op cit, p 36.

12. Davis, op cit, p 38.

13. Cragg, op cit, p 86.

14. See Ernst Troeltsch, *Christian Thought, Its History and Application* (University of London; London, 1923).

15. Raimund Panikkar, in Hick and Knitter (eds), *The Myth of Christian Uniqueness*, p 92.

16. Wilfred Cantwell Smith, 'Some Similarities and Differences Between Christianity and Islam: An Essay in Comparative Religion', in *The World of Islam; Studies in Honour of Philip K. Hitti*, edited James Kritzeck and R. Bayly Winder (Macmillan; London, 1960), p 49.

17. Raimundo Panikkar, 'The Relation of Christians to their Non-Christian Surroundings; in Joseph Neuner (ed), *Christian Revelation and World Religions* (Burns Oates; London, 1967), p 169.

18. Langdon Gilkey, 'Plurality and its Theological Implications', in Hick and Knitter, *The Myth of Christian Uniqueness*, pp 43, 47, 50.

19. Hick and Knitter, op cit, p 109.

20. Hick and Knitter, op cit, pp 187, 190.

21. Quoted in Robert H. Thouless, *An Introduction to the Psychology of Religion* (Cambridge University Press; Cambridge, 1971), p 116.

22. Walter M. Abbott, SJ, and Joseph Gallagher (eds), *The Documents of Vatican II* (Geoffrey Chapman; London, 1966), pp 662-3.

23. Davis, op cit, p 54.

24. Karl Barth, *Church Dogmatics, Vol I: The Doctrine of the Word of God* (T & T Clark; Edinburgh, 1956), second half-volume, pp 325, 327.

25. Ibid, pp 299-300.

26. Emil Brunner, *Revelation and Reason* (The Westminster Press; Philadelphia, 1946).

27. Clark H. Pinnock, *A Wideness in God's Mercy* (Zondervan; Grand Rapids, 1992), p 45.

28. Gavin D'Costa, *John Hick's Theology of Religions* (University Press of America; New York, 1987), p 103.

29. Harry Boer, in *Pentecost and Missions* (Eerdmans; Grand Rapids, 1961), contrasts the emphasis of the modern missionary movement on the Great Commission with 'the apparently complete absence of this motivation as a conscious factor in the missionary life of the early church' (p 15).

30. Pinnock, *op cit*, p 156.

31. Peter Beyerhaus, article in *Kerygma and Dogma*, (April-June 1969); pp 87-104.

CHAPTER EIGHT

DEVELOPING MINISTRY STRUCTURES TO WIN THEM BACK

IN CHAPTER 4 WE FOCUSED on the key issues which a church must address in order to experience the renewal necessary for spiritual vitality and clarified objectives. Such measures are directed towards the institutional factors which will renew the church for its challenging task of winning back an 'external constituency' which is not only increasing in numbers but at the same time further distancing itself from the churches. In Chapters 5, 6 and 7 we explored the three contextual factors of urbanization, secularization and religious pluralism which provided the ministry context in which the church's re-evangelizing strategy must be developed. This final chapter endeavours to provide the second stage in the renewal strategy, by suggesting structures and strategies for the church to address more effectively the problems of winning back a lost constituency and reaching out to those nominal Christians who have never been actively involved in a local church. The first stage dealt with the internal structures for church renewal. This second stage is concerned with strategies and structures to enable the church to engage with the world.

In attempting a response to the problem we must bear in mind the principal reasons for the unchurched becoming inactive, then distanced and, finally, dissociated. Many leave because they find the worship services predictable, incomprehensible or irrelevant to their world. Others leave because they are excluded from the fellowship circle, marginalized from the leadership, or because their skills and ministry concerns are ignored. Still others depart because of strained or broken relationships. There is not the willingness to work towards reconciliation between the offended parties, neither is there the community support to conciliate between the estranged individuals and bring about reconciliation for the health and strengthening of the wider fellowship.

Then there are the casualties who succumb to the pressures of the world around them and find they can no longer live by double standards: one representing the ideals of the church and the other representing the ethical norms of society, whether in the area of honesty in personal and financial dealings or in sexual behaviour. They are either excluded from the fellowship or take the initiative themselves to terminate their membership, either out of remorse or defiance. The tragedy is that for the majority of those individuals, the church provides no adequate support to work out the implications of the gospel in their particular context in order to face the pressing trials and seductive temptations which are prevalent in their working environment. Whatever the reason, most of the unchurched, who were formerly churched, have a negative impression of institutionalized religion.[1]

Some people may have drifted away for no strong negative reason. Their weekly schedule was upset by weekend work demands, family responsibilities, or leisure activities, so that church was crowded out in the competition to fit fresh activities into a limited time allotment. Or they simply moved away and failed to take the initiative to establish contact with a new church. It is this particular group of people who are most likely to respond positively to the survey question, 'If someone you knew and liked invited you to attend church with them, would you go?' No doubt such a question pricks the conscience and revives memories of happy times and eroded values.

The impact of materialism, secularism and pluralism have severely eroded the values which undergird the kingdom of God and compromised the total commitment required by the gospel to the sovereign rule of Christ over his kingdom. While the majority of unchurched people give the 'correct' answers, remembered from their churchgoing days, to questions of belief, these beliefs no longer represent a conviction sufficiently strong to be translated into specific commitments. They are also held alongside other views which are mutually incompatible, without any contradiction being recognized or consideration of consequence. If European and Australasian experience represents precedents, it is likely that, as nominality in the United States passes to a second and third generation, responses to questions relating to belief will become less orthodox.

In order for the lapsed and distanced from the churches to be won back, or their former church allegiance translated into personal commitment to Christ and incorporation into an active body of believers, the church will need to radically rethink its evangelistic strategies to re-engage the morally compromised, the spiritually confused and those who perceive themselves to be socially excluded by churchgoers.

CHURCHES MUST ADDRESS THE PRINCIPAL CAUSES WHICH INHIBIT THEM FROM RESPONDING TO THE CHALLENGE OF NOMINALITY

There are a range of issues which are typically ignored by the church because the cost of facing up to them is too high in terms of possibly antagonizing the congregation and putting jobs at risk. The following represent some of the most common factors which seriously inhibit the church's attempts to respond to the challenge to reach out to nominal Christians.

Confinement within the church premises

Most churches are over-preoccupied with what happens in the sanctuary and the church hall. The main concerns of church leaders is to organize events and run programmes which are attractive, relevant and sufficiently publicized to draw people on to their 'turf'. They are concerned to generate and maintain a centripetal dynamic. There is some justification for this way of thinking in that the presence of the people of God within a community should be meeting the needs of people and arousing curiosity. However, problems arise when this 'come-to-us' perception of ministry becomes the dominant one and is pursued over an extended period of time. Then there is a strong and almost inevitable tendency to create an ever widening cultural and communication gap between the church and that segment of the wider community which fails to respond to such invitations. In a highly secular environment the church must shift emphasis from a centripetal to a centrifugal ministry strategy.

Kennon Callahan has drawn attention to the fact that the day of the churched culture in the United States is over and that the day of the mission field has come. He identifies three factors which mark the unchurched culture:

1. The value of church is not among the major values of the culture.

2. A substantial number of persons are not seeking our churches on their own initiative.

3. By and large, persons live life as though the church did not substantially matter.[2]

Many leaders are still unable to hear and face up to Callahan's challenge to rethink their strategies to engage an unchurched culture, because the old ways are still working in significant numbers of churches. Among them are well-known mainline megachurches which attract already-churched people looking for inspiration through participation in a quality worship experience and through hearing able preaching. Then there are the newer independent congregations which are attracting people who have become bored, disillusioned and frustrated with their former congregations and are looking for churches with a more contemporary image and programmes which meet their life-stage and crisis needs.

It is these churches which provide the models for the struggling congregations who are looking for answers without having to face the more radical questions. If Christian leaders in the United States want some idea of where the cultural trends are leading, then Canada, Europe and Australasia might provide some salutary warnings.

Churches can either opt to concentrate their efforts on that section of the population which is prepared to take the initiative in checking out local churches in response to the invitations issued through advertising campaigns, TV and radio programmes and church members inviting friends to special events. Or they can direct their attention to the majority of the unchurched who are increasingly unlikely to respond to such invitations. This will entail a fundamental shift in strategy from concentrating on the church gathered, to resourcing the church in dispersion. The locus of outreach is no longer primarily the church building, but the communities where the church members live, work and socialize. It is a reinstatement of the centrifugal motion of mission, which entails going into all the world, as against the centripetal dynamic of attraction to a centralized church programme. Such journeying involves crossing cultural as well as geographical frontiers.

Programmes which are inwardly focused
The programme approach to ministry pursued by churches in North America had much to commend it in the post World War II years up to the end of the 1960s. During that period the USA was predominantly a

churched culture. There was a large churchgoing population and a significant 'external constituency' consisting of fringe persons who maintained some kind of lose association with the church and were favourably disposed towards institutionalized religion. The decade of the 40s, 50s and 60s were also a time of rapid suburban development and the desire to create residential communities which provided a social base from which to draw people into Adult Sunday School classes composed of others from their own neighbourhoods. These were the golden years of the Adult Sunday School movement which peaked in 1963 and then went into rapid decline.[3] The following decades have been characterized by a serious breakdown in community based on neighbourhood, due to increased mobility and the demise of the traditional family. The resulting social distancing meant that the Sunday School became largely ineffective as a means of evangelism and the reincorporation of the nominal and notional 'Christian' population.

Some of the most strident criticism of programme-based churches has come from Ralph Neighbour. He has raised a series of questions regarding the programme approach to ministry which require some serious reflection.

1. Are the staff of specialists equipping the saints for ministry or running programmes?
2. Does the work of the church specialists further their contact with the unchurched, or cut them off because their isn't enough time in their busy week to know the unconverted?
3. What percentage of the church membership is inactive?
4. Does the need to maintain a programme result in people being recruited regardless of their gifts or their abilities?
5. For how many hours a week does the main sanctuary stand empty, and what is the occupancy of the Sunday School classrooms? Could the Hilton Hotel survive with that level of occupancy?
6. In an average week how many unchurched persons enter the sanctuary, Sunday School, interest group or home group meeting?
7. How does the number calculated for question 6 compare with the total number at all meetings?[4]

Dependence upon inadequately trained professional leadership

A sanctuary-based, pulpit-focused and programme-oriented approach to ministry means an undue emphasis on the role of the professional Christian leader. This has created a bottle-neck in Christian ministry and led to the disempowerment of the laity. The professionals in ministry today have largely been trained in their seminaries, Bible Schools and Christian colleges to operate within a churched culture. Consequently, they feel most comfortable and competent when they are functioning within the institutional boundaries. They are able to respond most adequately to issues of church polity, liturgy, the pastoral needs of church members and Christian education. However, when confronted with a questioning, doubting or defiant dechurched or non-Christian society their professional competence quickly evaporates. The church programmes over which they have control then become their source of security and primary preoccupation.

Kennon Callahan draws a distinction between a local church and a mission outpost which is helpful at this point. In a 'mission outpost',

> leaders and pastors 'live out' much of their leadership and work in the world. By contrast, in the local church of the churched culture, leaders and pastors live out much of their work and leadership inside the safety and security of the local church.
>
> This is not accidental. With the best of intentions, good people in the church—pastors and leaders—have worked from the assumption that they must first tend to the needs of the church before they can tend to the needs of the world. The problem comes when they seldom or never get outside.[5]

Intimidated by a secular and pluralist society

If church leaders are not adequately trained to operate on the frontiers of faith in an unchurched mission environment, they are ill-prepared to equip people to operate outside the church context. They opt, therefore, to educate and train their people to work within their own sphere of operations. It is all too easy to perpetuate this insularity because, as we have noted in the quote from Callahan, the clergy are largely confined to the churched culture. It is the laity who are endeavouring to live out their faith and bear relevant witness in a world which operates on a very different value system and on premises regarding the nature of reality which are frequently antithetical to a theist position.

Preachers exhort their congregations to be faithful witnesses in their places of work, homes, neighbourhood and other spheres of influence, but they are not trained in the necessary apologetic and evangelistic skills to equip the laity to face such a daunting challenge. Furthermore, the vast majority of churches are not structured to provide the support groups and outreach teams to undertake the task. They still operate in a maintenance rather than a mission mode. In the long term the preachers' exhortations become counter-productive to the point where their repeated utterance is more a venting of the pastor's frustrations than a call to concerted action. Despite the rhetoric, the major emphasis is placed on enlisting and equipping the laity to ensure the continued function of the organization. Reacting to this persistent tendency towards ministerial introversion, one English clergy friend of long standing, Canon Harry Sutton, protested, 'What we need are not more mini-pastors, but more maxi-witnesses'. It is a high priority for the church to operate according to biblical priorities in any society which is predominantly unchurched.

In the previous two chapters we considered the two predominant influences in our society which the church must address on a broad front. It is only when the church is in responsible dialogue with the world, demonstrating the relevance of the biblical revelation to the multiplicity of issues which daily confront us, that nominal Christians will come to reconsider their position and identify with the believers who have re-established contact in the context of the environments where they live out their daily lives.

Too involved in running programmes to respond to felt needs

In the light of the above, churches first need to review their Christian education and spiritual formation programmes to determine their relevance for making disciples equipped to function in today's world, a world which looks very different from the world of yesterday. Secondly, there needs to be a balance between those programmes designed to meet the needs of existing members and those programmes designed to minister to the spiritual, social and material needs of the unchurched. There is a persistent bias to address the former, while neglecting or postponing the latter. The result of this imbalance is churches which are like a bakery renowned for its excellent bread, most of which is consumed by the employees of the bakery. The only outlet is a small shop located at the bakery where a few informed, discerning and sufficiently motivated customers take the trouble to visit the bakery in order to make their purchases.

Protestantism throughout the western world largely consists of small churches. Fifty per cent of churches have worship attendances of less than seventy-five people. Eighty per cent of churches have less than two hundred.[6] Small congregations attempting to operate as 'full service' churches through centrally based programmes invariably over-diversify and end up offering more than they can deliver. As a consequence, quality suffers and visitors in search of ministers who can meet their needs go elsewhere until they find churches with a greater range of attractive and competently run programmes. On this basis the small church cannot compete with the megachurch down the street or across town. Furthermore, the committed church members are exhausted trying to maintain their programmes and making repeated attempts to enlist reluctant 'volunteers' who are far from convinced that the activity for which their support is being enlisted is a worthwhile use of their time.

Programmes tend to take on a life and momentum of their own. New pastors soon discover that it is far easier to add a new programme than to 'axe' an existing one. Churches which suffer from trying to uphold precarious programmes are characterized by appeals to the congregations to show their support and loyalty by turning up to as many events on the church calendar as they can. The faithful supporters almost entirely consist of those members with a long commitment to the institution, the lonely and those who have retreated from the hazardous world outside to the security of the church.

The church in the 1990s needs to be far more focused, ensuring that each of its range of programmes contributes to the overall goal of equipping the people of God to survive and spiritually reproduce in an alien environment which is both hostile and potentially responsive. Barna Research has shown that the most cherished top three values are family, health and time. These are shared across the board in US society, whether the respondents are non-Christian, unchurched, churched or born-again.[7] We should not be surprised that one of the consequences is that, across the board, people are spending less time participating in church activities. According to the Barna Research,

> Overall, 44% of adults say they are giving the same amount
> of time to church endeavours this year as they did last year;
> 20% are giving more time; 33% are spending less time. This
> is a net loss of 13 percentage points in the proportion of
> people giving more to their church's life.[8]

No wonder so many churches are finding it increasingly difficult to sustain previous levels of commitment by the laity to running and supporting their programmes. The basic question which needs to be asked is: 'Are the church members there to support the programmes or are the programmes designed to support the people of God and equip them to survive and thrive as Christian disciples living as members of the kingdom of God in the world?' Discipleship requires maintaining a rhythm of the inward pull and the outward thrust. My wife discovered in the course of visiting unchurched neighbours that churchgoers were perceived as people too busy to have time for anyone beyond their church friends. The tendency is for people to have fewer and fewer non-church-going friends the more committed they become to their local church.

More concerned to gather a crowd and increase membership than with growing people and community building

In a situation of general church decline among the mainline denominations, there still remains a significant percentage of growing churches. For instance, in England, where overall adult church attendance has declined from 11.3 per cent in 1975 to 9.5 per cent in 1989 (an average loss of 28,000 persons per year) and where the number of churches has declined from 39,064 in 1979 to 38,607 in 1989, still 25 per cent of all English churches grew between 1985 and 1989, while 67 per cent remained static.[9] Furthermore, the data on the overall decline in church numbers is a net total and masks the fact that while some churches have been closed, other have been opened and are thriving today.

Despite the existence of growing congregations and newer movements, the overall churchgoing trends have continued to decline or remain static in the western world.[10] This fact forces us to face the question whether the growth patterns of certain 'successful' churches mainly represent their increased share of the churchgoing population market, or whether they are attracting significant numbers of the formerly-churched and never-churched to replace those who are being lost to the world. Regrettably, some so-called 'successful churches' are reluctant to undertake this kind of analysis even to the extent of failing to take account of their 'back door' losses. So long as there is net gain, there is little cause for concern.

Such attitudes reflect a churched-culture mentality. The focus of attention is on the numbers being gathered within the church, rather than on the impact being made outside the confines of the church premises. Once again Callahan provides some words of wisdom:

It is important, at this point, to note that the focus of

membership is a characteristic mark of a churched culture. When the nature of leadership is understood to be focused *inside* the church and when people in the culture are self-initiating their activity in the church, then membership becomes a mark of a 'successful church'. Statistics reporting membership numbers are pleasingly noted.

By contrast on a mission field the characteristic mark that is of predominant concern for the Christian church is salvation, not membership. On a mission field, the focus is on sharing the good news of the kingdom on winning persons for Christ. The central concern is helping persons to claim 'Jesus is Lord' in their lives, whether they become members of a specific denominational entity or not.

To be sure, salvation implies membership in the body of Christ. Certainly it is understood that they will look forward to being a part of some local congregation. But the focus is in the world more than in the church. The predominant focus is on mission, not membership.[11]

DECENTRALIZE IN ORDER TO IMPACT THE WORLD MORE EXTENSIVELY

Churches which are prepared to take seriously the cultural shift from being a predominantly church society to one which is unchurched must recognize their need to turn inside out! In other words, the focus of attention will not be on running programmes in order to gather the congregation together but on equipping the people of God to exercise its God-entrusted mission to the world. The gathering of the church will be to celebrate what God is doing through them in the world, to renew and refocus that mission and to equip the membership by providing personal support and training in line with their gifts. Sunday worship becomes a preparation for the week rather than a prologue to the week.

Church staff persons have a ministry focused not on running their programmes, but on recognizing the strategic placement of their members in society and helping them recognize and take full advantage of their opportunities for witness and service. In order for ministry to be dispersed and actualized where church members are located in their neighbourhood and work place, the following issues need to be addressed.

Provide support systems to facilitate witness in society

The existing congregation needs to be taught the basis of ministry as depicted in the New Testament: namely, that all people who are called to discipleship are also called to convey the message of Christ and to be part of the implementation of his purposes within the sphere of influence into which God has sovereignly placed them as his representatives. The widespread impression that ministry is primarily concerned with ordination and the pastoring of a congregation by hired professionals needs to be combated. This narrow ministry focus is but the tip of the iceberg. The task of the 'professionals' is to equip the whole people of God for their very diverse and dispersed ministries according to where the Lord has strategically deployed them to undertake his purposes in the world.

Such teaching needs to be regularly heard in the preaching or teaching ministry of the church and reinforced by group discussion and exploration of its concrete application in the life situations of the members. Their sphere of influence and ministry may be their residential neighbourhood, their place of work, their professional associations, their extended families, their leisure activities—anywhere that they are within friendship networks. Such has been the 'churchly' focus of ministry that the very concept of ministry in the market-place exercised by ordinary church members frequently comes as a startling revelation when such a vision is shared with the congregation.

The approach taken in advocating such a concept in public ministry should be one of teaching rather than exhortation. The latter approach will prove to be counter-productive, because all it is likely to achieve is the raising of frustration levels and the imputation of guilt. The deductive teaching approach needs to be complemented by an inductive modelling of the concepts through a variety of pilot projects undertaken by clusters of affinity groups within the congregation.

At the outset it is preferable to begin modestly and selectively with a few involved people from the congregation, rather than to restructure the entire congregation to become a ministry task force. Most churches do not have the trained leadership or ministry experience to embark on a multi-front campaign, and the bulk of the members are unlikely to be motivated until they hear the testimonies and see the evidence of such concepts actually working in the market-place. They do not want to hear from the pastoral staff, whom they regard as remote from the issues and pressures of the work place, but from lay persons like themselves, whom they respect personally and professionally and with whom they can identify.

The church leaders need to commit themselves to a ministry of intercession, enquiring from the lord of the harvest where the sowing and reaping may be done most productively and strategically. We want to go where he directs and be supportive of those representatives of the congregation who will be operating on the front line.

Alongside this prayer commitment, leaders need to be reviewing the congregation in order to discern where there are significant relational clusters of members. These may be in particular residential communities, professions, or places of work. Having identified the individuals concerned, they can be invited to an exploratory meeting to try and discover how they might organize themselves into a 'community of witness' in order to incarnate the ministry of Jesus in that location or social and professional context. We are not here talking about a clandestine infiltration or an open evangelistic assault on the unsuspecting. Rather the emphasis is on mutual support in working out the implications for Christian discipleship in that situation; how genuine care for colleagues can be expressed in response to their work pressures, family crises, personal goals and health concerns, etc. The goal of such communities is the multiplication of signs of the kingdom of God in that place. It is living out the Christian life for the benefit of the total community or business enterprise.

The organization and agenda for such communities of witness will vary according to context. Those who identify the issues and determine the agenda will be the individuals who belong to that environment rather than the church staff. The ministry staff do not act as experts imposing a predetermined programme, but rather serve as resource persons, providing biblical, theological and pastoral insights in response to the issues which are being raised by the group members. In terms of how those insights are to be contexualized, the lay persons will be the experts rather than the staff persons.

As such communities are formed, the problem will frequently arise of how individuals from other churches who work alongside church members might also participate in such communities of witness. This should be no problem, provided that they can share in the faith basis of the group and identify with its life-style values and ministry goals. If and when they introduce unchurched persons to the group, the church their invitees are most likely to attend is that of the person who invited them.

The communities of witness form a lay apostolate which will help churches to develop theologies and ministries of the laity and thereby release the church from its sanctuary confinement. For many years, critics of the western-based missionary enterprise have railed against the 'missionary compounds' established by European and North American missionaries in Africa and Asia. Yet, at the same time, we have been blind to the 'church compounds' which we have created in the missionary-sending countries. Missionaries have simply been reproducing overseas the 'come-to-us' ministry strategy of their home churches.

Now is the time to break out of the compound mentality here in the West, following the example set by many missionaries in the Two-Third's World! This is the only way in which the one hundred million unchurched Americans are likely to be affected by the gospel. Ensuring that the church is interacting with the world with a message which requires the adoption of a kingdom lifestyle will also make church members face up to the acute and widespread nominality problem, manifested by the fact that nine-tenths of the churchgoing population live according to values which are no different from the values of those who make no such commitment claims. The most hopeful route to personal renewal and transformation of the church is the pathway of mission in the world.

I am a firm believer in beginning small. That seems to be the kingdom way of doing things. Jesus represented the kingdom of God as the smallest of seeds growing into the biggest of bushes (Mt 13:31). The parable emphasizes that starting small is not to be confused with thinking small. Significant ministry concepts with global impact often arise out of unimpressive beginnings. There is value in starting small, firstly because lessons can then be learned along the way and incorporated to provide a firmer foundation for future growth based on the lessons of experience.

Secondly, starting small gives leaders time to accumulate experience on the basis of trial and error. It is preferable to make mistakes on a small rather than a large scale! The learning curve is at it steepest during the early stages in the development of an enterprise. If a large-scale project is launched by people with no previous experience, then the results can be catastrophic. Either it fails to get off the ground or, if it does become airborne, risks a devastating crash landing through the failure of untried components facing in-flight conditions for the first time.

Thirdly, time needs to be given to build a support and mentoring team to resource the leaders of the communities of witness. The disciplers themselves need to be discipled. Mentoring is a demanding task for the mentor as it entails providing a support for people whose gifts and calling are different from those of the church's pastoral staff, many of whom may have had significant experience in the secular work place or may have been away from that secular environment for many years. The role of the mentor is that of a listener and a theological and ministry resource person to help in the identification and exploration of faith issues. The mentor also serves as a liaison between that specific area of ministry and the broader ministry agenda of the church, thus ensuring that the group is not going off at a tangent.

Ensure that a decentralized approach to ministry does not result in the fragmentation of the congregation
The possibility of fragmentation must be recognized from the outset and measures taken to safeguard the church from such an unfortunate development. Some church leaders over-react to the extent that they opt for a regimented model of church life, with the result that the church operates more like a business machine than a life-pulsating body. The significance of the body metaphor as applied to the church is that the human body combines unity with diversity. Each individual, serving as a member within the body, does so without losing any sense of individuality. Discipleship with the New Testament is designed to grow people to their full potential in Christ and not to process them to conform to a particular personality type or assembly line operator in the spiritual reproduction enterprise. A functional church is one in which each member has both a location and function, and in which both leaders and members recognize each person's unique combination of personality, giftedness, experience and distinctive calling.

The basis of unity is both conceptual and relational. In Chapter 4, which discussed the internal aspects of church renewal for the restoration of nominal Christians, we emphasized the need for the church to develop a philosophy of ministry and a purpose statement. This is particularly needful when denominational loyalties have been eroded. Among Baby Boomers, for instance, the majority now worship in a church tradition other than the one in which they were raised.[12] People in search of a church are shopping around to find the kind of church which meets their personal and family needs, has worship styles with which they can relate and has an affirming ambiance which enables them to feel accepted.

A decentralized approach to ministry requires that the many groups involved in a multiplicity of ministries according to their social context, must all relate to a set of core values and common purpose. In other words, that there is a master 'battle plan' behind every local skirmish. In societies which are heterogeneous and highly mobile there is a felt need to be part of something bigger than the small group. They want to take their place within a significant movement which is intimately involved in society at large and effectively addressing contemporary issues. This is, in part, the explanation for the emergence of the megachurches in the last twenty years, which is bringing about a significant reconfiguration of the churchgoing population. Lyle Schaller maintains that in the United States over 50 per cent of churchgoers are attending 14 per cent of the largest churches.[13] However, some doubt is cast on the accuracy of this estimate through the research conducted by John Vaughan. His data, based on a study of the Church of God Anderson, Nazarene, Church of Christ, Disciples of Christ, Evangelical Free, Evangelical Lutheran Church of America, Presbyterian Church USA, Southern Presbyterian Church and United Methodist, reveals that their congregations with 350 plus attenders, a total of 7,452 churches, representing 6 per cent of their church total, account for just 17 per cent of attendance in those denominations. This percentage will increase by an unknown amount when the Pentecostal and independent charismatic megachurches are added. Whatever the true figure, it is clear that these growing megachurches are all characterized by a strong sense of purpose and congregational commitment to their ministry objectives and goals.

Where there is an absence of such a purpose statement the networking model quickly develops holes and eventually begins to fall apart. The issue is not simply whether or not such a purpose statement exists, but whether it is known, understood and owned by the church leaders and at least 75 per cent of the membership, and to what extent is it being translated into operational objectives and criteria for performance evaluation.

This brings us to the final consideration under this heading, namely the need for a relational, or organizational, basis for unity. Carl George, director of the Fuller Institute for Evangelism and Church Growth, has made a significant contribution in their area with his systems approach to ministry development, which he has described as the 'metachurch' model. The prefix 'meta' focuses on the need for a change of thinking in regard to the way ministry is conceptualized and structured. Carl George offers the following explanation of his term:

> The label *metachurch*, then, is quite distinct from mega-church. This new label allows for greater numbers, but its deepest focus is on change: pastors changing their minds about how ministry is to be done, and churches changing their organizational form in order to be free from size constraints. A metachurch pastor understands how a church can be structured so that its most fundamental spiritual and emotional support centers never become obsolete, no matter how large it becomes overall.[14]

George emphasizes the distinction between the 'megachurch' and the 'metachurch', by likening the former to an elephant and the latter to a field of mice, with each mouse representing 'a tiny, home-based cluster of believers'. The metachurch model is of great significance in regard to the reactivation of the nominal Christian, many of whom have been turned off by traditional models of ministry and styles of worship. In the traditional church the main entry points are the worship service and the Sunday School or Christian education programme. These are both based on church premises and operate on a 'come to us' philosophy of outreach. This is in contrast to the decentralized ministry model which operates on a New Testament mission strategy of outreach, sharing the good news and life in Christ in people's everyday world. It represents an incarnational, as distinct from an extractionist, approach to ministry. Each group of believers, which we have termed a 'community of witness', becomes a point of contact for the dechurched nominal and unchurched notional Christian. It provides an example of authentic Christian community with which the individual can identify, or presents a challenge which causes that person to become acutely aware of what he or she is missing by becoming inactive or isolationist.

The diagram on the following page illustrates the difference between the traditional, centralized approach to ministry and the decentralized approach of the metachurch, and emphasizes the multiplication of entry points into the corporate life of the church. In the metachurch illustration, the small groups (sometimes referred to as cell groups) are depicted as an 'X' representing the Roman numeral ten; this indicates the average number of persons in each small group. Notice also that the small groups are clustered in groups of five. Working with each cluster is a lay coach who provides support for the small group leaders, meeting

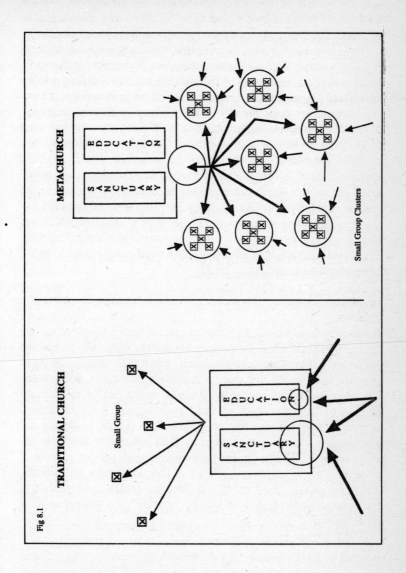

Fig 8.1

with the 'huddle' of five on a regular basis to provide support, problem solving and future planning, and to act as a two-way communication channel linking the church's leadership team with the group members.

The metachurch model ensures that the small group structure is regarded as the primary expression of the church's ministry in the world. Small groups are not viewed by the church leaders as appendages to the centralized programmes, but represent the church in dispersion, occupying strategic positions for day-to-day ministry in different contexts. Many efforts at developing an extensive small group ministry have come to grief due to lack of a clear purpose statement, a failure to select carefully, support adequately, or provide in-service training, and the absence of clear and short lines of communication linking the pastoral team and church board with the frontline of ministry manned by the clusters of small groups. Small groups have also suffered from the fact that they are often superimposed on an existing structure which was already proving burdensome for the committed members to maintain. The added expectation to get involved in a small group proved to be the straw which broke the camels back!

Develop contextualized approaches to witness in a variety of spheres of influence.

Nominality takes various forms and is present among people at varying distances from the life of the institutional church. With some people, the major obstacle preventing a reactivation of their faith, or their coming to personal faith for the first time, is principally attitudinal. With others, the major blocks are intellectual struggles or the lack of an adequate knowledge base on which to build their beliefs. A contextualized approach entails placing ourselves in their shoes in order to identify and address the issues which are influencing their lack of response to the life and message of the church. The following two grids provide a means of identifying where people are in terms of their knowledge and attitude, first to the message itself and then to the agent seeking to communicate the message, and indicate what kind of communication strategy needs to be developed.

Fig. 8.2. RELATING TO THE MESSAGE

KNOWLEDGE

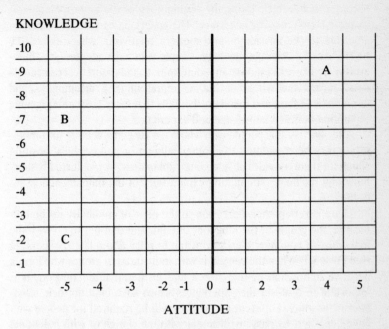

ATTITUDE

If you are seeking to relate the gospel to persons with little knowledge (A) who are eager to learn, clearly the strategy needs to be based on the provision of information together with opportunities to discuss its implications for living. Their curiosity has already been aroused and they are open to consider the gospel in relation to their deep-seated spiritual needs. However, in the case of those persons who have little information or are misinformed (B) and have a negative attitude, the approach will be one of exploding myths and misunderstandings, but in such a winsome way as not to alienate the person or group. It is no use winning the argument at the expense of losing the person.

People at position 'C' have considerable knowledge, which constitutes the principal reason for rejecting the content and implications of the message. In their case, time must be taken to discover the extent of their knowledge of the gospel and then to uncover reasons for their negative attitude. The obstacle may be intellectual, or the absence of spiritual insight, or a refusal to accept the implications of the message for personal living. Such persons require more opportunities for dialogue and the working through of a wide range of issues before the gospel becomes 'believable'. Using the terminology of the anthropologists, a 'paradigm shift' may be necessary. The gospel may no longer be believable due to the inroads of post-modern relativism, which denies the possibility of a cohesive ideology. People who have adopted post-modernism are likely to espouse an indeterminate and theoretical centrelessness, regard the whole of life as representing a meaningless and unpredictable flux, and maintain the view that there is an unbridgeable separation between knowledge and experience.

Alternatively, the people with whom we are endeavouring to communicate may be committed to another religion or philosophical position which for them provides an adequate explanation, or intellectually satisfying and spiritually stimulating exploration, of the fundamental issues of life.

There is yet another dimension to the issue of credibility in communicating the gospel of the kingdom of God, and that has to do with the individual or community endeavouring to relay and relate the message (see Fig 8.3.). When the contact is with individuals or groups who have a negative impression of the church and institutionalized religion, it is important to discover the experiences which have built up their resistance or hostility. Different approaches will be required for people who have been hurt by past involvement with the church or with individual Christians living inconsistent lives or displaying judgemental attitudes (A), than for the person whose opinions have been based on hearsay, without their having been personally involved in the church (B). The former will need the re-establishing of levels of trust, hopefully leading to the introduction of those who are 'once bitten, twice shy' to a small group of Christians with whom they can relate and who can provide an attractive example of authentic Christian community. 'B' may be even more open to accepting an invitation to attend a church which, by its spiritual vitality, relevant preaching and community life, breaks their negative stereotype.

Fig. 8.3 RELATING TO THE MESSENGER

KNOWLEDGE/EXPERIENCE

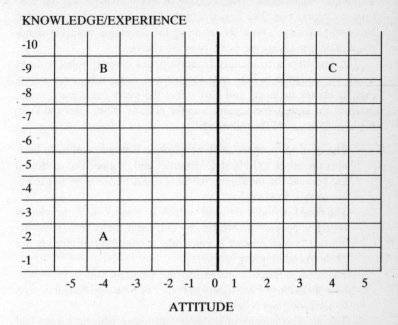

ATTITUDE

People occupying position 'C' on the grid, who already have an openness to any sincere Christian willing to communicate the message, primarily need the opportunity to get to know the witness more intimately and for the message to be reinforced through experience of the Christian community represented by the Christian advocate. Throughout this section we have noted the vital importance of strategically placed 'communities of witness', which are the very building blocks of the metachurch model.

Facilitate the realization of full ministry potential

During the past two decades there has been a plethora of books on every-member ministry. The case has been argued theologically, historically and from the standpoint of missiological urgency. The unresolved issue is how to make it happen. Established ministerial patterns have to be reconfigured in the face of resistance not only from some clergy who want to safeguard their own professional status, but from their congregations who insist on looking to the ordained minister to provide the many kinds of ministerial care to which they feel entitled. Lacking conflict management skills, many clergy have succumbed to pressure to fulfil traditional expectations. The breaking of this stereotype was our concern in Chapter 4 on 'The Renewal of the Church for the Restoration of Nominal Christians'. Now we return to the discussion from the standpoint of decentralizing the ministry of the church.

The first step is to identify leadership and ministry roles or tasks which are designed to deal with the issue of nominality, both among existing church members and also within the wider community, ie the inactive, the lapsed, the nominal and the notional. Such roles and tasks might include any of the following:

—The need to reconnect with people who have succumbed to business pressures and life-style priorities and dropped out of church life because the preaching, teaching and activities were not relevant to their working lives.
—The need to identify and establish contact with previously churched people who are moving into our ministry area, recognizing that if such contact is not made, a significant proportion are likely to end up going nowhere.
—The need to relate to and explain the Christian faith to those who have abandoned Christianity in favour of New Age teaching, cults or sects, or other religions.
—The need to engage in dialogue with those who no longer find Christianity intellectually tenable, because of scientific objections or the philosophical presuppositions of post-modernism.
—The need to establish 'communities of witness', providing a range of ministries readily available to peoples outside the church's normal sphere of influence, ie in distant residential communities, new housing developments, commercial centres, factories, etc.

These ministry challenges make us aware that the church must ensure that its members, already strategically placed to penetrate many of these segments of society—are suitable equipped for the task. They need to be clustered according to location and ministry opportunities so that a vision for outreach can be shared, resources identified and appropriate strategies developed. Such a mission-focused approach is a far cry from the concerns of those church leaders who are preoccupied with running their inward-looking, church-based programmes and in making constant appeals for volunteers to fill the vacant slots. Of course maintenance needs must be filled, but not at the expense of the congregation's mission outreach. And every existing programme must be re-examined periodically to ascertain whether the need for which it was created still exists, and to what extent the programme is providing an effective response.

In enlisting and empowering persons for ministry the inductive approach is usually to be preferred. This entails beginning to explore with the individual how they could be involved in ministry by starting with the interests, concerns and passions which God may already have laid upon their hearts. Secondly, the person's talents and gifting by the Holy Spirit need to be explored. This is usually best accomplished in a group setting where teaching is provided on the Holy Spirit's role in gifting every person to make a distinctive contribution to the internal and extended ministry of the Christian community. Then an indication is given of the variety and extent of the gifts of the Holy Spirit in order that the ascended Lord might continue his manifold ministries in his church and through his people to the world at large. Following that, the group members help one another to identify the particular gift which each member has, and pray for one another for the empowering of the Holy Spirit for service. The following provides an example of a form which might be used to facilitate the process of identifying a person's gifts and relating that gifting to a particular ministry area.

Fig. 8.4

WHAT IS GOD'S CALLING FOR THIS PERSON IN FURTHERING HIS KINGDOM?

1. What are this person's interests, concerns, or passion?
2. What are this person's talents and gifts?
3. What kind of temperament does this person have?
4. What previous experiences does this person have which may be of relevance for Christian ministry?
5. What is this person's level of spiritual maturity?
6. What is this person's time availability?
7. What tasks seem most appropriate for this individual, considering the above information?

Having assessed the above information, then match the profile with the roles or tasks which seem appropriate to the individuals interests, gifts and availability.

Fig. 8.5
JOB DESCRIPTION

1. Ministry description
2. Desired interest and motivation
3. Spiritual gifts/talents required
4. Temperament best suited
5. Level of spiritual maturity
6. Experience required/desired
7. Time needed weekly/monthly
8. Goals to be pursued
9. Ongoing support and accountability
10. Resources provided (human/material)

Some churches may wish to develop pro formas to process the deployment of church members in spheres of ministry according to God's gifts and calling. In other situations, such procedures would be regarded as intimidating or 'worldly' and therefore their use will be counter-productive. At least the issues listed need to be considered in placing or recognizing anyone in ministry, no matter whether the process is handled in an organized or informal manner.

It is sometimes advisable to provide two or three possibilities for the person being interviewed to consider. They are not then restricted to a 'Yes/No' decision but can compare options. Furthermore, it needs to be emphasized that the person should seek the guidance of God in making their decision. They are not saying 'Yes' to the church leader conducting the interview, but rather appreciating that the process is designed to help them discern the voice of God who is the one to whom they must respond in accepting any call to ministry.

Relate the circumference to the centre

By multiplying communities of witness the church creates outposts—or rather 'forward positions'—of the kingdom of God. The issue we now address is how these many small groups relate to the centre or base of operations. In the traditional model there were two points of entry, the worship service and, in the US, the Christian education programme; in the UK it is through a range of group activities. A key consideration is to ensure that the spiritual vitality present in the 'forward positions' is also in evidence at the operational base. If the centre lacks spiritual vitality and social relevance, the groups will be in danger of degenerating into protest groups with the risk that they will eventually dissociate themselves completely from the centre.

The purpose of the centre is not to frustrate initiatives on the front line, but to provide training and support for the people involved in those initiatives, to celebrate victories, to care for casualties and provide additional resources to meet the needs of people beyond the reach of church-based programmes who are being spiritually reactivated. Fig. 8.6 indicates the multiple entry points for people who have been drawn into a community of witness.

When the small group ministry has been developed to the point where the groups are functioning effectively as access points for nominal Christians, the church will need to provide alternative ways of relating to and being incorporated into the wider Christian community. The external constituency which has become distanced and in danger of becoming substantially reduced, is now being reactivated and enlarged.

The worship service develops a heightened sense of celebration as new people come who have already had their curiosity aroused or been restored to a vital faith within the context of the small groups. The worship time represents a gathering together of the teams which have been working in scattered and diverse situations for the cause of the gospel during the week. The members come together to rejoice at all that God is doing and to refocus their vision. It is also a time of reaping as the gospel is proclaimed in word and sacrament and people contacted through the 'communities of witness' are invited to make their public response in context of the great congregation.

People who have experienced an uplifting and challenging time of celebration are then likely to invite friends to accompany them on a future occasion. Not every newcomer will come via the cell group into the Sunday worship. There will need to be careful monitoring of the channels by which people are being introduced to the life of the church. Those who begin with the worship service need to be in a relational group within the first six weeks, otherwise they will remain on the fringes of the churches, a potential nominality problem in the making! The risk is lessened when the inviters are themselves in a small group which is open to new people, for they will then be able to invite friends to the group meeting as well as the worship service.

254 / *Winning Them Back*

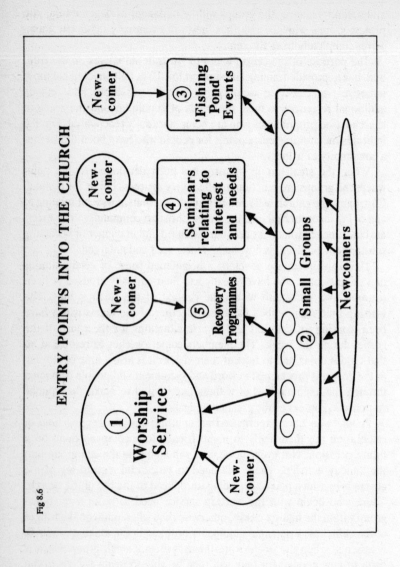

Fig 8.6

Such dynamics are not restricted to churches of megachurch proportions; they can be experienced by any size of church which has developed a number of 'communities of witness' which are functioning effectively as feeder cells. The point is that the metachurch model developed by Carl George removes many of the growth restrictions in traditional structures. In the case of churches which have grown so rapidly through this pattern of decentralized ministry that they have outgrown their sanctuary seating limits, celebration events will have to be held less frequently, possibly utilizing hired facilities.

In addition to hosting celebration worship services and music concerts, the church-based programmes and special events will also provide a variety of contact opportunities to supplement the work of the community-based small groups. These may be widely publicized social programmes and events of a recreational, entertainment or sporting nature. They provide opportunities for casual witness and ministry and serve as 'fishing ponds' in which new people can be invited to participate in a small group composed of people they previously met at the one-off event.

If the church is able to provide a gymnasium or sports field, or has access to a community facility, then people can become involved on a more regular basis in line with their sporting interests. Such relaxed, non-threatening contexts provide opportunities for friendships to be forged.

Another function provided by the 'centre' is to run seminars relating to the interests and needs of church members and the wider community. Seminars might be held on such diverse topics as : managing the family finances, potty training of toddlers, caring for elderly relatives, helping young children to know God, the questions about life teenagers are facing, financial planning for retirement, etc. Church leaders will learn what seminar topics to offer by keeping their ear to the ground to discover the questions people are asking and the pressing issues they are facing.

Yet another function of the centre is to operate a range of recovery programmes for hurting people. Sometimes such persons can be adequately cared for in the regular small groups. In other instances people with deep-seated problems will need specialist care. The group leaders must recognize the limitations of the group and be able to decide when problem people need to be referred to a support or recovery group led by an expert counsellor. They may be suffering acute depression, the results of sexual abuse during childhood, domestic violence, drug dependency, etc. If left in the regular small group environment the unmet needs of these people may derail the entire group. It is better if they can be part of a recovery programme consisting of people who have undergone similar experiences with whom they can relate. The last centralized function to be mentioned here is the provision of support and training for the leaders who are operating in the communities of witness and other programme areas. This is the concern of our next section.

Grow leadership able to sustain the growth momentum

A leader has been described as someone at least one step ahead of the rest. There is danger that, in the course of training, the leader moves too far ahead too quickly so that the trainee loses contact. In order to avoid people being trained out of a situation, rather than equipped for it, two educational principles need to be observed. One is 'learn on a need-to-know basis', and the other is 'learn a little, practise a lot'. When too much teaching is given up-front, some people are so intimidated by the amount they are supposed to know before they begin to function that they withdraw from the programme. The other response is to become so enamoured of the theory that those who qualify are no longer in touch with the people they are supposed to lead.

The emphasis in the metachurch model is placed on apprenticeship learning beginning with observation and then moving on to participation/reflection. This seems to be much closer to our Lord's discipling model as recorded in the Gospels. Each small group has a leader-in-training alongside the more experienced leader, who serves as coach to the novice. The leader is in a mentoring relationship with the trainees and gives them opportunities for leadership according to their level of spiritual maturity and technical competence.

The problem with this model, in cases where it constitutes the only method of training, is that the novice is likely to reproduce many of the mistakes, and be bound by the limitations, of the group leader. It therefore needs to be supplemented by training beyond the group context. Carl George argues the need for 'huddles' consisting of the leaders of five groups, with a leader responsible for each group cluster. He designates the cluster leader as an 'L', that is, a leader of fifty, whereas the cell group leader is an 'X', ie a leader of ten people. These leaders of group leaders will have previously proved themselves as small group leaders, thereby gaining credibility. The trainee leaders will also be invited to share alongside the group leaders. Carl George describes what happens in the huddle:

> Under the L's direction and diagnostic coaching, the X's report their activities celebrate their successes, identify their problems. They plan; they propose solutions to difficulties; they hold each other accountable; they exhort one another; and they pray together. This L-X team models the quality of caring desired in each X-led group.[15]

Huddles also provide an effective two-way communication channel to keep the senior leadership in touch with developments at the front line and enable the leadership to communicate church-wide visions and concerns.

As ministry expands among the people of God operating in the communities of witness, there will be an urgent need for ministerial training to be made widely available at that level. Some of this will be provided by the churches themselves but, in addition, there will be a need for a range of courses in pastoral care, evangelism and group dynamics as well as the more traditional biblical and theological disciplines. Here is a new market for seminaries which have educators on their faculties who can relate to this context and educational philosophy.

As increasing numbers of people become involved in ministry, the range of activities expands and their inter-relationship becomes increasingly complex, the senior leadership will need further in-service training in order to facilitate this creativity, while ensuring cohesion and quality control.

CONCLUSION

In the course of this book we have attempted to draw attention to the nominality problem by tracing its extent and complexity. We have described the ways in which sources in the church, society and the individual contribute and interact in generating the nominality syndrome. We have reviewed the three main societal factors of urbanization, secularization and relativist religious pluralism. The comprehensive nature of the challenge which nominality represents could stimulate a comprehensive transformation of the church, as it first endeavours to set its own house in order and then reaches out in its mission of restoring the lapsed, reactivating the faith of the nominal, bringing the notional to active faith for the first time, and then extending its outreach to those who do not as yet identify at all with the Christian message or relate to any community of believers. We should not be surprised that the challenge appears to be totally beyond our human resources. Mission is always like that, whether it be a ministry of restoration or salvation.

From the outset, Christ has made it clear that the church must not attempt to move forward in its own strength, but seek the anointing and filling of the Holy Spirit. Power for ministry is dependent upon the forging of an intimate relationship with the Lord as a vital prerequisite. Grasping for power without a deeply grounded experience of communion with God and reliance upon him, may be spectacular in the short-term but will be devastating in its long term consequences. There will be no significant restoration of 'nominal Christians' apart from the reproduction of 'normative Christians', understood not as finished products, but as persons who are themselves growing up in the unity of the faith and the knowledge of the Son of God, to maturity, to the measure of the full stature of Christ (Eph 4:13).

NOTES

1. The polls conducted by Barna Research indicate that only 20 per cent of the unchurched have much confidence in Christian churches; only 39 per cent believe the churches to be relevant (strongly agree—10%; agree somewhat—10%); and only 13 per cent would consider being part of a local church. See George Barna, *What Americans Believe* (Regal Books; Ventura, 1991), pp 163, 187.
2. Kennon L. Callahan, *Effective Church Leadership* (Harper and Row; San Francisco, 1990), pp 19-20
3. Win and Charles Arn, in *A New Vision for the Sunday School*, provide graphs which record the trends from 1915 to 1981. Their data is reproduced in Ralph W. Neighbour, Jr, *Where Do We Go From Here?* (Touch Publications; Houston, 1990), p 17.
4. Ralph W. Neighbour, Jr, *Where Do We Go From Here?* See pp 47-57, which provide the basis for this series of questions.
5. Callahan, op cit, p 30.
6. See Chapter 5, '*The Protestant Mindset and Urban Reality*', p 151.
7. George Barna, *What Americans Believe*, pp 152-158.
8. Ibid, p 68.
9. Peter Brierley, '*Christian' England* (MARC Europe; London, 1991), pp 30, 31, 64, 128.
10. The latest Barna research into churchgoing trends in the United States indicates an upturn from 43%-45% in the period 1986-90 to a high of 49%.

Whether this constitutes a change or is no more than a blip only time will tell. (See Barna, op cit, p 236).

11. Callahan, op cit, pp 23-24.
12. Doug Murren, *The Baby Boomerang* (Regal Books; Ventura, 1991), p 37; Lyle E. Schaller, *It's a Different World* (Abingdon Press; Nashville, 1987), pp 24-28.
13. Lyle E. Schaller, *The Multiple Staff and the Large Church* (Abingdon Press; Nashville, 1980), pp 28-44.
14. Carl George, *Prepare Your Church for the Future* (Fleming H. Revell; New York, 1991), pp 51-52.
15. Ibid, pp 139-140.

NOMINAL CHRISTIANS IN THE 1990s

by Peter Brierley

CONTENTS

NOMINAL CHRISTIANS IN THE 1990s

Introduction

The BA Sociology of Religion student I was teaching protested, 'But you can't have a nominal Christian. It's a contradiction in terms.' Doubtless very true, but that there are huge numbers of nominal Christians is also unfortunately undoubtedly true. And Ralph Winter, founder of the US School for World Mission, has shown there are more nominal Christians in Europe than in the rest of the world put together.[1]

The genesis of this paper has been the research that Eddie Gibbs has initiated which is described in this book *Winning Them Back*[2]. A detailed analysis of this survey is given below. Before we come to that, however, it is worth looking at other material on the same subject so that this study across the western world can be set in the context of what is actually happening in one part of the world.

Definitions

Eddie Gibbs gives detailed attention to the definition of nominality, and describes commitment to the local church in six groups—active regular, passive regular, occasional, lapsed, nominal and notional.[3] In this paper, the last two terms are defined as in the English Church Census Report *'Christian' England*, where nominal Christians are taken as 'church members who do not regularly attend church' and notional Christians are 'those who would say they were Christian but are neither church members nor regular churchgoers'.[4] This definition of nominality accords with that used by Australian researchers.[5] A more detailed definition by Dr David Barrett is given later in Section C.

A. Nominality in Europe

Great Britain

On these definitions, *'Christian' England* shows that in 1990 8% of the population of Great Britain (England, Wales and Scotland) were nominal Christians and 47% were notional. In 1980, using a similar analysis given in detail in *Church Nominalism: the Plague of the Twentieth Century?*[6], the percentages were 9% nominal and 47% notional. In other words, there was a small decrease of nominal Christians in Britain during the 1980s, but the proportion of notional Christians remained the same.

Church Nominalism explores some of the beliefs of nominal and notional Christians. Broadly speaking, they believe in God, believe that Jesus was at least an important man, view the Bible as an 'inspired' book (in the sense that Shakespeare is sometimes described as 'inspired'), want their children to be taught religious education (because of its ethics and moral values), and will certainly have thought about life after death even if they do not believe in it. What is missing from such a 'theology' is the absence of any belief in the Holy Spirit as a person who can indwell people, renewing and sanctifying them and bringing them ever more towards a likeness of Jesus Christ. If they are asked about the Holy Spirit, the most some will say is that 'it is a force for good', the word 'good' reflecting the word 'Holy'. The Scripture, 'they will hold to the outward form of our religion, but reject its real power' (2 Tim 3:5 *GNB*) summarizes their position precisely.

Austria

The *Austrian Christian Handbook*[7] gives similar figures. In 1990 13½% of the population were nominal Christians and 53½% were notional. In 1980 the percentages were 9½% and 55½% respectively, showing that in Austria's situation the amount of nominal Christianity has increased in the 1980s but there was a slight decrease in notional Christianity. An increasing secularization probably accounts for the decrease in notionalism. That more and more Roman Catholic church members are attending mass less and less accounts for the increase in nominality.

Other European countries
The religious attitude or aptitude of a population is explained in *'Christian' England* in five groups, two of which are nominal Christians and notional Christians. The other three are:

1. *New Christians*, that is, those who attend church regularly but are not yet church members. They may be just feeling their way in coming to church for the first time (and may not yet be Christian) or they may be lapsed attenders returning.
2. *Normal Christians*, who are both regular attenders and church members. Church membership means something different to different denominations. For Anglicans it is usually taken as those on the Electoral Roll. Those receiving adult baptism in a Baptist church usually become church members at the same time. In some Pentecostal churches, the ability to speak in tongues is required for membership. For Reformed and Roman Catholic churches, however, the concept of membership is different—essentially referring to all their baptized community. In order for their figures to have a similar meaning as for other churches, their numbers are reduced, differently country by country, but explained in the relevant *Christian Handbook*.
3. *Non-Christian people* are neither churchgoers nor church members and, if asked, would not call themselves Christian. They are not necessarily non-religious, however. Many will be Muslims, Hindus, Sikhs or members of other non-Christian religions, and others will be members of a non-Trinitarian church such as Jehovah's Witnesses, Mormons (Church of Jesus Christ of Latter Day Saints), Christadelphians and such like. The remainder will be agnostics, atheists and others who simply say they are not religious.

It is possible to work out the percentages of these five groups for those countries in Europe for which a *Christian Handbook* has been published. These handbooks collect and analyse each country's church data in the same way and, particularly, seek to get details of all the different denominational groups within a country, the large majority of which are usually very small. Whilst insignificant by themselves, collectively they can make up several percentage points in terms of church membership of a population. Because of this common basis in compilation, reasonable comparisons can be made across the countries.

The figures are given in Table 1 overleaf. A number of assumptions have had to be made, however. The Spanish[8] figures assume the same attendance/community ratio as in Austria. The percentage going to church in Denmark[9] is assumed to be the same in 1980 and 1990 as it was in 1985. In Denmark, Finland[10] and Norway[11], it is assumed that all Free Church members attend church and only they attend these churches. In 1990 figures have to be estimated throughout for The Netherlands[12]. The attendance/membership ratio in The Netherlands and in French-speaking Switzerland[13] is assumed to be the same as in France[14], denomination by denomination. In Northern Ireland[15] and the Republic of Ireland[15], attendance/membership proportions are assumed as in England, with the Roman Catholic percentage being doubled. New Christians in Northern Ireland are assumed to have the same new/attenders ratio as in England in 1990, and half that in 1980. For the Republic the ratio is assumed to be similar to another major Roman Catholic country, Austria. The results are given below:

Table 1: Religious structure of various countries in 1980 and 1990

	New		Normal		Nominal		Notional		Non-Christian		Total Population
	1980 %	1990 %	1980 %	1990 %	1980 %	1990 %	1980 %	1990 %	1980 %	1990 %	1990 millions
Austria	½	½	26½	21½	9½	13½	55½	53½	8	11	7.6
France	½	½	12½	12½	9½	8½	63½	63½	14	15	55.4
French-speaking Switzerland	½	½	16½	14½	9½	8½	68½	60½	5	16	1.5
Spain	0	0	19	20	8	4	51	45	22	31	40.1
Denmark	0	0	5	5	20	18	65	68	10	9	5.1
Finland	0	0	5	5	28	23	60	63	7	9	5.0
Norway	0	0	5	5	26	27	60	54	9	14	4.2
The Netherlands	1	1	28	27	29	23	5	8	37	41	15.2
Great Britain	3	1	8	9	9	8	47	47	33	35	56.0
Northern Ireland	6½	4½	42½	40½	20½	15½	20½	20½	10	19	1.6
Republic of Ireland	1	1	63	50	22	31	12	15	2	3	3.5
Total all these countries	1	½	15	14½	12	10	50	49	22	26	195.2

This table is very interesting in what is reveals. In the traditional Roman Catholic countries (Austria, France, The Netherlands, French-speaking

Switzerland, Spain and the Republic of Ireland) the proportion of new Christians in the churches is minimal, and most of these are likely to be in the rapidly expanding Protestant churches, a feature of all these countries. In Scandinavia the numbers of new Christians are virtually zero, reflecting the very high proportion who are baptized as church members in these countries. In the Protestant countries of Great Britain and Northern Ireland, the numbers are slightly higher, but noticeably falling in both Great Britain and Northern Ireland—the churches in these countries are attracting fewer people. How improve the image?

The high churchgoing in Roman Catholic countries is seen in the large numbers in the 'Normal' columns, and the low church attendance in Scandinavia is also clearly seen. The experience of Great Britain and Northern Ireland is very different here. Both parts of Ireland have exceptionally high proportions of their population attending church regularly (45% and 51% North and Republic respectively in 1990), and Great Britain shows itself in the table to be much like Scandinavia— much smaller numbers of regular churchgoers. This reflects the problem of nominality and notionalism.

The proportions of nominal Christians are relatively low in Roman Catholic countries (because so many Catholics still attend mass), though in The Netherlands and the two Irelands the nominal proportions are high, showing the disaffection with the Catholic church and some of its policies in these countries—the issues of family planning and abortion are especially strong in both. There are many more nominal Christians in the Scandinavian countries. The direction of change is interesting also. Nominality is increasing in Austria and the Republic of Ireland (quite substantially in both), and slightly in Norway (within the margins of error in the figures). But nominality is declining elsewhere, in both Roman Catholic and Protestant countries. It is declining sharply in Finland, The Netherlands, Spain and Northern Ireland.

Notional Christianity is substantial from this table. Overall, half the population in these countries, and in Scandinavia, France and French-speaking Switzerland substantially more than half are notional Christians. It is only much smaller in The Netherlands, where the non-Christian group is huge. Notionalism is static or declining across these countries, except for small increases in Denmark, Finland, The Netherlands and the Republic of Ireland.

The non-Christians account for a quarter of the population on average in these countries, a figure which varies widely, however. For all except Spain, The Netherlands and Great Britain, the percentage is less that 20%. In the Republic of Ireland it is exceptionally low at 3% in 1990. But, except for Denmark, the percentage is increasing. In French-speaking Switzerland, Spain, Norway and Northern Ireland the percentage has increased very markedly in the 1980s. (It should be noted that Jehovah's Witnesses, Mormons and so on would not accept the description 'non-Christian' though they would 'non-Trinitarian'.)

What then in essence does this table tell us? That nominal Christians are a significant part of the population in these countries, and in some countries where either baptismal policy or disillusionment is high, the figures are substantial—about a quarter of the population. Generally though, nominality is declining, but declining slowly, suggesting that it is (literally) dying out gradually. Studies in England suggest that many of the nominal Christians are older Christians (over 45 in this context). The previous Bishop of Southwark once remarked, 'We have moved from where Christianity is culture to where Christianity is choice', and this statement includes a covert age-analysis, for those to whom Christianity is culture tend to be over 45 and those for whom Christianity is choice are largely under 45. What is happening is that the older Christians for whom Christianity is culture, who include many nominal Christians, are declining slowly as they are 'promoted to glory' as the Salvation Army puts it.

Table 1 thus shows a slowly declining nominality, a substantial but static notionalism, a decline in basic church attendance (partly because churches are less attractive to people), and an increasing but substantial number of non-Christians. We are becoming more secular.

But this analysis is at best highly superficial. Table 1 tells us what is happening but not really *why* it is happening. Partly this is because so little data is available. It may also be that the categories used are too all-embracing. Peter Kuzmic, in an excellent paper 'Christian Mission in Europe'[16] recalls the 'Nominalism Today' workshop held at the Lausanne II Congress in Manila in 1989, where four types of nominality were suggested: the 'ethnic-religious identity' nominal, the second generation nominal, the ritualistic nominal, and the syncretistic nominal. Some of these descriptions would overlap with the notional Christians. Peter Kuzmic indicates that in Europe:

> all four types of nominals exist and should become priority concern for intentional and comprehensive programmes of evangelization. Awakening the religiously indifferent and

those who have found false security in a superficially sacra-
mentalistic, cultural and/or nationalistic and yet only nominal
Christianity is a very complex challenge. Evangelism in
Europe must also take into account large numbers of those
who have been 'disappointed by Christianity or have remained
at a level of a merely psychological piety or legal morality'.[17]

What is hidden in this analysis is the theological component. What are
the beliefs of nominal and notional Christians now? Are they changing?
Has the wide sweep of the New Age Movement made substantial
inroads into people's basic beliefs? Why are the churches becoming less
attractive? It was to answer such questions as these that Eddie Gibbs
initiated his survey, and to this we must now turn.

B. Nominality across the western world

Methodology

Eddie Gibbs asked a few ministers of relatively large churches in different countries if they would help him with his nominality study. The
sample is therefore not random, but the instructions given to each
church asked them to interview those who had not been in church for at
least a year. Altogether 308 completed questionnaires were returned
from churches in Australia, England, Scotland and the United States.

The questionnaire asked basic questions of age, gender, marital
status, the environment in which people were born and where they now
lived, and for how long, and how much they had moved. It also asked
about occupation (to get social class) and education. It then moved on to
church commitment, and frequency of attendance, or how long since
they attended, looking at the principal reasons for stopping going. It
looked in some depth at their belief, and their religious actions and
practices outside church attendance, and finally asked a few straightfor-
ward questions on Bible content. A copy of the questionnaire is available from the Christian Research Association in London.

The sample

The questionnaires were completed evenly by gender—49% men and
51% women, reflecting the population proportions, with slightly more
men in the United States, and slightly fewer in Australia, but not
significantly so.

Just under one third (31%) of the forms were completed in Scotland, with a further quarter (25%) in England, just over a quarter (28%) in Australia, and the remaining one in six (16%) in the United States. Just over half (56%) therefore are directly British. Only 4% of the sample were over 75 years of age, too few to form a separate category, so they have been combined with those aged 66-75. Whilst the average age was 44, this did vary significantly across the countries as Table 2 shows.

Table 2: Age of respondent by country of residence

Age	18-25 %	26-35 %	36-45 %	46-55 %	56-65 %	Over 65 %	Total (=100%)	Average age
Scotland	7	18	19	25	12	19	88	48
Australia	17	28	19	18	12	6	83	40
England	12	22	24	18	9	15	76	44
USA	10	28	17	17	11	15	46	45
All countries	12	23	20	20	11	14	293	44

Table 2 shows that the sample was rather younger in Australia and rather older in Scotland, and this will need to be borne in mind when analysing by age. But all countries covered all ages, enabling comparisons to be made across each.

Only 2% of those interviewed were separated, too few to justify separate analysis, so these have been added to the 5% who were divorced. 6% of the sample were widowed, 17% were single, and the remaining 70% were married. These figures did not vary significantly by country, suggesting perhaps that life experiences of marriage, break-up and widowhood are similar across the western world in the early 1990s.

The sample showed a movement towards city life in the adult years: 36% were raised in a city, but 46% now lived in one. On the other hand, 39% were born in a rural area or village, and 36% still lived in such. It was those in towns who changed: 25% were born there, but only 18% now lived in one. There was, however, a fairly heavy inbuilt stability, as only 43% of the sample had changed the type of environment in which they now lived from where they had been raised. Of this 43%, 16% had moved towards a greater urban life, and 27% towards a more rural life. This interesting pattern, at divergence with so many population trends across the world, is mainly because in Britain many people are moving out of the city into more rural, or at least commuter rural, areas. The detailed figures are given in Table 3 below.

Table 3: The environment in which people were raised and now live

Where now living	Where raised				All areas
	Rural area %	Village %	Town %	City %	
Rural area	10	1	1	1	13
Village	6	8	7	2	23
Town	3	1	10	4	18
City	4	6	7	29	46
All areas	23	16	25	36	287 (=100%)

The sample thus has a clear dominance of urban living with almost half now living in a city, and almost two-thirds (64%) living in either a town or a city. A town in this context was defined as having a population of at least 3,000 people, and a city as at least 100,000 people.

Respondents had moved to their present location on average 14 years ago, suggesting stability for church involvement. One-third (31%) moved up to five years ago, 11% 6-10 years ago, 21% 11-20 years ago, and 37% over 20 years ago. Thus roughly one-third of people had been in their present house for up to five years, one-third 6-20 years, and one-third longer.

How many times had people moved their place of residence more then 3 miles or 5 kilometres? On average four times. It was slightly less in the United States (three times) and slightly more in Australia (five times). There was however a solid core of people who had moved many times—one-fifth (20%) had moved at least seven times, and one-twelfth (8%) had moved more than ten times.

Church involvement for such people is therefore difficult, since they have a relatively short time to get known. How do churches really spot newcomers? What kind of incorporation procedures does this suggest they need? One church in Surrey has a system whereby a member of the congregation calls within one month of anyone moving into their town (identified as the 'For Sale' notice is changed to 'Sold'). I asked the minister if it had any effect. 'Rather!', he replied, 'We are getting so many newcomers we are having to build an extension to accommodate them all!' Details of movements are given in Table 4.

Table 4: Number of times people have significantly changed residence by country of residence

	Number of times changed residence					Total (=100%)	Average number
	None %	1-3 %	4-6 %	7-10 %	More than 10 times %		
United States	20	43	24	7	6	46	3.4
Scotland	16	36	36	9	3	91	3.7
England	13	41	23	11	12	73	4.4
Australia	11	26	33	19	11	82	5.1
All Countries	14	36	30	12	8	292	4.2

The amount of movement suggested by this study is considerable, and is perhaps a key finding in its implications for church life and for evangelism.

Asking information about occupation in order to determine social class did not work well in an international context. Occupation skill levels vary, and therefore coding on a British occupational norm is invalid. In any case, the figures did not vary significantly by country, though the United States respondents had slightly fewer professionals than the others. The results did reflect the traditional imbalance between the different social groups. Working class people were completely misrepresented according to population proportions. Only one unskilled person was interviewed and only 23 partly skilled. Eight people (3%) simply stated they were retired without giving their former occupation. Just over one-third of the sample (35%) were professionals, just under a quarter (23%) were intermediate and almost a third (31%) were skilled. These results confirm the bias the church has towards the middle and more professional classes, and how we reach others outside these groups will not be discerned from these results. An altogether different study is needed to ascertain the aspiration beliefs and religious practices of those who are partly skilled or unskilled. The question was asked of both partners if married, but the results were similar—a slightly smaller proportion of professional wives and rather more in the skilled category.

Education beyond the Secondary or High School level had been undertaken by nearly two-thirds (63%) of respondents. 3% had a postgraduate qualification, 30% had graduated from university, 30% had been to a technical college or studied at night school, and the remaining 37% had done none of these. There were rather more amongst the Scottish and American respondents who had no further qualifications, balanced by rather fewer English and Australian. These results confirm the answers given to the occupation question and show that those involved with the church tend to have more academic qualifications then others. Is intelligence a prior requirement for church commitment?! These findings are not unexpected, but they are disturbing. Insofar as this study looks at those who have left the church it also means that some of the dissenters, as it were, are those with good brains who presumably therefore drift away for intellectual as well as emotional or other reasons.

The answers given to the so-called 'control' questions highlight the importance of forming personal relationships with people as quickly as possible, communicating a reasoned faith, and being aware that the audience being reached is only one part of the entire population. These findings may not be revolutionary, but they are important. They form the basis of the need to look at respondent's church commitment, which now follows.

Church commitment

A little under a third (31%) of respondents declared themselves to be 'a strongly committed Christian', and almost half (49%) indicated that they were 'a Christian, but not very committed'. One person in eight in the sample (12%) was uncertain whether they were a Christian or not. One person in 25 (4%) said they were 'no longer a Christian' and a similar proportion (4%) indicated that they 'never have been a Christian'. For analysis purposes these last two groups have been added together because their numbers are too small otherwise. These proportions did not vary significantly across the four countries, suggesting that the sampling instructions were sufficiently explicit. Slightly more Americans indicated they were not very committed Christians, rather than unsure, and rather more of the English declared they were no longer Christian rather then uncommitted.

How often did respondents attend church? On average just a little less than once a fortnight, 20 times a year. The Australians, Scots and Americans were less (17, 19 and 19 times respectively) and the English more (26 times), but these did not vary significantly by country. Altogether three in every seven (42%) said they never went to church, one-and-a-half in seven (21%) said they attended only on special occasions, one in seven reckoned on going once or twice a month, and the remaining one-and-a-half in seven would go weekly. As the average figures indicate, the Americans were weak on weekly attendance, the English stronger. Americans tended to go just once or twice a month. What did vary, of course, was churchgoing frequency by commitment to Christianity, and this is given in Table 5 below.

Table 5: Churchgoing by Christian commitment

Christian commitment	Frequency of church attendance				Total (=100%)	Average per year
	Weekly %	Once/twice a month %	Only special occasions %	Never %		
Strong	77	19	1	3	92	43
Weak	13	27	55	5	150	13
Unsure	3	9	70	18	33	5
No longer/never	—	—	61	39	23	1
Overall	31	20	40	9	298	20

This is a fascinating table. It shows that even the strongly committed Christian reckons on attending church weekly only three-quarters (77%) of the time, and 4%, or one person in twenty-five, never attend or do so only on special occasions! Could this be incipient nominality? That some strongly committed Christians should in current practice attend church so infrequently suggests something is wrong. This table gives no answers to the obvious question 'What?' but these figures do suggest the importance of measuring the regularity of church attendance.

Even more astonishing are those labelled 'not very' in Table 5, who agree they are Christian even if not very committed. That tentative commitment is extremely weak—half only go to church on special occasions (55%), and one in twenty (5%) never go at all. That doesn't say much for the strength of a weak commitment, and the figures again underline the usefulness of looking at church attendance frequency.

Those who are not sure if they are or are not Christians, the 'not sure' in Table 5, do not reckon on going to church except on special occasions for nearly three-quarters of them (70%), and one in six (18%) never go. One in eight (12%) go either weekly or once or twice a month.

As might be expected, those who are no longer Christians, or who have never been Christians, rarely go to church. But three in five (61%) still reckon on going on special occasions. In other words, those outside the church still come sometimes, and the festivals are therefore extremely important events for nominal people. This is the reverse of the nominality described above; those outside come occasionally, whereas those inside do not always go regularly. This finding mirrors that obtained in the *Lifestyle Survey* of the Church of Scotland[18] and in the *Scottish Church and Social Concerns Survey*[19], both of which analysed church attendance patterns for church and non-church members. Both found that non-church members would reckon on attending church: nine times a year and five times a year respectively.

Table 5 is an important table for the study of nominality. It throws up the question, 'What really is Christian commitment?' and it also suggests that looking at churchgoing regularity can be an important measure of it, though this does not give any indication of causation. The correlation between frequency and commitment is -0.58, and future tables focus on frequency of attendance as a main variable rather then commitment (one is measurable, the other is not).

Stopping attending church

Were there times in the lives of respondents when they had stopped going to church for at least a year and then started attending again? For over half the answer was 'YES' (55%), and 2% of these had not yet reached a place when they had started to attend again (these are omitted in the answers to relevant questions). For the remainder, 45%, they continued to attend church. How do these answers vary by churchgoing frequency? Table 6 gives the answer.

Table 6: Tendency to stop going to church by frequency of attendance

Ever stopped attending?	Frequency of church attendance				Total (=100%)	Average per year
	Weekly %	Once/twice a month %	Only special occasions %	Never %		
YES	26	22	44	8	158	18
NO	37	19	35	9	136	23
Both groups	31	20	40	9	294	20

Those who have left and subsequently returned tend to go to church slightly less now then those who have never left. The difference is however not great, though those who have left and returned are less likely to attend every week, and more likely to go only on special occasions. In other words, once the commitment is broken it is difficult to recover it. Two-thirds (66%) of those who have returned attend only once or twice a month or on special occasions, against 54% of those who have never left. These differences are small, though significant. What in some ways is more alarming in both Table 6 and Table 5, is just how much churchgoing takes place outside regular weekly attendance. Three in every five (60%) attend less frequently then once a week. This reinforces the earlier finding of the importance of measuring church-going regularity, but it also indicates that nominality (as reflected in church attendance) is very much bound up with the question of commit-ment, as already noted.

Did people stay away from church for as long as a year more than once? Yes, some did, in fact one person in five (19%), and one person in twenty-five (4%) stayed away three times or more. The average number of times away was 1.2, a figure which varied across the different coun-tries. Scotland was lowest at 1.1, followed by Australia at 1.2, England at 1.3 and the United States at 1.4. This perhaps supports the finding above that Americans tend to go to church weekly less than the other coun-tries, and they tend to stop going more. Is there again a link between regular weekly attendance and sustained commitment?

How old were those respondents who stopped attending for a period, when they stopped? They ranged from 1 year old to 68 years of age, with an average of 24, the Australians being a little younger at 22 on average and the Americans a little older at 26 years. But these averages are misleading because of a small number at higher ages which extends the average. The modal range is 15-19 when 36% leave, and the median age (the age below which 50% have left, and 50% leave above it) is 19.8 years, and it is frightening to think that half of those who leave the church do so before the age of 20. The median age for Australians is 18.6 years, for the English 19.0, for the Scots 20.8, and for the Americans 22.1 years.

For those who twice stopped going, the average age they stopped the second time was 30 years of age, and for the half dozen who had tried three times, the third time they gave up was at an average age of 34 years. There is a clear progression here, as one would expect.

The detailed age breakdowns for these three groups is given in Table 7 and the data for those leaving church for the first time illustrated in Figure 1.

Table 7: Age at which respondents stopped attending church

Total	Under 10 %	10-14 %	15-19 %	20-24 %	25-29 %	30-34 %	35-39 %	40-49 %	50-59 %	60 or over %	(=100%)
First time	3	12	35	18	7	9	2	6	5	3	152
Second time	0	7	3	28	21	10	18	7	3	3	29
Third time	0	0	16	0	17	17	17	33	0	0	6

Fig 1: Age at which respondents stopped attending church

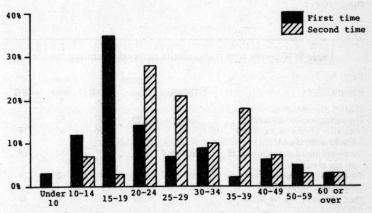

How long were those who left the church away from it? The question asked respondents to indicate if they stopped attending church 'for one or more years', but in fact the average length of time away from the church was eight years. Lose a person, and you lose them for a long time! The proportions for different lengths are given in Table 8.

Table 8: Number of years absent from the church

Time	Percentage
1 or 2 years	20%
3-5 years	33%
6-10 years	25%
11-15 years	9%
16-20 years	8%
Over 20 years	5%

Table 8 shows that half of those who leave the church return within five years, but one person in 8 (13%) does not come back until after at least sixteen years. The English Church Census found that a curious phenomenon occurred in the 1980s. There was an upsurge in women aged 45 and over coming into the church[20]; could this reflect a group of women (over 40,000) who had left disillusioned perhaps in the 1960s?

It is important to identify why people cease churchgoing, and the questionnaire suggested thirteen reasons and gave space to write in others (which was hardly used). Against each reason the respondent was asked to indicate whether that reason had been a major or a minor influence, and the age at which they left for that reason. Table 9 gives the answers.

Table 9: Reasons why respondents stopped attending church

Reasons in full	Abbreviation	Average Age	Total %	Influence Major %	Minor %
The worship service was boring	Boredom	20	67	50	17
I moved out of the area and did not look for a new church		21	65	46	19
There were few other people there of my age or background	Loneliness	21	61	33	28
The church programmes did not meet my personal/family needs	Irrelevant	22	76	52	24
The congregation was not welcoming		22	45	26	19
I had serious doubts about the Christian religion		23	67	48	19
I had a disagreement with the minister/pastor	Doubts	23	22	13	9
I was ill for a long time		23	11	8	3
I disagreed/could not live by the church's moral teaching	Morality	24	51	31	20
The church was demanding too much from me		26	48	25	23
I was expected to make too many commitments	Over-committed	26	47	21	26
I had a disagreement with a church member/members		26	27	18	9
I was looking after my elderly/dying parent/relative	Family	29	13	8	5

This is a highly significant table, and shows a gradual progression of distancing as the age progresses. It explains also why so many leave in their teens and early twenties (the ages given above are average ages).

It suggests that boredom is the initial factor, followed by loneliness or indifference if one moves away (a common occurrence). The lack of relevance of the church and a discourteous congregation do not encourage people to stay. If a person is able to endure boredom, irrelevance and loneliness, then they may find that they cannot abide the church's teaching. First they have doubts, and then openly disagree with the moral teaching and expectations of the church. It is particularly interesting that this reason averages in the mid-twenties, when the pressure of cohabitation is very high (it peaks in the early twenties). Doubtless many cohabitees, feeling uneasy within themselves because of their lifestyle, 'blame' the church for being 'out-of-date', and leave.

Even for those who accept the tenets of the Christian faith and its moral and ethical teaching, it is all too easy to get sucked into the church's programme, especially if someone is young (mid-twenties), perhaps with no family to look after, perhaps with plenty of financial resources (two salaries if married), and then they react because their needs for leisure, relief from the pressure, or perhaps growing demands from a young family or advancement at work, mean that they simply stop attending church. The church asked too much of them, and did not recognize their own needs whilst they were busy meeting the needs of others. On average this group left at age 26.

In 1992 March for Jesus in Britain conducted a simultaneous Roadshow, which included interviewing people. 2,400 mostly young people (46% were aged 13-17) were thus contacted. The key reaction to church is that it was 'boring'.[21]

How far were the reasons why respondents stopped attending church related to the number of years since they had last moved? Were relative newcomers more likely to stop attending? The only factor where this proved important was in the welcome given by the congregation. For those who had last moved up to ten years ago this was a major influence for 36%, against 12% for those who had last moved more than ten years ago. So hard can it be to get accepted!

It might be thought that with this survey concentrating on whether or not people stopped attending church, this change of behaviour might be significant with various beliefs. However, of the 25 statements listed in Table 10, all but one did not vary significantly by whether a person had stopped going to church or had not. The exception is a critical exception, though—was the Bible uniquely inspired by God? 64% of those who had never stopped going to church (or at least not for a year or more) believed the Bible was uniquely inspired, against 49% who believed the same but had stopped attending. Biblical inspiration is a key differential.

Table 9 is a catalogue of disasters, many of which the church could overcome with foresight. Making services attractive has been mentioned previously (the whole image issue), and it ought to be possible to have a welcoming system operating even if the numbers of young people in their early twenties is relatively small. It is easy to decry the irrelevance of the church; indeed Robin Gamble has written a book with that very title[22]. How do you help a church become more relevant? Robin Gamble makes some suggestions, and so does Eddie Gibbs in this book[23].

It was noted in the discussion prior to Table 7 that because a few older people stop attending the church, the average age becomes misleading, and using the median age would be more appropriate. That is also true in Table 9, where the average age has only been indicated because of consistency. To get the median age, that is the age at which most of these arguments are likely to be strongest, as a rule of thumb reduce the average age by four years. It then becomes clear that boredom, loneliness, irrelevance and disagreement are key features for disaffected teenagers.

There were four reasons where the results were highly significantly different from those given in Table 9 when country variations were considered. On average the worship was boring for 67% of respondents. It was, however, considered boring by 91% of English respondents and 83% of Scottish. Clearly boredom is a British disease, and one in which we could look both to Australia and the United States, which have much higher percentages of their populations in church, to learn how to make church services more interesting. So many teenagers say 'it is boring', that we smile at hearing the same phrase again. But they mean it, and if we want to keep them, we need to change!

Almost two-thirds of respondents said that doubts about the Christian religion influenced them to stop attending church. In Scotland this 65% became 86%. What is causing that to be so dominant in Scotland?

One-quarter (27%) of the sample said that having disagreements with church members influenced them to stop going to church. In Australia this registered at 58%. A detailed study of Australian church life by Peter Kaldor[24] has shown that much 'switching' between denominations takes place. Could internal squabbles be a powerful motivating factor behind this behaviour?

Overall, the fact that some respondents were expected to make too many commitments influenced 47% to leave the church. In England the proportion thus influenced was no less than 80%! Here then is another major reason in English church life why so many in their twenties especially stop going to church. The church dominates their lives. Doubtless because keen folks with energy are in short supply, they are asked (or volunteer) to do many things. Ultimately, however, the sheer pressure means they react, and they tend to react by leaving the church and stopping attending altogether. This is an important finding, and suggests the urgency of teaching being given about priorities in life (and practised in the church context!). Priorities need to involve ourselves and our time with God, our commitments to our church and family, and the needs of our work, leisure and home. Few churches perhaps give instruction on this. The MARC Europe 'Effective Use of Time' Seminar, which includes teaching on priorities, has for a long time been the most popular it has held. If pastors need to learn priorities, how much more do their church members!

Nominal belief
What do church members believe? It would sometimes be nice to know! To find out more of what this sample believed twenty-five statements were given and respondents asked to indicate whether they agreed or disagreed with each, or whether they were unsure. To prevent any kind of automatic answering of the question some statements were deliberately put into the negative for those would answer orthodoxly (for example, one statement was 'Jesus was not the unique Son of God'). These questions have been transposed in the analysis below for simplicity in understanding. Altogether thirteen were put negatively in this way; those interested in seeing exactly which statements were amended should consult the full questionnaire; they are asterisked (*) in the list below.

Table 10: Respondents religious beliefs and opinions

Statement	Agree %	Unsure %	Disagree %
*1 God does exist; therefore all religions are not a waste of time	87	11	2
2 By prayer we can communicate with God	79	12	9
*3 Jesus' death on the cross has meaning for today	79	15	6
4 Jesus was the Divine Son of God	75	17	8
*5 Jesus was the unique Son of God	72	21	7
6 God is three Persons: Father, Son and Holy Spirit	70	15	15
*7 The Bible is largely relevant in today's world	68	21	11
8 God holds humans responsible for their actions	67	19	14
*9 Praying about things will alter the outcome	64	24	12
*10 The stories of Jesus recorded in the Bible were not invented by his followers	63	25	12
11 There is life after death	62	26	12
*12 The soul does not return to earth in different human bodies or forms of life	61	31	8
13 The miracles recorded in the Bible actually happened	60	33	7
14 God is a Personal Being	58	21	21
15 The Bible is uniquely inspired by God	58	23	19
16 The only way God can forgive our sins is through Jesus Christ	58	24	18
*17 The universe did not come into existence by chance	58	28	14
18 There is good in all religions, but the nature of God is revealed most truly in Christianity	56	24	20
*19 There is a way of knowing God personally while we are on earth	55	23	22
20 Humans are uniquely made in the image of God	52	27	21
*21 All religions are not valid paths to the one Truth	47	21	32
*22 We cannnot learn as much about God from the Muslim, Buddhist and Hindu scriptures as from the Bible	44	34	22
*23 Humans did not evolve from apes by the process of evolution	40	26	34
24 The devil actually exists as a real being	36	26	38
*25 God is not a cosmic energy or a life force	32	36	32

This is an interesting list. Note the ones which are agreed about by most—the four accepted by at least three-quarters of respondents. These cover the existence of God, the power of prayer, the relevance of the cross and the personhood of Jesus. In some ways it could be argued that these four facets are the heart of the gospel. If people are becoming nominal or notional Christians it is not because they disbelieve in the crucial tenets of the Christian faith. It is not the message which is driving them out.

Note too the main areas of disagreement. There are four which mustered at least a quarter of respondents. Not all agree that Christianity is unique (item 21), nor that God is not a cosmic energy (item 25—as many agree on this as disagree, the only one which is equal). Certainly not all agree on creation (item 23), nor that the devil exists (item 24, the only one where those disagreeing exceed those agreeing). The New Age argues all four of these, and it may be that in these replies we are seeing the influence of that movement—small, and at the end of the scale, but likely to grow. Maybe some are leaving the church because they are being weaned away by alternative theologies, with a secular or occult genesis. This suggests how much the church needs to be on its guard against all apostasy, and meet spurious claims with the truth of God.

Ten of the statements have a score of 25% or higher in the 'Unsure' column. People are uncertain about the Bible (items 10, 13 and 22), immortality (items 11 and 12), creation (items 17, 20 and 23) and personal human beings (items 24 and 25). These are key doctrines which need re-emphasizing in today's churches if people are not going to drift away— remember these are the highest scores of a sample roughly half of whom *have* left the churches, and about which they were the most uncertain. Something for the next sermon series?

These twenty-five items may be grouped in a number of ways. Common themes around seven subjects are given in Table 11, together with the average percentage of those agreeing given in Table 10. The fourth column, labelled 'Score' is derived from all three figures for each item in Table in the following manner:

$$\text{Score} = [\text{Agree \% minus Disagree \%}]/[\text{Unsure \%}]$$

There is nothing special about such a formula, except that it treats all in the same way and uses all three scores.

Table 11: Summary of beliefs and opinions

Abbreviation	Statement included	Average of agree's	Score
Christ	3, 4, 5	75%	4.0
Prayer	2, 9	72%	4.0
God	1, 6, 14, 25	62%	3.3
Eternity	11, 12, 17	60%	1.7
Bible	7, 10, 13, 15, 22	59%	1.7
Salvation	8, 16, 19, 24	54%	1.5
Uniqueness	18, 20, 21, 23	49%	0.9

These three groups might be summarized as God, Faith and Uniqueness, and it is that order of importance that counts for those who have left the church. The most basic fundamentals are still in position, but the remainder has slipped. This is what notional Christianity is all about—no churchgoing or church membership but still a willingness to be called Christian. These people all believe in God, and accept Jesus as special, but the details of the faith are unknown, and the uniqueness of Christianity is far from acceptance.

More detailed analysis of these results was undertaken, by multiplying the score given above by average church attendance per year (called 'certainty' in the Table below). These figures were then analysed by variance across group and country, with the following results:

Table 12: Probability of certainty and country beliefs

Group	Certainty		Country	
	F value	Probability	F value	Probability
Christ	1.24	0.354	5.90	0.032
Prayer	1.56	0.300	1.35	0.406
God	2.25	0.152	1.95	0.192
Eternity	0.66	0.551	4.15	0.065
Bible	1.79	0.196	2.59	0.101
Salvation	4.44	0.036	7.78	0.007
Uniqueness	0.67	0.592	2.51	0.125

The F values in the above table are the key numbers emerging from the analysis of variance and the probability of these occurring by chance are given. The table shows that only three results are statistically significant, that is when the probability value is less that 0.05. Two these three come in the Salvation row, and one in the Christ row.

The Salvation 'certainty' significance indicates that the percentage of those unsure and disagreeing are important in assessing where people stand, which is not the case with any other group, for which just the proportion agreeing is sufficient. The Salvation 'certainty' figure is made significant by the high proportion of people disagreeing with the statement that 'the devil actually exists as a real being'. In other words, this particular statement is of crucial importance in evaluating what people believe, and since half of these respondents have left the church at some stage, it may be presumed that belief in the devil or not was a key part of their theology, as it were.

The two country significances are for Christ and Salvation, and in both instances it is the high values emerging from the United States which cause the significance. In other words, Americans reacted to these groups of statements quite differently from respondents in Britain and Australia. The key difference is that Americans almost entirely *agreed* with these statements, whereas in Britain and Australia there was a much higher number of those who disagreed or who were unsure. Americans therefore strongly agree that Jesus' death has meaning for today, that Jesus was the Divine Son of God, that Jesus was the unique Son of God, that God holds humans responsible for their actions, that the only way that God can forgive our sins is through Jesus Christ and that there is a way of knowing God personally while we are on earth. (The last statement on the devil as a real being is not specially different for Americans.) All these statements are clear orthodox statements and reflect the exposure of many Americans to the gospel message through church, television and in other ways. Americans are more orthodox in their beliefs than respondents in other countries—but that didn't stop many of these respondents from leaving the church. In other words, orthodoxy of doctrine may be very important, but intellectual assent does not necessarily lead to greater commitment or staying power.

That the basic facts of the gospel are better known to Americans than Australians and the British again says something about the teaching programme that churches need to engage in. Philip Margesson would extend this comment to Europe generally. Philip is president of the European Co-ordinating Committee of the Christian and Missionary Alliance, and in a recent interview said:

> There is little acknowledgement of the gospel in Europe today. Just as the word 'missionary' is usually associated with sending people to lesser-developed countries, so is the word 'unreached'. This tends to divert people's attention away from the needs of the continent of Europe, where most of our neighbours are untouched by the gospel, even though they may have roots in the Christian position.[25]

Nominal belief by environment

There is another significant variation in Table 10 between those who currently live in a rural area or town, and those living in a village or city.

The latter have a remarkable degree of agreement with the overall percentages given in Table 10 for 'Agree', whereas this is not true of the former, those in rural areas or towns.

Using the groups in Table 11, two of the statements relating to Christ vary significantly by where respondents lived. That Jesus' death on the cross has meaning for today (statement 3) was agreed by 97% of those in rural areas, but only 71% of those in towns. That Jesus was the Divine Son of God (statement 4) was agreed by 95% of those in rural areas, but only 70% of those in towns. There was no significant variation for statement 5. With regard to God, statement 6 about the Trinity was agreed by 92% of rural people, 59% of those in towns. Other statements about God were not significantly different.

On the question of eternity, two statements of the three had significant variations. That there is life after death (statement 11) was agreed by 72% of rural people, but only 49% of those in towns. That the universe did not happen by chance (statement 17) was agreed by 84% of rural people, but only 48% of those in towns.

Finally, on two salvation statements there was a significant difference also. That Jesus is the only way by which God can forgive us (statement 16) was agreed by 74% of rural people, but 48% of those in towns. That there is a way of knowing God personally (statement 19) was agreed by 74% of those now living in rural areas, but only 46% of those living in towns.

We thus have environmental differences in the broad areas of Jesus Christ, God, Eternity and Salvation, but not other areas. These differences are all in the direction of a much higher degree of affirmation by those in rural areas, and much less by those living in towns, with those living in villages or the city being close to the norm in each case. Someone once said, 'You are nearer God's heart in a garden than anywhere else on earth', suggesting the power of nature to reflect the actuality and attributes of the Creator. This may explain the higher rural percentages, where one is undoubtedly closer to nature. Why those in towns should be so much less in agreement than those in cities, however, is not clear.

This section has identified key statements for nominal and notional Christians. Many orthodox beliefs about Christianity are current amongst those who were once ex-churchgoers. God, prayer, the person and work of Jesus are generally accepted; the creation, the devil, the uniqueness of Christianity, God as a life-force are more controversial, with more disagreement than in other areas. Uncertainty is seen about the Bible, immortality, creation and personal eternal beliefs. Belief or not in the devil is a crucial turning point for many.

It has also been seen that the Americans are much more orthodox in their beliefs than the British or Australians, and probably many others in Europe. Clear teaching on key doctrines is important—we need to be 'ready to make your defence' (1 Pet 3:15 *NRSV*)—but, since this study is about those who have left the church, more than intellectual correctness is needed to retain church commitment.

Christian practice

In order to assess differences on Christian practice, as opposed to Christian belief, a number of statements were made and respondents asked to indicate whether these were true of them frequently, sometimes, rarely or never. Altogether twenty-two statements were made, and the large majority answered them all.

In order to evaluate the large number of percentages generated by these questions, a simple 'scoring' system has been used, whereby an answer of 'frequently' scores +2, 'sometimes' +1, 'rarely' −1, and 'never' −2. On this basis, the replies given are shown in descending order in Table 13.

The asterisked (*) item has had its percentages entered the other way round, as this was the sole example of a statement whose answers could be expected to go normally in the other direction.

There are four items where the score is over +1.0. Respondents were keen on justice and helping others. They also acknowledged that both their parents and grandparents attend(ed) church. These are scarcely hallmarks of the religious! They could be anyone, and these statements simply say that for these respondents religious items were less important than social issues or parental example.

There were three items which scored very negatively, with scores lower than −1.0. These concerned personal evangelism either in the church or with the church, and trying to mobilize the church to take political action. All were definitely not on!

Table 13: Respondent's Christian practice

Practice	Score	Frequently %	Sometimes %	Rarely %	Never %
1 When I see people treated unfairly I want to do something about it	+1.5	60	36	2	2
2 I am happy to help anyone, especially those who don't go to church, in any way I can	+1.3	52	37	6	5
3 One or more of my grandparents attend/ed church	+1.3	67	18	5	10
4 One or more of my parents attend/ed church	+1.1	59	20	9	12
5 I support financially religious causes	+0.6	33	37	15	15
6 What I learn from the Bible influences my daily life	+0.6	33	37	13	17
7 I spend time in private prayer to God on a daily basis	+0.4	37	27	13	23
8 I pray for guidance before making important decisions	+0.4	34	30	16	20
9 I sense the presence of God in a special way	+0.2	23	38	15	24
10 I feel nearer to God when I meet with sincere Christians	+0.2	26	33	14	27
11 I feel that I have met with God in my private devotions	0.0	24	30	18	28
12 I feel that I have met with God in the worship service	−0.1	21	29	18	32
13 I sense God brings me into contact with individuals who he wants me to help or who he sends to help me	−0.1	15	37	18	30
14 I tell others about my faith in Christ	−0.3	10	36	21	33
15 I attend at least one church meeting apart from worship services	−0.4	23	14	22	41
16 I am actively involved in doing things in my church	−0.4	23	17	20	40
17 I read portions of the Bible on a daily basis	−0.4	20	18	22	40
18 I pray with other people from my church	−0.6	20	14	14	52
19 I read horoscopes	−0.6	7	26	30	37
20 I invite non-churchgoing friends to come to church with me	−1.2	2	17	24	57
21 I am involved in a church outreach activity intended to reach non-churchgoers	−1.4	4	10	17	69
22 I encourage my church to get involved in political issues (eg, prayer, writing letters, etc)	−1.5	4	8	15	73

Table 14: Church involvement by Commitment

Practice	Strongly committed	Not very committed	Not sure if Christian	No longer Christian	Never a Christian
15 Attend a church meeting	+1.2	−0.9	−1.6	−1.9	−1.7
16 Active in church	+1.1	−0.8	−1.6	−1.8	−2.0
18 Pray with others	+1.1	−1.1	−1.8	−2.0	−1.8
20 Invite friends	+0.5	−1.4	−1.8	−2.0	−2.0
21 Outreach	−0.5	−1.7	−1.9	−2.0	−2.0

Similar analyses on practice as were undertaken for beliefs did not work so well because of a number of opposites implicit in Table 13. For example, item 6 indicates that what people learn from the Bible influences their life, yet item 17 negatively reports on the daily reading of the Bible. Whilst both are doubtless true expressions of reality, the linking of these items together simply creates a tension that the analysis of variance programme cannot resolve. The same is true of some of the statements of God and prayer.

There are two items where the United States differs from the other western countries. More American respondents than others claimed to pray daily (38% against 35%), and more Americans felt the presence of God than others (33% against 22%).

Those most involved with the church, as might be expected, are the committed Christians. This shows up with certain statements, as given in Table 14.

This table is instructive in that it shows clearly the dividing line between being involved with the church and its activities and the degree to which one is committed to being a Christian. Only the strongly committed engage in meaningful activity outside the worship services, and not all of these are too keen on outright evangelism! The scores in Table 14 are only positive in the first column, and from Table 5 we know that these are the folk who mostly attend church every week (over three-quarters). It suggests that it is not just church attendance, but regular church attendance, and especially weekly church attendance, which both builds commitment and gives man- and woman-power for activities.

There was very little variation across these figures by gender or marital status. Married people were most likely to attend a meeting other than the worship service than singles (27% against 18%). Likewise the environment where the respondent was born or now lived made little difference.

290 / *Winning Them Back*

Those who had moved less than six years ago were more inclined to be involved in the local church (46% against 32% for those who had lived there longer). This again underlines the importance of catching people whilst they are still relatively new to an area. It did not matter how many times people had moved—this made no difference to their involvement.

Nor were there any significant variations by social class in terms of Christian practice, as given by this dominantly middle-class sample. Nor, interestingly, was there any difference according to the respondent's level of education.

In summary, therefore, the results of this study show, across the four countries that:

1. Females are not more involved than males in church activities.
2. Married people are not more likely to be involved in church activities than single people. There were too few separated, divorced and widowed people to comment.
3. The frequency with which people move does not make them more or less likely to be involved in church activities.
4. Blue collar workers are not less likely to be involved in church activities, but the definition of 'blue collar' varies nationally.
5. Those who received less education are not less likely to be involved in church activities.
6. It is not true that those who are only occasional churchgoers or who never attend are more likely to describe themselves as not Christians or unsure whether they are or not. Some said they were strongly committed Christians!
7. People who have moved frequently are not less likely to be involved in church activities.

Those who attend church on special occasions or who never attend are, however, less orthodox in their beliefs than regular attenders, and are less likely to have a devotional life, experience the presence of God, relate their faith to their daily life, have basic Christian knowledge and believe in the devil.

Significant variations in Christian practice
Were there then no significant variations at all? The answer is YES for four of the control variables used in this study—country, age, where now living, and whether they had left the church. To these we now turn.

There were variations by country of respondents who *frequently* undertook certain practices, however, and these are given below; the asterisk (*) denotes the figure(s) which is specially different.

Table 15: Christian practice across different countries

Practice		Scotland %	United States %	England %	Australia %
4	One parent attends	66	70	44*	61
5	Support financially	33	30	45*	24
9	Presence of God	14	40*	18	30
11	Private devotions	16*	33	25	26
12	Meet God in worship	13*	27	29	20
13	God brings people	10	29*	10	22*
16	Actively involved	22	17	30*	14
18	Pray with others	14*	18	30	23
19	Read horoscopes	13*	14*	1	4

Table 15 shows that English people's parents attended church less frequently than those in other countries—nominality is not something of this generation! English people tend to give more regularly to religious causes than others, and say they are actively involved in their church life. Americans, however, sense the presence of God more frequently than others, and believe (with the Australians) that God brings people to them for help (the divine sovereignty). They, with the Scottish, read their horoscopes more. The Scottish pray and meet with God in worship far less frequently than people of other nations.

The percentages in the above table are those which correspond to respondents frequently undertaking the activity mentioned. Thus it is not to be thought that many religious or quasi-religious people in England do not read their horoscopes—the sample simply claimed that they did not do so frequently.

There is the occasional significant variation by age, as given below, again using the frequently undertaken percentages, except for the last two which are *never* undertaken.

Table 16: Christian practice across different ages

Practice	Country	18-25 %	26-35 %	36-45 %	46-55 %	56-65 %	66 & over %	Overall %
15 Attend meeting outside worship	Scot	0	13	12	23	40	59	26
16 Actively involved	Scot	0	16	5	21	16	47	22
	Aust	14	35	19	7	30	0	21
18 Pray with others	Aust	21	35	6	13	20	33	21
Never undertaken								
20 Invite friends to church	Scot	83	69	65	70	80	38	65
21 Involved in outreach	USA	40	54	100	75	100	33	67

Table 16 shows Scottish older people (56 or over) coming to church meetings outside the worship service and being actively involved in the church. In Australia, however, it tends to be those who are 26-35 or 56-65 who are more actively involved. It is the same age groups who are more likely to pray with others too. This is an interesting pair of ages— do they represent young marrieds and their parents?

Table 16 also shows that younger people (under 26) and those aged 56-65 tend never to invite their friends to church. In the United States, it is those aged 36-45 and 56-65 who reckon never to be involved with outreach. The age group 56-65 shows up as being special across these different countries—is this the time for turning again to Christianity or turning away?

As with Christian belief, so some Christian practice varied with the environment in which people currently lived, with the rural areas again being offset against towns. With some practices, those living in rural areas scored the highest, and those living in the town the lowest. There are five which varied significantly:

Table 17: Christian practice across different environments

Practice	Rural score	Town score	Overall score
11 Meet God in my private devotions	+0.7	−0.4	0.0
13 Sense God sends me people to help	+0.4	−0.4	−0.1
14 Tell others about faith in Christ	+0.2	−0.7	−0.3
16 Actively involved in church	0.0	−0.6	−0.4
17 Read Bible daily	0.0	−0.8	−0.4

For these five statements, the rural score was highest across the four environments and the town score was the lowest (lowest equal to the city in statement 16). These statements could be taken to suggest a deeper spirituality in rural people, and more committed activity amongst rural church people, with the opposite for those in towns. Why might this be so? Do the towns lack the anonymity of the city and the closeness of village and rural life? Are you simply branded as 'different' in a town setting, without neighbours or others having a real opportunity to observe the reality of a person's faith in action?

Some Christian practice also varied according to whether or not a person had left the church at some time. This is not surprising, though the extent to which it was significant was interesting—out of the twenty-two statements, Christian practice only varied significantly in four statements! In other words, whether a person had left the church and returned or had continued in their churchgoing tended to make little difference in their walk as a Christian. So much for the impact of going to church! However, the four areas where there was a difference are actually very important, and return again to the heart of commitment and spirituality. The relevant scores are given in Table 18 below.

Table 18: Christian practice across churchgoing

Practice	Stopped attending church but returned	Have not stopped going to church	Overall
6 Bible influences life	+0.4	+0.7	+0.6
12 Meet God in worship service	−0.5	0.0	−0.1
14 Tell others about faith in Christ	−0.4	−0.1	−0.3
18 Pray with other people	−0.9	−0.3	−0.6

Witness, worship, united prayer and obedience to the Scriptures could easily be regarded as the heart of what it means to be a Christian. What these figures suggest is that those who have left the church at some stage and returned never perhaps seem to regain either the depth of their former commitment (or at least the commitment of others who have not left) nor their spirituality either. Leaving the church might therefore be likened to creating a scar in one's spiritual life—you can function after the operation but the skin is never quite the same. Something, perhaps intangible, has gone. 'Once bitten, twice shy' is an oft-used saying—maybe it applies in the spiritual realm too.

It is important therefore for the church to do everything it can to retain those who attend. This is not just important for the church but for the people themselves. Both lose out if they leave. How to stop people leaving needs to get far greater priority attention in many churches.

In Australia 54% of churchgoers have become nominal[26]. A detailed study of nominalism in this country, *Faith without the Church*, confirms many of the trends seen in this study. They have summarized their results as follows:

> Few nominals have totally rejected the Christian faith, but they are far less certain in their affirmation of it than those who attend regularly. In general, they place greater emphasis on faith as supporting moral standards, and comparatively less emphasis on personal access to God.[27]

What emerges from this rather scattered evidence? That Christian practice tends not to vary with most factors of person, housing movement, or social factors. It does vary a little by nationality, perhaps because of the different traditions inherent in the Christian way of life in each community. It varies sporadically with age but not in any uniform way. The elderly are more active than the young, but this is not a surprise. It varies by environment and commitment to churchgoing, especially across those factors where truth faith is more evident.

The types of activity which do generate variations relate to active involvement with the church, attending meetings outside worship, praying and talking with others, and sensing the presence of God either privately or corporately. Many of these activities are associated with intensity of commitment, and it is this factor above all others which tends to be causational in the behavioural manifestation of a Christian faith. This is not a new finding, as Roozen and Carroll found in 1980 [28]. In their study of regular churchgoers and the unchurched, they found it was the items which measured commitment that made the greatest difference between them. This after all is not over-surprising, but it is good to have one's feelings sometimes rooted in facts!

It could be thought that parental influence might have been higher. But this is diminishing, as was also found in the 1982 *Leeds Common Religion Project* [29]. Scores for attendance patterns from answers to Statements (3) and (4) are given below.

Table 19: Influence of parents and grandparents

Respondents who attend church	Attendance patterns of:	
	Grandparents	Parents
Weekly	+1.6	+1.4
Once/Twice a month	+1.6	+1.1
On special occasions	+1.2	+1.0
Never	−0.1	−0.1

These scores come, as before, from taking 'frequently' as +2 down to 'never' as −2. They suggest a declining influence between grandparent and parent, but only a small one. The Leeds Project, as with this study, showed that the largest change comes between the parent and the present generation.

Biblical knowledge
The questionnaire also explored respondent's biblical knowledge in an elementary way by asking five questions about the New Testament focusing around the ministry of Jesus in the Gospels. Where was He born? Who preached the Sermon on the Mount? What does 'Golgotha' mean? What was Zacchaeus' occupation? Who wrote the four Gospels? Answers were simply assessed as right or wrong. Everybody completed at least some of these questions—or tried to! A few omitted answering one or two they found particularly difficult.

The answers reveal a woeful ignorance of even the most basic biblical facts. 59% (of the 98% answering this particular question) knew who preached the Sermon on the Mount—as well as Jesus, Moses, Elijah and John the Baptist where strong contenders! 87% knew that Jesus was born in Bethlehem, Jerusalem and Nazareth being alternatives offered. Only two people didn't attempt to answer this question. Likewise 85% knew the names of the four Gospels, though a few got confused with Thomas and Peter, and five didn't answer. What 'Golgotha' means was more difficult, and only answered correctly by 49% of those answering the question; 6% (including one-sixth of the Australians) didn't even attempt it. Likewise, Zacchaeus' occupation proved hard—55% got it right and 7% (including one-fifth of the Australians) didn't try this final question.

Such results can hardly inspire confidence in the reasons behind deeper questions; if 87% say that God exists, what do they mean by that? 79% said that Jesus' death on the cross had meaning for today (Table 10); how many could explain correctly what that meaning was? Including such questions was very useful in a study of this nature, and helps in understanding the perceptions respondents may have of major aspects of knowledge of the Christian faith.

Overall, 67% of these questions where answered correctly by those attempting answers. Everyone in the English sample answered each of the five questions, though not always correctly. Of the answers, the English got most correct—72%, followed closely by the Scots at 70% and the Australians at 68%. But these countries were all way ahead of the Americans at 54%. This result is interesting. Americans go to church more[30], they are more orthodox in their beliefs (discussion after Table 12), but they actually have less biblical knowledge, as judged by these five questions. And this, despite the many adult Sunday Schools run by American churches!

Where did the Americans fall down? Primarily on the answers the other countries found easiest—who preached the Sermon on the Mount, where Jesus was born, and naming the four Gospels. Although the other two questions were generally answered badly, the Americans did not answer them significantly worse. The detailed percentages of the number of correct answers (out of those answering each question) is given by country in Table 20.

Table 20: Correct answers to biblical knowledge by country

Question	England %	Scotland %	Australia %	United States %	Overall %	Overall Number
Jesus' birthplace	88	88	93	69	87	265
Gospel writers	90	87	89	69	85	259
Sermon on Mount	71	64	54	39	59	178
Zacchaeus' job	58	59	49	50	55	157
Meaning Golgotha	55	51	46	43	49	142
Average all questions	72	70	68	54	67	1001

It can be seen from this table that English respondents did particularly well on who preached the Sermon on the Mount (compared with other countries), and so did the Scots. Australians were strong on the birthplace of Jesus but weaker on Zacchaeus' occupation, where the Americans were strong.

As might otherwise be expected, those who came to church most frequently got more answers correct than those who didn't. Weekly attenders got 82% of the answers right, those who came once or twice a month 71%, while special-occasion-only people scored 58%. But those who never came to church still scored 46%, reflecting a relatively high residual knowledge of some aspects of the New Testament. This bears out the 'theology' of nominal and notional Christians (briefly outlined in the discussion under Great Britain in the first section). How did this basic knowledge vary by country by frequency of attendance? The next table indicates this.

Table 21: Correct answers by country and churchgoing

Churchgoing frequency	England %	Scotland %	Australia %	United States %	Overall %	Average sample
Weekly	95	84	86	39	82	94
Once/twice monthly	78	72	73	62	71	59
Special occasions	50	65	56	61	58	120
Never	50	39	52	15	46	25
Overall	72	70	68	54	67	298

This table is consistent with earlier comments, with the higher percentage for 'special occasions' or 'never' perhaps reflecting the strength of the religious education that many respondents would have had at school. If the survey was repeated in say ten or twenty years time the results could well be quite different, especially in Britain with the changing nature of religious education in schools.

It is the United States which has quite different percentages in Table 21. The regular weekly churchgoers were particularly low in Bible knowledge (and this was true across all questions, with the meaning of 'Golgotha' actually scoring best at 62%). Those who go only once or twice a month answered much better, and this suggests that the sample may have been selected untypically in this aspect, in that of the fourteen American weekly churchgoers a much higher percentage was ignorant, and in this context this only means half a dozen people. The much lower percentage in the American column for those who never go to church is significant, and perhaps suggests that those really outside the church in America are just that—really outside. They have less biblical knowledge, especially as religious education is not taught in school. This kind of low percentage is what may obtain in Britain and Australia in the future. The nominal issue in the United States therefore starts with a different base of elementary religious knowledge, and this difference is clearly an important perception for practical purposes.

The environment and churchgoing differences seen in belief and practice did not emerge with knowledge. More rural people got the birthplace of Jesus wrong than those from urban areas, but those who had stopped going to church got as many correct answers as those who kept on going.

This section highlights therefore the general paucity of relatively simple biblical knowledge, even amongst weekly churchgoers who, nevertheless, know more than those who attended less frequently. It also shows that British and Australian respondents generally had a much higher knowledge than the Americans, and this has very real implications for reaching out to nominal Christians.

SUMMARY

This section has been concerned with analysing the survey undertaken by Professor Eddie Gibbs. What are the main conclusions emerging from it? They may be summarized as follows:

1. The key characteristics when assessing Christian beliefs, practices and knowledge were the frequency of church attendance, nationality, and to some extent age, environment and whether people stopped going, and in that order of importance. The value therefore of denominations regularly collecting and publishing church attendance figures cannot be stressed too highly.
2. Church attendance could be used as a proxy for Christian commitment.
3. If people stopped going to church for at least a year, the length of time they were away averaged 8 years, but with half under 6 years, and an eighth over 15 years.
4. Half of those who left did so before they were 20 years of age and a further sixth before they were 25.
5. People left because they were bored, lonely, found it irrelevant, had doubts, or disagreed with the moral teaching—in that order by age.
6. Widely accepted beliefs relate to the existence of God, the power of prayer, the relevance of the cross and the personhood of Jesus.
7. Disagreement centres around the uniqueness of Christianity, the

nature of God, creation and the existence of the devil. This last was highly significant, and is an important item to note.

8. People were unsure about the Bible's authority, immortality, creation and personal eternal beings (the devil emerging again here, too).

9. Americans tended to be much more orthodox in their beliefs than either the British (in Scotland or England) or the Australians.

10. Respondents acknowledged their parental example in churchgoing even if they did not follow it. Their parents went slightly less than their grandparents, but the transition to the present generation is the greater difference.

11. Justice and helping others were thought specially important by most respondents. Evangelism and getting the church involved politically were definitely out of season!

12. There was a sharp difference between those who were strongly committed Christians and the rest. The committed went to church meetings during the week, were actively involved in their church, prayed with others, and invited others to come to church, but even these did not reckon on personal evangelism.

13. The elderly tend to be more actively involved in their church.

14. Bible knowledge was not strong, especially in the United States. Weekly churchgoers knew more than others, but there was a high residual or retentive factor operating amongst the British and Australians.

15. Those living in rural areas tended to have a more committed and spiritual Christianity than those in towns.

16. Those who stopped going to church and returned lost out on key aspects of Christian discipleship.

What do these sixteen points suggest by way of action? They demonstrate the *importance of this kind of research*, and especially the value of international research. Far too little of this is done by Christian organizations, and it was done in this instance through the personal acquaintances built up by Eddie Gibbs in his extensive travels.

It highlights the need for *teaching basic doctrines*, so that people know why they believe what they believe. They might not be so uncertain then! This especially applied to teaching about the nature of God, and the future eternal state—immortality and the devil are not widely accepted. This suggests that teaching needs to focus especially on the eternal domain, more than much teaching currently does. This might then act as a spur to encouraging more personal evangelism, weak even amongst the strongly committed.

It also suggests that *different strategies need to be adopted* in the United States from the other countries surveyed here. The study suggests a weak orthodox shell of knowledge in the States without basic information to hold it up. Perhaps this is why the New Age Movement there is particularly making so much headway. It also acts as a powerful warning to those in Britain and Australia that teaching children basic knowledge of the Scriptures is highly important—the information imparted seems to last a long time (a life time?), if this study has been correctly interpreted.

The survey also underlines both *the importance of strong commitment*, which is crucial for much church activity, and the peril of asking people to be too committed—many leave because of the demands made on them. What actually is expected of a church member? What might be, as it were, a typical Job Description? What might reasonably be expected and what not? Some churches do draw up such a list, but they are few. More could do so with profit—in effect, thinking through the implications of Christian commitment.

The results also indicate the *value of retaining those who come to church*. Finding those who are becoming dissatisfied—either with the church or with their own Christian walk—is vitally important if people are not to leave and stay a long time in desert places.

C. Nominality worldwide

The Rev Dr David Barrett's massive volume *World Christian Encyclopaedia*[31] contains detailed church statistics for every country in the world. Essentially compiled in the 1970s, some of the figures and trends need updating now, but it still contains a vast amount of useful information. In particular, Barrett analyses each country's Christian population in three ways relevant to this paper. He details the number of nominal Christians, the number of practising Christians, and the number of non-practising Christians. These three groups together give the total number of Christians in a country. The definitions he employs are not the same as those used in the earlier parts of this paper. Practising Christians, for example, are defined as those who go to church at least once a year. Nominal Christians are defined as professing Christians who are unaffiliated or unchurched, that is, not affiliated to churches, nor in contact with them, nor attached to them, nor associated with them, nor known to them nor on their rolls or books. They are therefore Christians who are outside or who have rejected the institutional churches or are otherwise not on the records of organised Christianity, who may individually be Christians but who are not part of the corporate life, community or fellowship of the churches, and who therefore from the churches' point of view are regarded as Christians in name only, whilst at the same time often maintaining Christian beliefs and Christian values. Nominal Christians, in other words, are Christians who, for reasons good or bad, do not belong to the visible and organised community of believers. They are sometimes called the latent church as opposed to the manifest church which asserts Jesus as the Christ (Paul Tillich, et al).

Non-practising Christians are defined as 'affiliated Christians who take no part in their churches' ongoing activities, and who are inactive and non-attending, or who describe themselves as such. They are sometimes termed 'dormant Christians'.[32]

In terms of the usage in this paper, David Barrett's 'non-practising' would conform to our 'nominal' and his 'nominal' would conform to our 'notional', and for conformity his figures are so interpreted below. The total figures in these three dimensions for the world are given in Table 22.

Table 22: Practising, nominal and notional Christians worldwide

Type	1900 millions	Annual rate of Change %	1970 millions	Annual rate of Change %	1985 millions	Annual rate of Change %	2000 millions
Practising	469	+0.9	884	+1.4	1,090	+1.3	1,330
Nominal	52	+2.2	248	+2.0	336	+2.9	514
Notional	37	+1.2	85	+2.5	123	+2.4	175
Total world	558	+1.1	1,217	+1.6	1,549	+1.8	2,019

The total numbers represent 34% of the world's population in 1900 and 1970, falling to 33% in 1985 and 32% in the year 2000, though David Barrett has since revised his figures to take account of the massive turning to Christianity in China in the 1980s especially and puts the percentage now in 2000 at 34%.[33]

The percentages show the rate of change per year, and all in the latter part of the twentieth century are increasing faster than they were in the first 70 years. But it will be noticed that the rates of increase for both nominal and notional Christians are higher than for practising Christians. This means that the proportion of the world's Christians who are nominal or notional is increasing and this is reflected in Table 23.

Table 23: Proportions of practising, nominal and notional Christians

Type	1900 %	1970 %	1985 %	2000 %
Practising	84	73	70	66
Nominal	9	20	22	25
Notional	7	7	8	9
Total world (=100%)	558m	1,217m	1,549m	2,019m

Table 23 indicates that whilst the proportions of both nominal and notional Christians are increasing, it is the nominal Christians who are increasing fastest. Table 1 showed that nominal Christians were declining in many parts of Europe; if true for the whole continent then it can only mean that nominal Christians are increasing elsewhere. Europe has exported its problem to the rest of the world! This is not good news, but it begs the question, where in the world is it happening?

David Barrett analyses his figures continent by continent, and these are given in Table 24. The Table shows that:

1. Between 1990 and 1970 nominal Christians increased more than notional Christians in every continent.
2. Notional Christians increased faster than nominal Christians between 1970 and 1985 in Africa, South Asia, Europe and Latin America.
3. These trends continued between 1985 and 2000 except in Africa. So notional Christianity is increasing especially in South Asia, Europe and Latin America. This does not contradict the earlier comments on Europe, although Table 1 shows notional Christianity static between 1980 and 1990.
4. Nominal Christianity is increasing especially fast in Africa and Asia (South and East).

Table 24: Practising, nominal and notional Christians:
Numbers and percentage changes by continent 1900-2000

All figures are in millions; all percentage changes per annum

	Africa	South Asia	East Asia	Old USSR	Europe	North America	Latin America	World
1900 numbers								
Practising	7.82	14.95	5.33	87.30	246.29	56.59	50.98	469.26
Nominal	0.94	1.40	0.75	9.70	27.49	2.98	9.04	52.31
Notional	1.18	0.57	0.93	7.99	4.60	19.24	1.98	36.49
Total	9.94	16.92	7.01	104.99	278.38	78.81	62.00	558.06
1900-1970 change								
Practising	+3.6%	+2.1%	+1.8%	−0.4%	+0.3%	+1.4%	+1.8%	+0.9%
Nominal	+4.8%	+3.3%	+3.0%	+1.1%	+1.6%	+2.5%	+3.2%	+2.2%
Notional	+4.6%	+1.2%	+2.6%	−9.1%	+0.8%	+0.9%	+1.4%	+1.2%
1970 numbers								
Practising	90.73	62.72	18.77	64.51	312.91	152.31	182.07	884.02
Nominal	25.19	14.05	5.95	21.50	84.20	16.93	79.96	247.79
Notional	27.04	1.35	5.80	0.0	8.02	37.20	5.35	84.77
Total	142.96	78.12	30.52	86.01	405.13	206.44	267.38	1216.58
1970-1985 change								
Practising	+3.4%	+3.1%	+2.7%	+1.4%	0.0%	+0.3%	+2.4%	+1.4%
Nominal	+3.4%	+3.4%	+2.0%	+0.3%	+0.7%	+2.3%	+2.9%	+2.0%
Notional	+3.5%	+5.0%	+1.8%	—	+4.1%	+1.0%	+3.5%	+2.5%
1985 numbers								
Practising	149.64	99.83	28.19	79.58	311.87	160.04	261.19	1090.34
Nominal	41.44	23.27	8.05	22.59	94.36	23.81	122.06	335.58
Notional	45.20	2.82	7.62	0.0	14.69	43.39	8.95	122.67
Total	236.28	125.91	43.86	102.17	420.93	227.24	392.20	1548.59
1985-2000 change								
Practising	+3.0%	+2.0%	+1.7%	+1.2%	−0.4%	+0.4%	+2.3%	+1.3%
Nominal	+5.3%	+5.3%	+3.1%	+0.3%	+1.5%	+1.8%	+2.9%	+2.9%
Notional	+2.9%	+6.0%	+2.6%	—	+2.1%	+1.3%	+3.8%	+2.4%
2000 numbers								
Practising	234.43	135.19	36.15	94.48	293.08	169.96	367.04	1330.32
Nominal	89.49	50.28	12.77	23.62	118.37	31.30	188.45	514.29
Notional	69.41	6.79	11.16	0.0	19.95	52.33	15.67	175.31
Total	393.33	192.26	60.08	118.10	431.40	253.59	571.16	2019.92

Why should nominality be strong in Africa? Perhaps because of the rapid expansion of the church in that vast land. The table suggests it is likely to be more of a problem as the century closes, perhaps because of the scarcity of trained teachers.

Why should nominality be especially a problem in Asia? In South Asia, the table has high increases in nominality throughout the century. Perhaps this reflects denominational, geographical or cultural factors. In East Asia the increasing nominality perhaps reflects the expansion of the church in China, and the small number of trained teachers.

Table 25: Practising, nominal and notional Christians:
Percentages of total numbers by continent 1900-2000

Each column of percentages adds downwards within each year and continent

	Africa	South Asia	East Asia	Old USSR	Europe	North America	Latin America	World
1900								
Practising	79%	89%	76%	83%	88%	72%	82%	84%
Nominal	9%	8%	11%	9%	10%	4%	15%	9%
Notional	12%	3%	13%	8%	2%	24%	3%	7%
Total (=100%)	9.94	16.92	7.01	104.99	278.38	78.81	62.00	558.06
1970								
Practising	63%	80%	62%	75%	77%	74%	68%	73%
Nominal	18%	18%	19%	25%	21%	8%	30%	20%
Notional	19%	2%	19%	0%	2%	18%	2%	7%
Total (=100%)	142.96	78.12	30.52	86.01	405.13	206.44	267.38	1216.58
1985								
Practising	63%	79%	64%	78%	74%	70%	67%	70%
Nominal	18%	19%	18%	22%	22%	11%	31%	22%
Notional	19%	2%	18%	0%	4%	19%	2%	8%
Total (=100%)	236.28	125.91	43.86	102.17	420.93	227.24	392.20	1548.59
2000								
Practising	59%	70%	60%	80%	68%	67%	64%	66%
Nominal	23%	26%	21%	20%	27%	12%	33%	25%
Notional	18%	4%	19%	0%	5%	21%	3%	9%
Total (=100%)	393.33	192.26	60.08	118.10	431.40	253.59	571.16	2019.92

Table 25 converts the numbers in Table 24 into percentages in an analogous way to those given in Table 23. They show a steady increase in the proportion of nominal Christians per continent in every continent except the old USSR where the percentage decreases, undoubtedly due to Communist rule, and people becoming more willing to speak out there.

Notional Christian proportions do not generally increase in the same way, but fluctuate much more, and tend to be similar across the century. This stability reflects the finding in Europe in Table 1, and suggests that fringe Christians—the 'latent church' as David Barrett calls them—tend to be much the same over time, though the proportions vary quite considerably from continent to continent. Notional Christians are strongest in North America, East Asia and Africa, and are much stronger than nominal Christians in North America. In East Asia and Africa the proportions are generally similar. In other parts of the world, nominal Christians are much more numerous, especially in Europe and in Latin America where, in both continents, there are huge numbers of nominal Roman Catholics.

CONCLUSION

What is the answer to nominality? There is no one answer, and no simple answer. It will vary by denomination, nationality, theology and opportunity that committed church people have. It is also, I suspect, related to the values held by the population and the image they have of the church, church leaders and its moral code. All are changing, not least the basic values in society. We are moving towards qualitative alternatives to our quantitative mode. Economic development, technological development, media expansion, more international contacts, the increasing mobility of people, increasing competition in business, the changes in our social structures, new hopes, the changes in our beliefs and norms, are all happening. People need training for change. In a sense, nominality starts as people drift away, perhaps either refusing to change with the church, or reacting adversely to changes being incorporated. What are some of the values driving these changes? A speaker from Gallup, talking on the findings of their European Values Study, gave the following list [34]:

Table 26: Old and new values (Europe)

Old values	New values
Economic and social security	Creativity
Political activity	Environmental activity
Community	Independence
Old (hard) technology	New (soft) technology
Position of authority	Self-authoritative

Table 26 lists value changes as perceived from European research. But the Europeans are not the only ones to have researched this. George Barna, amongst others, has researched similarly in the United States. His conclusions are given in Table 27 [35]:

Table 27: Old and new values (United States)

Old values	New values
Quantity of possessions	Quality of possessions
Money	Time
Old traditions	New traditions
Commitment	Flexibility
Group identity	Individualism
Trusting people	Proven integrity
Satisfaction through work	Satisfaction through leisure

The two lists are dissimilar in their detail, but similar in their suggestion of quite radical change being expected in the 1990s. This has to include attitudes to the church and religion. The New Age Movement is perhaps only the forerunner of other such searches for reality. That need (and its value) is *not* going to change. We therefore have to work out anew how to bring eternal non-changing reality to a temporary and fast-changing world. And the key issue here is *commitment*.

How might such commitment come about? In an article in *Management Today* [36] five items were suggested for creating commitment in a business. It would be interesting to apply these to the church today:

1. An awareness of the overriding importance of company missions or goals. (Hence the setting of Christians goals, identifying how they might be accomplished, communicating the same, and setting priorities within them.)

2. A massive increase in the disclosure of information. (Hence more research? Certainly more factual rather than suppositional articles in the Christian press, though there has been some increase in this in the 1980s.)
3. The devolving of responsibility for quality to the shop floor. (Hence involving laypeople in radical leadership and responsible decisions.)
4. Reassertion by management of its basic right to manage. (Hence a recovery of authority by senior church leadership? Certainly a recovery of the lordship of Christ, and the practical implications of this.)
5. A major move away from 'them and us' by the reduction of obvious status differentials between employees. (Hence exit the parsonic management style—and even the parson?!)

Nominality eats at the heart of Christianity; we must recover the heart.

NOTES

1. Ralph Winter, *Unreached Peoples'81*, C. Peter Wagner and Edward R. Dayton, David C. Cook; Elgin, Illinois, 1981, p 141.
2. Professor Eddie Gibbs, *Winning Them Back,* Monarch Publications, MARC imprint; Tunbridge Wells, Kent 1993.
3. Ibid, Fig 1.4
4. Peter Brierley, *'Christian' England*, MARC Europe; London, 1991, pp 201 and 202.
5. Peter Bentley, 'Tricia Blombery and Philip Hughes, *Faith Without the Church? Nominalism in Australian Christianity*, Christian Research Association; Victoria and New South Wales, Australia 1992, p 25.
6. Peter Brierley, *Church Nominalism: the plague of the twentieth century?*, MARC Monograph No 2; London, 1985.
7. Dr Robert Schlarb, Heinz Gerhardt, and Lindsey Mansfield (data compilation), Mary Lawson (editor), *Christliches Handbuch für Österreich Kirchen und Missionen* (Austrian Christian Handbook for churches and missions), MARC Europe; London, 1991.
8. Gabino Campos (data compilation), Mary Lawson (editor), *Compendio Cristiano Español: Iglesias y Misiones* (Spanish Christian Handbook of churches and missions), MARC Europe; London, 1991.
9. Peter Lodberg and Flemming Kramp (data compilation), Peter Brierley (editor), *Dansk Kirkehåndbog* (Danish Christian Handbook), Scandinavia, Copenhagen and MARC Europe; London, 1989.
10. Dr Harri Heino) data compilation), Peter Brierley (editor), *Suomen kristilliset kirkot ja yhteisöt* (Finnish Christian Handbook Part 1: Churches), Suomen Kirkon Seurakuntatoiminnan Keskusliitto, Helsinki, and MARC Europe; London, 1988.
11. Dr Dagfinn Solheim and Rev Ingunn Fokestad (data compilation), Peter Brierley (editor), *Norsk Håndbok for Kirke og Misjon* (Norwegeian

Handbook for Churches and Missions), Lunde Forlag, Oslo, and MARC Europe; London, 1990.

12. Drs Edith Merckx-Stringer (data compilation), Peter Brierley (editor), *Handboek van Chrisitelijk Nederland* Netherlands Christian Handbook), Uitgeversmaatschappij J H Kok BV, Kampen, Evangelishche Alliantie, Driebergen, The Netherlands, and MARC Europe; London, 1986.

13. Peter Brierley (editor), *Le Christianism en Suisse Romande* (Christian Handbook of French-Speaking Switzerland), MARC Europe; London, 1990.

14. Action Recherche Croissance (data compilation), Philippa King (editor), *La France Chrétienne Première Partie: Les Églises* (French Christian Handbook Part 1: Churches), MARC Europe; London, 1989.

15. Val Hiscock, Peter Brierley, Boyd Myers and Lindsey Mansfield (editors), *Irish Christian Handbook* (Lamhleabhar Chriostai na hEireann), MARC Europe; London, 1992.

16. Peter Kuzmic, 'Christian Mission in Europe', chapter in a Festschrift for Dr Gerald Anderson published in *Toward Century 21 in Christian Mission*, Eerdmans; USA, 1992.

17. Gerhard Weber, 'Home Mission: Where do we stand? Where do we go?' in *Mission and Evangelism, Report of a Regional Consultation,* Loccum, 1978, Vol 4, pp 72-88.

18. Dr Alex Robertson (academic consultant), *Lifestyle Survey*, Church of Scotland Board of Social Responsibility; Edinburgh, Scotland, 1987.

19. Boyd Myers, *Scottish Church and Social Concerns Survey*, MARC Europe; 1992.

20. Op cit (item 4) Table 31 p 82.

21. Brian Clews, UK Co-ordinator, *March for Jesus Roadshow*, Opinion Poll Results and Press Release, May 1992.

22. Robin Gamble, *The Irrelevant Church*, Monarch Publications; Tunbridge Wells, Kent, 1991.

23. Op cit (item 2).

24. Peter Kaldor, *Religious Musical Chairs*, Report No 5 from the 1986 Joint Churches Census, Research Division, Uniting Board of Mission; 1988.

25. Philip Margesson, article in *Alliance Life,* March 4th 1992, p 16.

26. Op cit (item 5), p 33.

27. Op cit (item 5), p 70.

28. David A. Roozen and Jackson W. Carroll, *Recent Trends in Church Membership and Participation*, c 1980, and quoted in item 5 above.

29. A discussion of some of the findings of the *Leeds Common Religion Project*, which has yet to be published, are given in item 5 above, pp 16-18.

30. Op cit (item 4) p 59.

31. Rev Dr David B. Barrett, *World Christian Encyclopaedia*, Oxford University Press; Oxford, 1982.

32. Ibid, pp 51 and 52.

33. Rev Dr David B. Barrett, *International Bulletin of Missionary Research*, January 1991.

34. Director of Research, Gallup Social Surveys, Helsinki, Finland, speaking at a seminar in Helsinki on 3rd April 1992. The European Values Study was undertaken in Europe in the 1980s.

35. George Barna, *The Frog in the Kettle*, Regal Books; California, USA, 1990, p 33.

36. *Management Today*, British Institute of Management; London, November 1984 issue, also quoted in item 5, pp 25, 26.

BIBLIOGRAPHY

Abbott, Walter M., S J and Joseph Gallagher. *The Documents of Vatican II*. Geoffrey Chapman; London, 1966.

Arn, Win. *The Pastors Church Growth Handbook*. Church Growth Press; Pasadena, 1979.

Barna, George. *User Friendly Churches*. Regal Books; Ventura, 1991.

Barna, George. *What Americans Believe*. Regal Books, Ventura, 1991.

Barrett, David. *World Christian Encyclopedia*. Oxford University Press; Nairobi, 1982.

Barth, Karl. *Church Dogmatics, Volume I: The Doctrine of the Word of God*. Edited by G. W. Bromley and T. F. Torrance. T & T Clark; Edinburgh, 1956.

Berger, Peter. *The Sacred Canopy*. Doubleday and Co. Inc; Garden City, New York, 1967. Published in the UK under the title *The Social Reality of Religion*. Faber and Faber; 1969, and Penguin Books; 1973.

Berger, Peter. *A Rumour of Angels*. Doubleday and Co. Inc; Garden City, New York, 1969.

Bellah, Robert, et al. *Habits of the Heart*. Harper and Row; New York, 1985.

Beyerhaus, Peter. *Kerygma and Dogma*. April-June, 1969.

Boer, Harry. *Pentecost and Missions*. Eerdmans; Grand Rapids, 1961.

Brierley, Peter. *'Christian' England*. Eltham, London; MARC Europe, 1991.

Brierley, Peter. *Church Nominalism: The Plague of the Twentieth Century?*. MARC Monograph No 2. MARC Europe; London, 1985.

Brunner, Emile. *Revelation and Reason*. 1946.

Callahan, Kennon L. *Effective Church Leadership*. Harper and Row; San Francisco, 1990.

Capra, Fritjof. *Tao of Physics*. Shambhala; Berkeley, 1975.

Chandler, Russell. *Understanding the New Age*. Word Books; Dallas, 1988.

Christian Witness to Nominal Christians Among Protestant Christians. Lausanne Occasional Papers No.232; Thailand Report, 1980.

Connell, Richard J. *Substance and Modern Science*. Center for Thomistic Studies, and Notre Dame University Press; Houston, 1988.

Connor, Steven. *Postmodern Culture*. Blackwell; Oxford, 1989.

Cragg, Kenneth. *The Christ and the Faiths*. SPCK; London, 1986.

Davis, Charles. *Christ and the World Religions*. Hodder & Stoughton; London 1970.

D'Costa, Gavin. *John Hick's Theology of Religions*. University Press of America; New York, 1987.

De Pree, Max. *Leadership is an Art*. Doubleday and Co. Inc; New York, 1989.

Durkheim, Emile. *Socialism*. Collier Books; New York, 1962.

Edwards, David. *Religion and Change*. Hodder & Stoughton; London 1969.

Fishman, Robert. *Bourgeois Utopias*. Basic Books Inc; New York, 1978.

Gallup Report. *Religion in America—50 years 1935-1985*. No. 236, May 1985.

Gay, John D. *The Geography of Religion in England*. Duckworth; London, 1971.

George, Carl. *Prepare Your Church for the Future*. Fleming H. Revell; Tarry-town, New York, 1991.

George, Carl and Bob Logan. *Leading and Managing Your Local Church*. Fleming H. Revell; Old Tappan, NJ, 1987.

Gibbs, Eddie. *The God Who Communicates*. Hodder & Stoughton; London, 1985.

Gibbs, Eddie. *Followed or Pushed?* MARC Europe; 1987.

Greeley, Andrew. *The Persistence of Religion*. 1973.

Guinness, Os. *The Gravedigger File*. InterVarsity Press; Downers Grove, 1983.

Hale, J. Russell. *The Unchurched—Who They Are and Why They Stay Away*. Harper and Row; San Francisco, 1980.

Hick, John and Paul F. Knitter (eds). *The Myth of Christian Uniqueness*. Orbis Books; Maryknoll, 1987.

Joslin, Roy. *Urban Harvest*. Evangelical Press; Welwyn, 1982.

Kaldor, Peter, Vaughan Bowie, Glenn Farquar-Nichol, (eds). *Green Shoots in the Concrete*. Scaffold; NSW, Australia, 1985.

Kelly, Dean M. *Why Conservative Churches are Growing*. Harper and Row; New York, 1977.

Kraft, Charles. *Communication Theory for Christian Witness*. Abingdon Press; Nashville, 1983.

Kritzeck, James and R. Bayly Winder. *The World of Islam, Studies in Honour of Philip K Hitti*. MacMillan; London, 1960.

Kumar, Krishan. *Prophecy and Progress—The Sociology of Industrial Society*. Penguin Books; Harmondsworth, 1978, 1986.

Kurtz, Paul. *In Defense of Secular Humanism*. Prometheus Press; Buffalo, New York, 1983.

Leon, Arnold E. *Secularization—Science without God?* Westminster Press; Phil-adelphia, 1967.

Luecke, David. *Evangelical Style and Lutheran Substance*. Concordia; St. Louis, 1988.

MARC Europe, *Prospects for the Eighties*, 1980; *Prospects for Wales*, 1983; *Prospects for Scotland*, 1985; *Prospects for the Nineties*, 1991.

Marty, Martin. *The Modern Schism: Three Paths to the Secular*. SCM Press; London, 1969.

Marty, Martin. *Pilgrims in Their Own Land*. Little Brown and Co; Boston, 1984.

MacKay, Donald. *The Clockwork Image: A Christian Perspective on Science*. InterVarsity Press; Downers Grove, 1979.

Murren, Doug. *The Baby Boomerang*. Regal Books; Ventura, 1991.

Neighbour Ralph. Jr., *Where Do We Go From Here?* Touch Publications; Houston, 1990.

Newbigin, Lesslie. *Foolishness to the Greeks*. Eerdmans; Grand Rapids, 1989.

Newbigin, Lesslie. *The Gospel in a Pluralist Society*. Eerdmans; Grand Rapids, 1989.

Ogilvy, David. *On Advertising*. Random House; New York, 1985.

Orr, J. Edwin. *The Light of the Nations*. Paternoster Press. London, 1965.

Oswald, Roy M. *How to Prevent Lay Leader Burnout*. The Alban Institute; Washington DC, 1984, 1986.

Pinnock, Clark H. *A Wideness in God's Mercy*. Zondervan; Grand Rapids, 1992.

Population Reference Bureau. *World Urbanization, 1800-2000*. Washington, 1971.

Reid, Gavin. *To Reach a Nation*. Hodder & Stoughton; London, 1987.

Rothauge, Arlin, J. *Sizing Up a Congregation*. The Episcopal Church Center; 815 Second Avenue, New York, NY. No date.

Savage, John S. *The Apathetic and Bored Church Member*. LEAD Consultants; Pittsford, NY, 1976.

Schaller, Lyle. *The Multiple Staff and the Larger Church*. Abingdon Press, Nashville, 1980.

Schaller, Lyle. *Activating the Passive Church*. Abingdon Press, Nashville, 1983.

Schaller, Lyle. *It's a Different World*. Abingdon Press, Nashville, 1989.

Smart, Ninian. *The Yogi and the Devotee*. Allen Unwin; London, 1968.

Snyder, Howard A. *Liberating the Church*. InterVarsity Press; Downers Grove, 1983.

Stark, Rodney, and William Sims Bainbridge. *The Future of Religion: Secularization and Renewal and Cult Formation*. University of California Press; Berkeley, 1985.

Stark, Rodney, and Charles Y. Glock. *American Piety: The Nature of Religious Commitment*. University of California Press; Berkeley, 1968.

Theilicke, Helmut (trans. Geoffrey W. Bromiley). *The Evangelical Faith*. Eerdmans; Grand Rapids, 1974.

Thouless, Robert H. *An Introduction to the Psychology of Religion*. Cambridge University Press; Cambridge, 1971.

Tonnies, Ferdinand. *Communities and Society*. Harper and Row; New York, 1963.

Troeltsch, Ernst. *Christian Thought, Its History and Application*. 1923

Wagner, C. Peter. *Your Church Can Be Healthy*. Abingdon Press; Nashville, 1979.

Webber, Robert E. *Secular Humanism: Threat and Challenge*. Zondervan; Grand Rapids, 1982.

Wickham, Edward. *Church and People in an Industrial City*. Lutterworth Press, 1953.

INDEX OF SUBJECTS

INDEX OF AUTHORS AND PERSONAL NAMES

British Church Growth Association

The British Church Growth Association was formed in September 1981 by a widely representative group of Christians committed to church growth either as researchers, teachers, practitioners or consultants.

The BCGA aims to help and encourage the church in Britain to move into growth in every dimension. The facilities and resources of the BCGA are available to researchers, consultants, teachers, practitioners and those just setting out in church growth thinking. The Association endeavours to offer practical help as well as encouraging and initiating church growth thinking and research.

Membership of the BCGA is open to both individuals and organizations interested in or involved in the theory or practice of church growth. On payment of an annual subscription members are entitled to receive the *Church Growth Digest* (the journal of the Association) four times a year, information about activities through the Newsletters, special discounts on conferences and books, membership of the Church Growth Book Service, voting rights to elect members to the Council every two years, links with other researchers, teachers, practitioners, and consultants on a regional or national level as well as help or advice on allied matters.

Further information about the Association and membership is available from the Secretary, British Church Growth Association, 3a Newnham Street, Bedford, MK4 2JR, Tel: 0234 32705.